1st Workshop on Argumentation Mining 2014

Held at ACL 2014

Baltimore, Maryland, USA
26 June 2014

ISBN: 978-1-63439-201-3

Printed from e-media with permission by:

Curran Associates, Inc.
57 Morehouse Lane
Red Hook, NY 12571

Some format issues inherent in the e-media version may also appear in this print version.

Printed by Curran Associates, Inc. (2014)

For permission requests, please contact the Association for Computational Linguistics at the address below.

Association for Computational Linguistics
209 N. Eighth Street
Stroudsburg, Pennsylvania 18360

Phone: 1-570-476-8006
Fax: 1-570-476-0860

acl@aclweb.org

Additional copies of this publication are available from:

Curran Associates, Inc.
57 Morehouse Lane
Red Hook, NY 12571 USA
Phone: 845-758-0400
Fax: 845-758-2634
Email: curran@proceedings.com
Web: www.proceedings.com

Introduction

Argumentation mining is a relatively new challenge in corpus-based discourse analysis that involves automatically identifying argumentative structures within a document, e.g. the premises, conclusion, and argumentation scheme of each argument, as well as argument-subargument and argument-counterargument relationships between pairs of arguments. Proposed applications of argumentation mining include improving information retrieval and information extraction, as well as providing end-user visualization and summarization of arguments. Sources of interest include not only formal genres, but also a variety of informal genres such as microtext, spoken meeting transcripts, and product reviews. In instructional contexts where argumentation is a pedagogically important tool for conveying and assessing students' command of course material, the written and diagrammed arguments of students (and the mappings between them) are educational data that can be mined for purposes of assessment and instruction. This is especially important given the wide-spread adoption of computer-supported peer review, computerized essay grading, and large-scale online courses and MOOCs.

Success in argumentation mining will require interdisciplinary approaches informed by natural language processing technology, theories of semantics, pragmatics and discourse, knowledge of discourse of domains such as law and science, artificial intelligence, argumentation theory, and computational models of argumentation. In addition, it will require creation and annotation of high-quality corpora of argumentation from different types of sources in different domains.

The goal of this workshop is to provide the first research forum devoted to argumentation mining in all domains of discourse. Suggested topics include but are not limited to:

- Automatic identification of argument elements (e.g., premises and conclusion; data, claim and warrant), argumentation schemes, relationships between arguments in a document, and relationships to discourse goals (e.g. stages of a "critical discussion") and/or rhetorical strategies;
- Creation/evaluation of argument annotation schemes, relationship of argument annotation to linguistic and discourse structure annotation schemes, (semi)automatic argument annotation methods and tools, and creation/annotation of high-quality shared argumentation corpora;
- Processing strategies integrating NLP methods and AI models developed for argumentation such as argumentation frameworks; and
- Applications of argument/argumentation mining to, e.g., mining requirements and technical documents, analysis of arguments in dialogue (meetings, etc.), opinion analysis and mining consumer reviews, evaluation of students' written arguments and argument diagrams, and information access (retrieval, extraction, summarization, and visualization) in scientific and legal documents.

Organizers:

Nancy Green, University of North Carolina Greensboro (USA)
Kevin Ashley, University of Pittsburgh (USA)
Diane Litman, University of Pittsburgh (USA)
Chris Reed, University of Dundee (UK)
Vern Walker, Hofstra University (USA)

Program Committee:

Elena Cabrio, INRIA Sophia-Antipolis Méditerranée (France)
Giuseppe Carenini, University of British Columbia (Canada)
Chrysanne Dimarco, University of Waterloo (Canada)
Floriana Grasso, University of Liverpool (UK)
Graeme Hirst, University of Toronto (Canada)
Maria Liakata, University of Warwick (UK)
Collin Lynch, University of Pittsburgh (USA)
Robert Mercer, University of Western Ontario (Canada)
Raquel Mochales-Palau, Katholieke Universiteit Leuven (Belgium)
Patrick Saint-Dizier, Institut de Recherches en Informatique de Toulouse (France)
Manfred Stede, Universitat Potsdam (Germany)
Joel Tetreault, Yahoo! Labs (USA)
Serena Villata, INRIA Sophia-Antipolis Méditerranée (France)
Adam Wyner, University of Aberdeen (UK)

Table of Contents

Conference Program

Thursday June 26, 2014

Session 1: Papers

8:30–9:00 *Annotating Patterns of Reasoning about Medical Theories of Causation in Vaccine Cases: Toward a Type System for Arguments*
Vern Walker, Karina Vazirova and Cass Sanford

9:00–9:30 *Towards Creation of a Corpus for Argumentation Mining the Biomedical Genetics Research Literature*
Nancy Green

9:30–10:00 *An automated method to build a corpus of rhetorically-classified sentences in biomedical texts*
Hospice Houngbo and Robert Mercer

10:00–10:30 *Ontology-Based Argument Mining and Automatic Essay Scoring*
Nathan Ong, Diane Litman and Alexandra Brusilovsky

10:30–11:00 Coffee

Session 2: Papers

10:30–11:00 *Identifying Appropriate Support for Propositions in Online User Comments*
Joonsuk Park and Claire Cardie

11:00–11:30 *Analyzing Argumentative Discourse Units in Online Interactions*
Debanjan Ghosh, Smaranda Muresan, Nina Wacholder, Mark Aakhus and Matthew Mitsui

11:30–12:00 *Back up your Stance: Recognizing Arguments in Online Discussions*
Filip Boltužić and Jan Šnajder

12:00–12:30 *Automated argumentation mining to the rescue? Envisioning argumentation and decision-making support for debates in open online collaboration communities*
Jodi Schneider

12:30–14:00 Lunch

Thursday June 26, 2014 (continued)

Session 3: Papers

14:00–14:20 *A Benchmark Dataset for Automatic Detection of Claims and Evidence in the Context of Controversial Topics*
Ehud Aharoni, Anatoly Polnarov, Tamar Lavee, Daniel Hershcovich, Ran Levy, Ruty Rinott, Dan Gutfreund and Noam Slonim

14:20–14:40 *Applying Argumentation Schemes for Essay Scoring*
Yi Song, Michael Heilman, Beata Beigman Klebanov and Paul Deane

14:40–15:00 *Mining Arguments From 19th Century Philosophical Texts Using Topic Based Modelling*
John Lawrence, Chris Reed, Colin Allen, Simon McAlister and Andrew Ravenscroft

15:00–15:20 *Towards segment-based recognition of argumentation structure in short texts*
Andreas Peldszus

15:30–16:00 Coffee

Session 4: Posters

16:00–17:00 Poster session

Titles That Announce Argumentative Claims in Biomedical Research Articles
Heather Graves, Roger Graves, Robert Mercer and Mahzereen Akter

Extracting Higher Order Relations From Biomedical Text
Syeed Ibn Faiz and Robert Mercer

Survey in sentiment, polarity and function analysis of citation
Myriam Hernández A. and José M. Gómez

Indicators of Argument-conclusion Relationships. An Approach for Argumentation Mining in German Discourses
Bianka Trevisan, Eva Dickmeis, Eva-Maria Jakobs and Thomas Niehr

Extracting Imperatives from Wikipedia Article for Deletion Discussions
Fiona Mao, Robert Mercer and Lu Xiao

Requirement Mining in Technical Documents
Juyeon Kang and Patrick Saint-Dizier

Thursday June 26, 2014 (continued)

Annotating Patterns of Reasoning about Medical Theories of Causation in Vaccine Cases: Toward a Type System for Arguments

Vern R. Walker
Director,
Research Laboratory for Law, Logic & Technology
Maurice A. Deane School of Law at Hofstra University
Hempstead, New York, USA
Vern.R.Walker@Hofstra.edu

Karina Vazirova
Protocols Coordinator,
Research Laboratory for Law, Logic & Technology
Maurice A. Deane School of Law at Hofstra University
Hempstead, New York, USA

Cass Sanford
Researcher,
Research Laboratory for Law, Logic & Technology
Maurice A. Deane School of Law at Hofstra University
Hempstead, New York, USA

Abstract

Automated argumentation mining requires an adequate type system or annotation scheme for classifying the patterns of argument that succeed or fail in a corpus of legal documents. Moreover, there must be a reliable and accurate method for classifying the arguments found in natural language legal documents. Without an adequate and operational type system, we are unlikely to reach consensus on argument corpora that can function as a gold standard. This paper reports the preliminary results of research to annotate a sample of representative judicial decisions for the reasoning of the factfinder. The decisions report whether the evidence adduced by the petitioner adequately supports the claim that a medical theory causally links some type of vaccine with various types of injuries or adverse medical conditions. This paper summarizes and discusses some patterns of reasoning that we are finding, using examples from the corpus. The pattern types and examples presented here demonstrate the difficulty of developing a type or annotation system for characterizing the logically important patterns of reasoning.

1 Introduction

This paper reports the preliminary results of research by the Research Laboratory for Law, Logic & Technology (LLT Lab) on a corpus of judicial decisions that we have annotated for patterns of argumentation. We first describe the sample of judicial decisions, and report the frequency of argument types using a coarse typology based on logical connectives. We then discuss three additional approaches to a finer-grained typology, based on types of inference, types of evidence, and types of evidentiary discrepancies. We conclude by discussing our working hypotheses for developing a type system for arguments, as well as discussing prior related work.

2 The Sample of Vaccine-Injury Compensation Decisions

The research in this paper is based on a sample of 10 judicial decisions in the United States, in which the petitioner was seeking compensation, under the National Vaccine Injury Compensation Program (NVICP), for injuries allegedly caused by a covered vaccine (Ashley and Walker 2013; Walker 2009; Walker et al. 2011, 2013). The sample is part of the Vaccine/Injury Project Corpus (V/IP Corpus), which comprises every decision filed during a 2-year period (a total of 35 decision texts, typically 15 to 40 pages each) that applied a 3-prong test of causation, enunciated by a federal court in *Althen* (2005). These decisions are authored by special masters attached to the Court of Federal Claims, who function as factfinders in contested cases. According to the

Proceedings of the First Workshop on Argumentation Mining, pages 1–10,
Baltimore, Maryland USA, June 26, 2014.

Althen test, in order to prevail the petitioner must establish three propositions, each by a preponderance of the evidence: (1) that a "medical theory causally connects" the type of vaccine with the type of injury; (2) that there was a "logical sequence of cause and effect" between the particular vaccination and the particular injury; and (3) that a "proximate temporal relationship" existed between the vaccination and the injury. Proving these causation conditions generally requires integrating expert, scientific evidence with non-expert evidence, and reconciling scientific standards of proof with non-scientific (legal or common-sense) standards of proof. In 5 of the decisions, the petitioner succeeded in proving all three *Althen* conditions and ultimately won the case (*Cusati*, *Roper*, *Casey*, *Werderitsh*, and *Stewart*), while in the remaining 5 cases the petitioner lost on the *Althen* first condition and the government won the case (*Meyers*, *Sawyer*, *Wolfe*, *Thomas*, and *Walton*).

This paper examines patterns of argument and reasoning found in the factfinding portions of these vaccine-compensation cases. And we have examined primarily the patterns of reasoning provided by the factfinder in support of the findings of fact. There are several reasons for taking this approach. First, focusing on the reported findings and reasoning of the factfinder also provides information about which arguments were successful (persuasive) and which were not. Second, in writing a decision, the factfinder is more likely to report her own reasoning with more care and detail than she might use in relating the argument of a witness or party. Third, in probably many situations, the reasoning reported by a factfinder was in fact also an argument made originally by a party, which was then adopted by the factfinder. Fourth, in most decisions it is easier to identify and count *all* of the reported findings and reasons of the factfinder, because they are often gathered together in a "Discussion" section of the decision; by contrast, counting the total number of arguments of the parties is more difficult.

Moreover, we have limited ourselves in this paper primarily to patterns that address the first of these *Althen* conditions: that is, whether there was at the time of the litigation a medical theory that causally linked the type of vaccine involved with the type of injury alleged. We have selected this issue for this paper because it involves an issue and style of proof that is general in nature, and less dependent upon the plausibility of particular facts that are peculiar to the specific case. Indeed, proving that "the vaccine can cause this type of injury, at least sometimes" is likely to exhibit patterns of reasoning common in many domains, both inside and outside of law.

In general, we expect both the arguments by the parties or witnesses and the reasoning given by the factfinder for a finding of fact to exhibit the same "argument patterns." That is, we expect the same types of patterns to occur, whether a party puts forth an argument for the factfinder to adopt, or the factfinder reports certain reasoning as being persuasive. As a matter of terminology, the term "argument" is typically applied to the argumentative reasoning of a party, whether or not it proves to be persuasive to the factfinder, and the term "reasoning" is often reserved for the supporting reasoning provided by the legal decision maker. However, from the perspective of exhibiting reasoning patterns, we consider "arguments" and "reasoning" to be equivalent – the only difference being attribution (the agent using the pattern, or to whom the pattern is attributed).

3 The Frequency of Arguments in the Sample Cases

In order to provide quality assurance in identifying the structure of the factfinder's reasoning, our methodology integrated analyses by three annotators in three steps. First, a student researcher trained in the LLT Lab's logic modeling protocols annotated a legal decision for elements of the factfinder's reasoning. Second, another student (who was usually more experienced than the first student) then reviewed those annotations, and the two researchers reached a consensus on any discrepancies. Third, Lab Director Walker performed an independent analysis, and he and the two student researchers discussed and documented any annotation issues, and decided on the final annotations. The resulting "logic model" of the reasoning for a single case integrates numerous units of reasoning into a single logical structure, with each unit consisting of one conclusion and one or more immediately supporting reasons (premises).

Walker et al. (2011, pp. 296-300) provide details on the default-logic framework and on the logical connectives used in the LLT Lab's logic models to connect the supporting reasons (premises) to the conclusion. Because evidentiary propositions (both conclusions and premises) have plausibility-values based on a seven-valued scale (from "highly plausible" through "undecided" to "highly implausible"), the logical connectives must operate on a many-valued scale. The four logical connectives we use in our logic models are:

- "MIN" assigns to the conclusion the *lowest* plausibility-value possessed by any of its supporting premises (MIN functions like a conjunctive AND);
- "MAX" assigns to the conclusion the *highest* plausibility-value possessed by any of its supporting premises (MAX functions like a disjunctive OR);
- "EVIDENCE FACTORS" merely lists relevant reasons or premises, but does not provide a computable formula for producing a plausibility-value for the conclusion as a function of the values of the premises; and
- "REBUT" assigns to the conclusion a degree of implausibility inverse to the degree of plausibility of the rebutting (defeating) premise, when (but only when) the rebutting premise is plausible to some degree (for example, if the rebutting premise is "highly plausible," then the conclusion is "highly implausible"; but if the rebutting premise is only "slightly plausible," then the conclusion is only "slightly implausible").

Using the kind of logical connective employed as a coarse typology, we can classify the arguments found within the factfinding. Table 1 summarizes the results of the argument frequencies within the LLT Lab's logic models for the 10 decisions in the sample, under *Althen* Prong 1 only, by type of connective. A single argument is defined as a single conclusion supported by an immediate level of reasoning – that is, a single conclusion supported by one or more premises or reasons. Where a single conclusion rests on both *prima facie* supporting premises and a defeater, we classified that argument by the connective occurring in the *prima facie* line of reasoning. In Table 1, for example, the reasoning of the factfinder under *Althen* Prong 1 in the *Roper* decision consisted of 7 arguments containing the EVIDENCE FACTORS connective, 2 arguments connected by MIN, and 1 argument connected by REBUT. The numeral "1" in square brackets in the REBUT column of Table 1 indicates that there was a second REBUT connective in the decision, but it occurred as a defeater attached to some other *prima facie* line of reasoning.

Name of Case (Filing Date)	Prong-1 Finding	EVIDENCE FACTOR Args	MIN Args	MAX Args	REBUT Args
Cusati (9/22/05)	For petitioner	5			
Roper (12/9/05)	For petitioner	7	2		1 [1]
Casey (12/12/05)	For petitioner		4	1	
Werderitsh (5/26/06)	For petitioner	2			3 [1]
Stewart (3/19/07)	For petitioner	5			
Meyers (5/22/06)	For government	5			[1]
Sawyer (6/22/06)	For government	10	1		[1]
Wolfe (11/9/06)	For government	5			[1]
Thomas (1/23/07)	For government	3			1
Walton (4/30/07)	For government	14	1		1 [3]

Table 1. Frequency of Arguments in Ten-Case Sample under *Althen* Prong 1, by Type of Connective

An examination of the results in Table 1 shows one reason why we regard this classification of arguments by logical connective as providing only a high-level or coarse typology, but not an adequately informative or useful typology. By far the most common form of argument stated is simply a conclusion, supported by a list of relevant considerations (the arguments containing simply the EVIDENCE FACTORS connective). In these arguments, no other structure is expressly indicated, beyond a listing of supporting reasons. Nearly 79% of the arguments (56 out of 71) contained no internal truth-functional structure, but were merely lists of supporting information considered by the fact-finder to be relevant to drawing that conclusion. This provides motivation for developing a more informative typology for arguments or reasoning patterns, beyond the connectives normally used in propositional logic.

However, we express a word of caution about maintaining descriptive accuracy in annotation. We have considered it critical to annotate patterns of reasoning in a way that accurately represents the reported reasoning of the factfinder. If there exists no semantic cue indicating a more structured form than merely a list of supporting reasons, then we believe that accurate annotation would represent the list form of the original document. It might be possible to *interpret* a list as a more structured line of reasoning, but the *data themselves* (as contrasted with the interpretation of those data) should not be contaminated with information not already expressed in the original source. Thus, we believe that it should always be possible to distinguish between annotations that are strictly faithful to the text in representing the author's stated meaning, and annotations that add the interpretations of commentators. The kind of type system we are discussing in this paper is the former kind, with which we can accurately capture the meaning of the author of the text.

4 Patterns by Types of Inference

This section discusses the possible approach of identifying patterns of argumentation or reasoning that exhibit some type of inference from premises to conclusion (beyond the propositional connectives discussed in Section 3). This approach would draw upon inference methods studied in fields other than law, such as deductive logic, probability or statistics, science or medicine. We discuss some of these types of inference that we find in the vaccine cases.

4.1 Deductive Reasoning

Occasionally reasoning is deductive in form – that is, if the premises are true then the conclusion must be true as well, and the sole avenue for undermining the argument is attacking the truth of the premises (Copi and Cohen 1998, p. 25). In such patterns, the supporting reasons are not merely a list, but rather a list of jointly sufficient reasons for drawing the inference as a necessary conclusion. For example, in *Casey* (p. 26), the conclusion that the varicella vaccine can negatively affect the nervous system was supported by a conjunction of two causal relations: that the vaccine can cause a direct viral infection, and that a direct viral infection can negatively affect the nervous system.

Deductive patterns of reasoning, however, would have premises connected to the conclusion by the propositional connective MIN, because the conclusion would be true (or plausible) *whenever all* of the premises are true (plausible). At most, therefore, 8 of the 71 arguments found in the 10 sample cases would be deductive in form. We find that it is extremely rare for the factfinders in the vaccine cases to explicitly lay out reasoning in a deductively valid format.

4.2 Probabilistic or Statistical Reasoning

Reasoning that is probabilistic or statistical in form could be sub-divided into many types – e.g., reasoning based on premises that are explicitly regarded as merely probable, or reasoning proceeding from a premise that most (or some percentage of) members of one class are members of another class. For example, in *Sawyer* (p. 10), the petitioner's expert relied on the generalization that "it would be reasonable for someone with [the petitioner's] condition to have some days that are less painful than others, but it should generally be a constant pain." And in *Walton* (p. 33), when the petitioner's expert argued that the MMR vaccine can cause myocarditis, the government's expert rebutted that if it were possible, then "we would have seen it by now because millions of doses of the vaccine have been given and this has not been reported."

4.3 Scientific or Medical Reasoning

While deductive and probabilistic inferences do not rely upon methods developed within any particular discipline, legal factfinders are often persuaded by inference methods familiar from science or medicine. For example, in *Walton* (p. 35), an expert for the petitioner and an expert for the government agreed that "an acute reaction from a vaccine-caused myocarditis would be expected to manifest within days to two weeks of infection." Yet the petitioner's "symptoms occurred well over three weeks after her vaccination." The special master found that "[p]erhaps the most significant problem" with the petitioner's theory of causation was "the lack of temporal connection between the MMR vaccination and evidence of a cardiac illness."

Scientific, medical and other expert witnesses sometimes reach a conclusion by balancing various factors and arriving at a considered professional judgment, and this process itself might be persuasive to the legal factfinder. For example, the opinions of two medical experts that the special master found credible in *Stewart* (pp. 36, 38) were supported by lists of reasons. An expert's scientific argument may be presented in a way that lends itself to a legal and logical structure, providing an expert judgment in weighing the same evidence that the Special Master can rely on in reaching a conclusion.

Sometimes the appeal to scientific reasoning is mediated by evidence that scientists themselves have already reached a conclusion on the issue. In *Meyers* (p. 10), the special master noted that the "scientific community has rejected [the expert's] theories as detailed in his articles because the human studies that have been conducted do not support his conclusions and his analytical methods do not comport with the *Daubert* requirement of reliability." *Daubert* was a decision by the U.S. Supreme Court discussing factors relevant to assessing the evidentiary reliability of a scientific expert opinion in court.

5 Patterns by Types of Evidence

This section discusses another approach to classifying patterns of argument and reasoning, one that is based upon the type of evidence in one or more of the premises. The form of reasoning or inference that relies on that evidence to arrive at a conclusion can be varied (as discussed in Section 4).

This section illustrates some of the types of evidence we find recurring in vaccine cases.

5.1 Legal Precedent as Basis

One of the most common patterns of legal reasoning involves the citation of prior legal decisions as precedents. Precedent-based reasoning occurs when judges or factfinders utilize prior cases as providing a binding rule or applicable principle, or as providing guidance by analogy to explain or justify an outcome in the undecided matter before them (Cross et al., 2010, pp. 490-512; Levi 1949, pp. 8-27).

In vaccine decisions, the special masters have utilized precedent-based reasoning in various ways. In *Wolfe* (pp. 9-11), for example, the petitioner's expert based his theory of causation solely on the temporal relationship between the vaccination and the onset of the injury, together with a lack of alternative theories of causation. The special master found that argument to fall short of the established burden, citing the Federal Circuit's decision in *Grant* (p. 1148) for the proposition that mere temporal relationship and lack of alternative causes is not enough to create a *prima facie* case. In *Werderitsh* (p. 44), the government challenged the petitioner's *prima facie* case by pointing to "the failure of valid epidemiologic studies to show a relationship" and "the absence of the knowledge of the appropriate biologic mechanisms responsible." The special master countered that "[l]egally, the absence of epidemiologic support for linking hepatitis B vaccine and MS, and the lack of identification of the specific biologic mechanism at work if hepatitis B vaccine causes MS do not prevent petitioner from satisfying her burden of proof," citing the Federal Circuit's decision in *Knudsen*.

5.2 Legal Policy as Basis

Sometimes an important basis for the reasoning is not merely a precedent, but an authoritatively established legal policy that is considered operative. For example, in *Casey* (p. 26), the special master decided that the petitioner "provided sufficient proof of a medical theory of causation," and explained in part that "[i]t is precisely because individuals experience adverse reactions to safe vaccines on rare occasions that Congress created the Vaccine Program." It is possible, for example, that a weaker statistical inference (Section 4.2) might combine with a policy objective to produce a persuasive argument.

5.3 Medical or Scientific Studies as Basis

In vaccine decisions, it is often the case that arguments are based upon medical or scientific studies, either published in medical or scientific journals or reported in medical treatises. For example, in *Stewart* (pp. 38-39), the special master relied in part on medical literature reporting a connection between the hepatitis A virus and cerebellar ataxia, in finding for the petitioner in a case involving hepatitis A vaccine and the same adverse medical condition. On the other hand, in *Meyers* (pp. 12-14), the special master refused to credit an expert opinion that was based on articles and reports that failed to address the relevant vaccine or injuries in the case. And in *Werderitsh* (p. 43), the special master was not persuaded by an article whose authors admitted that their study was small and its statistical power was reduced.

5.4 Case Reports as Basis

A case report is a descriptive study of a single patient's experience (Cetrulo 2013). Such anecdotal evidence is extremely weak evidence of causation, due to the lack of a control group for testing comparisons (Kaye et al., 2014). However, despite their obvious statistical shortcomings, case reports have been utilized by special masers in their reasoning. In *Roper* (pp. 5-9), the special master explicitly addressed the inability of case reports to provide "scientific certainty" by noting that the petitioner's burden is subject to a much lower "more probable than not" standard, and that accumulated circumstantial evidence of probability can become sufficient to prove causation. In *Stewart* (p. 36), the special master found the case report filed by the government to be relevant for showing a plausible medical theory. And in *Werderitsh* (p. 46), the special master was convinced of causation in large part by the expert's analogy with another vaccine case, and by the similarity of the timing pattern of the relevant symptoms in the two cases.

5.5 Fact Testimony as Basis

We mention here reliance upon the fact testimony of a lay witness as an evidentiary basis, although this is less common when the issue is the existence of a medical theory.

6 Patterns Based on Evidentiary Discrepancies

This section discusses a third approach to classifying patterns of argumentation and reasoning, one that is based on the insight that in law, perhaps more than in other domains involving fact-finding, cases are often decided primarily by resolving inconsistencies or discrepancies in the evidence. When the parties or their expert witnesses agree on a proposition, then the legal fact-finder generally accepts that proposition as uncontested fact, for purposes of the litigation. For example, in *Cusati* (pp. 11-14), the opposing parties' experts agreed on the fact that the MMR vaccine causes fever, and, in turn, that fever causes seizures. The special master utilized that consensus as part of the basis for concluding that the petitioner had met the *prima facie* standard with respect to causation. Similarly, in *Casey* (p. 26), all experts agreed that the temporal sequence of petitioner's symptoms was appropriate. The special master deemed that consensus entirely determinative as to the third condition of *Althen* and did not even engage in further temporal analysis.

6.1 Credibility of Source: Expert vs. Expert

When opposing expert witnesses disagree on some proposition or issue within their expertise, then one approach of the decision maker is to weigh the credibility of the experts, either individually or in comparison. For example, in *Sawyer* (pp. 16-20), the special master found the expert to be so unreliable that this ultimately became the main basis for the decision: "This is a case of unreliable expert testimony." The special master devoted 4½ pages of his single-spaced decision to detailing his supporting reasoning. In *Stewart* (pp. 41-42), the special master looked to the lack of credibility of the government's expert in reaching a finding for the petitioner. The expert was found to be "less than candid or credible" due to an insistence on an assumption that was directly contradicted by medical records, and his failure to take videotape evidence sufficiently into account. And in *Walton* (p. 35), the special master discussed why she "found Dr. Charash [the petitioner's expert] to be far less persuasive than Dr. Glezen or Dr. Brinker [experts for the government]."

6.2 Credibility of Source: Inadequate Explanation

Sometimes the credibility of a source is predicated upon that source's taking irrelevant factors into account, or failing to take relevant factors into account. In *Walton* (p. 35), for example, the petitioner's expert "relied upon assertions of fact not supported by contemporaneous medical records, failed to address the significance of negative cardiac testing, relied upon a temporal relationship between vaccination and onset of symptoms not established by the evidence, failed to demonstrate any support for his theories in research, and failed to address the contrary research evidence submitted by respondent's experts."

7 Discussion: Developing a Type System for Arguments

Our objective is to develop a type system for argument patterns using high-level categories such as those illustrated in Sections 4-6, and developing sub-types based on lower-level categories. The features of sub-categories that are important are those that help to identify arguments that were successful or unsuccessful in the vaccine cases. For example, under the category of medical or scientific studies as basis (see Section 5.3 above), a sub-category might be studies that report negative results (no evidence of a statistically significant causal relationship), and important features might include sample size and statistical power (see *Werderitsh*, p. 43). In developing a type system, we have formulated several working hypotheses from the approaches and examples discussed above.

First, it might be difficult to construct a well-defined taxonomy for types of argument patterns in a specific legal domain. That is, it might not be feasible to devise a classification system under which every argument instance would fit in one and only one category, even in principle. An argument instance might well fit under multiple categories. Moreover, this theoretical point is quite separate from the difficulty of devising a methodology for reliably and accurately placing each argument instance into the correct category.

As a result, it might be more realistic to develop a list of significant categories and features of arguments, and to score a profile for any particular argument instance on those categories and features. For example, an argument instance might involve a combination of attacking the credibility of a source through inadequate explanation (Section 6.2), by relying on a scientific study (Section 5.3) while employing probabilistic reasoning (Seciton 4.2). Then, instead of an identity relation (two arguments being "the same type"), a fuzzier relation of similarity might be useful, computed as a function of the profile scores of two argument instances.

Second, we cannot exclude the possibility that the optimal list of argument categories and features might be in part a function of the task to be performed, and some a priori list might not be optimal for all uses. This is an empirical question that remains to be answered.

Third, if it proves to be the case that the optimal list of argument categories and features is both a function of the task to be performed and widely variant from domain area to domain area, then the most promising approach might be machine learning on training texts that have been only lightly parsed in standard ways. That is, a coarser-grained semantic markup (e.g., sentences or clauses tagged merely as "evidence" and "finding," or "premise" and "conclusion") might be less costly to achieve, might have higher inter-annotator reliability, and might be entirely adequate for machine learning. In order to test this hypothesis, however, we still need to develop an adequate annotation scheme and a gold standard corpus of argument patterns.

Finally, once an adequate annotation scheme is developed, we will face the challenge of outcome evaluation. Argument patterns may differ in weight with respect to the overall conclusion and ultimate outcome of the case. For example, in the context of vaccine decisions, a finding that petitioner's expert was entirely unreliable may singlehandedly support dismissal of the entire claim (see *Sawyer*, pp. 16-20). In addition, it is far from clear whether case reports alone can support a medical theory connecting the vaccine to the injury (see *Roper*, pp. 5-9; *Stewart*, p. 36). Thus, comparative research and assignment of weights to argument patterns may be useful.

In addition to keeping these working hypotheses in mind, when deciding upon the tentative adoption of any annotation scheme or type system, we give consideration to: (1) the cost (in terms of both resources and risk of error) of manually applying the scheme to the number of legal documents needed to allow machine training and testing; (2) the feasibility of successfully automating the detection and annotation of new texts using the scheme; (3) the adequacy of the scheme as a means of performing various tasks, such as generating new arguments in new cases, or predicting ultimate case outcomes; and (4) the interoperability of the scheme with existing ontologies and datasets. Although many researchers have tested systems for automatically annotating legal texts (see references discussed in Section 8), we believe that critical work remains to be done on empirically developing an annotation scheme that is adequate for representing natural language arguments in legal texts, for the purpose of assisting in the generation of new arguments in new cases.

8 Prior Related Work

Our strategic approach is both empirical and logical in nature. Our approach is empirical because we consider it crucial to use a corpus of diverse and linguistically rich legal decisions to gain insights into actual argument patterns. We also take the typical approach of logic in looking for patterns of successful and unsuccessful argument at a "local" level, in the relationships among premises and conclusions (the distinction between "local" and "global" is due to Mochales and Moens, 2011, pp. 3-8). Local argument patterns (which frequently occur within a single paragraph) are distinguished from the global argument pattern that supports the ultimate decision on a claim (often the conclusion of an entire decision) (*id.*). We briefly mention here recent research bearing on our work.

Mochales and Moens (2011, pp. 5-6; 2008, pp. 12-14) annotated a corpus of 47 judicial decisions from the European Court of Human Rights using a system of argumentation schemes developed by Walton (1996; Walton et al., 2008). They focused on "The Law" sections of the judicial opinions, which discuss the arguments of the parties and the court's reasons supporting its decision. Thus, their focal point within the judicial decisions is similar to that in our study of the vaccine cases (factfinder reasoning) and their attention to the local argument patterns is similar to ours. One major difference might be that the reasoning in our judicial decisions usually rests heavily upon scientific and medical evidence, including expert opinions.

Saravanan and Ravindran (2010, pp. 47-53, 65-66) manually annotated sentences in a corpus of 200 decisions (approximately 16,000 sentences) from Indian courts using a "rhetorical" annotation scheme containing 7 categories: "identifying the case," "establishing facts of the case," "arguing the case," "history of the case," "arguments (analysis)," "ratio decidendi (ratio of the decision)," and "final decision (disposal)." It is unclear how many of these rhetorical categories will play a role in defining useful local argument patterns in U.S. cases.

Ashley and Brüninghaus (2009, pp. 132-43; Brüninghaus and Ashley 2005, pp. 65-67) investigated 146 cases involving trade secret misappropriation. "Squibs" of these cases (manually prepared textual descriptions of the case facts) contained sentences that were manually annotated with respect to being positive instances of 26 factors (a positive instance was a sentence "from which it could be reasonably inferred" that the factor "applied in the case"). A "factor" is a category of facts that helps to predict the case outcome for either the plaintiff or the defendant – for example, Factor F4 represents the fact pattern in which the defendant entered into a non-disclosure agreement with the plaintiff, and F4 favors an ultimate decision for the plaintiff. Chorley and Bench-Capon (2005) supplemented these factors with "values," in the context of building a "theory." Wyner and Peters (2010) selected 39 of these cases and a limited number of base factors, and developed semantically salient terms and synonyms for these factors. Even assuming that case squibs retain the linguistic richness of the original documents and contain a sufficient number of negative instances (sentences that are irrelevant to argumentation), the goal of annotating sentences for factors is to predict the ultimate outcome in domain cases, and such factors may or may not be relevant to local argument patterns within the case.

Biagioli et al. (2005), using a dataset of paragraphs selected from Italian legislative texts, classified the paragraphs into eleven types of legislative "provision" (e.g., definition, obligation, prohibition, permission). Each type of provision takes various arguments – for example, the provision type "obligation" takes as arguments the "addressee," the "action," and a "third-party." Such types of provisions might well appear in local argument patterns, which apply legal rules to evidence in a particular case.

Wyner et al. (2013, p. 167) annotated intellectual property appellate cases using 32 annotations, which were selected as being "those used in practice in the analysis of cases in law schools." Annotation types ranged from "Judge Name" to "Legal Facts" ("the legally relevant facts of the case that are used in arguing the issues"). While some of these annotation types might be relevant to local argument patterns, others probably are not.

9 Conclusion

We have reported the preliminary results of our efforts to develop an adequate type system or annotation scheme for marking up successful and unsuccessful patterns of argument in U.S. judicial decisions. We are working from a corpus of vaccine-injury compensation cases that report factfinding about causation, based on both scientific and non-scientific evidence and reasoning. We have summarized and illustrated the patterns of reasoning we are finding, and have discussed our strategy for future research. What seems clear is that the task of developing an adequate type or annotation system is both difficult and important. Without an adequate and operational type system, we are unlikely to reach consensus on argument corpora that can function as a gold standard, or to make robust and useful progress on automating the annotation of judicial decisions for argumentation.

References

Althen v. Secretary of Health and Human Services, 418 F.3d 1274 (Fed.Cir. 2005).

Ashley Kevin D., and Stefanie Brüninghaus. 2009. Automatically classifying texts and predicting outcomes. *Artificial Intelligence and Law* 17:125-165.

Ashley, Kevin D., and Vern R. Walker. 2013. From Information Retrieval (IR) to Argument Retrieval (AR) for Legal Cases: Report on a Baseline Study. *Proceedings of the 26th International Conference on Legal Knowledge and Information Systems (JURIX 2013)* (Kevin D. Ashley, ed.): 29-38.

Biagioli, C., E. Francesconi, A. Passerini, S. Montemagni, and C. Soria. 2005. Automatic semantics extraction in law documents. *Proceedings of tenth international conference on artificial intelligence and law* (ICAIL-05): 133-40. ACM: New York.

Brüninghaus, Stefanie, and Kevin D. Ashley. 2005. Generating Legal Arguments and Predictions from Case Texts. *Proceedings of tenth international conference on artificial intelligence and law* (ICAIL-05): 65-74. ACM: New York.

Casey v. Secretary of Health and Human Services, No. 97-612V (Office of Special Masters, United States Court of Federal Claims, December 12, 2005).

Cetrulo, Lawrence G. 2013. Case Reports. *Toxic Torts Litigation Guide* 1: §5:33. Westlaw, Thomson Reuters.

Chorley, Alison, and Trevor Bench-Capon. 2005. An empirical investigation of reasoning with legal cases through theory construction and application. *Artificial Intelligence and Law* 13:323-371.

Copi, Irving M., and Carl Cohen. 1998. *Introduction to Logic* (Tenth Edition). Prentice Hall, Upper Saddle River, New Jersey.

Cross, Frank B., James F. Spriggs II, Timothy R. Johnson, and Paul J. Wahlbeck. 2010. Citations in the U.S. Supreme Court: An Empirical Study of Their Use and Significance. *University of Illinois Law Review* 2010: 489-575.

Cusati v. Secretary of Health and Human Services, No. 99-0492V (Office of Special Masters, United States Court of Federal Claims, September 22, 2005).

Daubert v. Merrell Dow Pharmaceuticals, Inc., 509 U.S. 579 (1993).

Grant v. Secretary of the Department of Health and Human Services, 956 F.2d 1144 (Fed. Cir. 1992).

Kaye, David H., David E. Bernstein, and Jennifer L. Mnookin. 2014. Types of Causal Studies. *The New Wigmore: A Treatise on Evidence: Expert Evidence* §12.5.1. CCH Incorporated, Aspen Publishers.

Knudsen v. Secretary of the Department of Health and Human Services, 35 F.3d 543 (Fed. Cir. 1994).

Levi, Edward H. 1949. *An Introduction to Legal Reasoning*. The University of Chicago Press, Chicago, Illinois.

Meyers v. Secretary of the Department of Health and Human Services, No. 04-1771V (Office of Special Masters, United States Court of Federal Claims, May 22, 2006).

Mochales, Raquel, and Marie-Francine Moens. 2008. Study on the Structure of Argumentation in Case Law. *Legal Knowledge and Information Systems* (Jurix 2008) (E. Francesconi, G. Sartor, D. Tiscornia, eds.): 11-20. IOS Press.

Mochales, Raquel, and Marie-Francine Moens. 2011. Argumentation mining. *Artificial Intelligence and Law* 19:1-22.

Roper v. Secretary of Health and Human Services, No. 00-407V (Office of Special Masters, United States Court of Federal Claims, December 9, 2005).

Saravanan, M., and B. Ravindran. 2010. Identification of Rhetorical Roles for Segmentation and Summarization of a Legal Judgment. *Artificial Intelligence and Law* 18: 45-76.

Sawyer v. Secretary of the Department of Health and Human Services, No. 03-2524V (Office of Special Masters, United States Court of Federal Claims, June 22, 2006).

Stewart v. Secretary of the Department of Health and Human Services, No. 06-287V (Office of Special Masters, United States Court of Federal Claims, March 19, 2007).

Thomas v. Secretary of the Department of Health and Human Services, No. 01-645V (Office of Special Masters, United States Court of Federal Claims, January 23, 2007).

Walker, Vern R. 1996. Preponderance, Probability and Warranted Factfinding. *Brooklyn Law Review* 62: 1075-1136.

Walker, Vern R. 2003. Epistemic and Non-epistemic Aspects of the Factfinding Process in Law. *American Philosophical Association Newsletter on Law and Philosophy* 3(1): 132-136.

Walker, Vern R. 2007. A default-logic paradigm for legal fact-finding. *Jurimetrics* 47: 193-243.

Walker, Vern R. 2009. Designing factfinding for cross-border healthcare. *Opinio Juris in Comparatione* 3, paper n. 1, 1-40.

Walker, Vern R., Nathaniel Carie, Courtney C. DeWitt, and Eric Lesh. 2011. A framework for the extraction and modeling of fact-finding reasoning from legal decisions: lessons from the Vaccine/Injury Project Corpus. *Artificial Intelligence and Law* 19:291-331.

Walker, Vern R., Chan Hee Park, Philip H. Hwang, Arthur John, Evgeny I. Krasnov and Keith Langlais. 2013. A process approach to inferences of causation: empirical research from vaccine cases in the USA. *Law, Probability and Risk* 12(3-4): 189-205.

Walton v. Secretary of the Department of Health and Human Services, No. 04-503V (Office of Special Masters, United States Court of Federal Claims, April 30, 2007).

Walton, Douglas N. 1996. *Argumentation Schemes for Presumptive Reasoning*. Lawrence Erlbaum Associates, Publishers, Mahwah, New Jersey.

Walton, Douglas, Chris Reed, and Fabrizio Macagno. 2008. *Argumentation Schemes*. Cambridge University Press, Cambridge, UK.

Werderitsh v. Secretary of the Department of Health and Human Services, No. 99-319V (Office of Special Masters, United States Court of Federal Claims, May 26, 2006).

Wolfe v. Secretary of Health and Human Services, No. 05-0878V (Office of Special Masters, United States Court of Federal Claims, November 9, 2006).

Wyner, Adam, and Wim Peters. 2010. Lexical Semantics and Expert Legal Knowledge towards the Identification of Legal Case Factors. *Legal Knowledge and Information Systems* (Jurix 2010) (Radboud G.F. Winkels, ed.): 127-36. IOS Press.

Wyner, Adam, Wim Peters, and Daniel Katz. 2013. A Case Study on Legal Case Annotation. *Proceedings of the 26th International Conference on Legal Knowledge and Information Systems (JURIX 2013)* (Kevin D. Ashley, ed.): 165-74.

Towards Creation of a Corpus for Argumentation Mining the Biomedical Genetics Research Literature

Nancy L. Green
Dept. of Computer Science
U. of N. Carolina Greensboro
Greensboro, NC 27402, USA
nlgreen@uncg.edu

Abstract

Argumentation mining involves automatically identifying the premises, conclusion, and type of each argument as well as relationships between pairs of arguments in a document. We describe our plan to create a corpus from the biomedical genetics research literature, annotated to support argumentation mining research. We discuss the argumentation elements to be annotated, theoretical challenges, and practical issues in creating such a corpus.

1 Introduction

Argumentation mining is a relatively new challenge in corpus-based discourse analysis that involves automatically identifying argumentation within a document, i.e., the premises, conclusion, and type of each argument, as well as relationships between pairs of arguments in the document. To date, researchers have investigated methods for argumentation mining of non-scientific text and dialogue. However, the lack of appropriately annotated corpora has hindered research on argumentation mining of scientific research articles. Using the term 'argument' in a related but different sense than here, researchers have investigated annotation of scientific abstracts and full-text articles (e.g. Teufel, 2002; Mizuta et al., 2005; Liakata et al., 2012). However, the annotated corpora they have created are not designed for argumentation mining in the above sense.

Our goal is to create a freely available corpus of open-access, full-text scientific articles from the biomedical genetics research literature, annotated to support argumentation mining research. The corpus also would provide a rich new resource for researchers in related areas including information retrieval, information extraction, summarization, and question-answering. There is a critical need for automated analysis of the rapidly growing genetics research literature. Availability of the corpus should promote the development of computational tools for use by biomedical and genetics researchers. In the future, e.g., a tool enabled by argumentation mining could be used to automatically summarize arguments in the research literature that a certain genetic mutation is a cause of breast cancer. Methods developed from experimentation with this corpus should be adaptable to other scientific domains as well.

Section 2 of this paper discusses some terms from argumentation theory that are relevant to our goals and surveys related work. Section 3 discusses examples of argumentation in the target literature. The next three sections discuss challenges, practical issues, and future plans for creating the corpus.

2 Background

2.1 Argumentation Theory

Traditionally, an argument is said to consist of a set of ***premises*** and a ***conclusion***, and a formal model such as deductive logic is used to determine whether the argument is valid. An argument can be attacked by refuting a premise or by presenting an argument for a conclusion in contradiction to the original conclusion. However Toulmin (1998), who was concerned with modeling arguments in fields such as law and science, argued that logical validity is too restrictive a criterion for determining argument acceptability. Toulmin distinguished two types of premis-

Proceedings of the First Workshop on Argumentation Mining, pages 11–18,
Baltimore, Maryland USA, June 26, 2014. ©2014 Association for Computational Linguistics

es: ***data***, i.e., observations or conclusions of other arguments, and ***warrant***, i.e., a field-dependent accepted principle (such as a legal rule or a "law" of science).

Argumentation schemes are abstract descriptions of forms of argument that are used to construct acceptable arguments in everyday conversation, law, and science (Walton et al., 2008). Argumentation schemes may describe non-deductively valid arguments, and their conclusions may be retracted when more information is obtained. For example, an abductive argumentation scheme, often used in genetic counseling (Green et al., 2011), is reasoning from observations to a hypothesized cause. ***Critical questions*** associated with argumentation schemes play an important role in evaluating argument acceptability (Walton et al., 2008). For example, one of the critical questions of the abductive argumentation scheme is whether there is an alternative, more plausible explanation for the observation used as a premise. An ***enthymeme*** is an argument with implicit premises or conclusion. Argumentation schemes are sometimes useful in reconstruction of missing components of enthymemes.

2.2 Argumentation Corpora

A corpus of genetic counseling patient letters was analyzed in several ways to design a computational model for generation of arguments from healthcare experts to patients (Green et al., 2011). An annotation scheme was developed to describe the conceptual model of genetic disease and inheritance communicated to patients (Green, 2005a). Formal argumentation schemes describing arguments found in the corpus were defined (Green et al., 2011). Analyses of pragmatic features included rhetorical relations (Green, 2010a), ordering constraints and discourse markers (Green et al., 2011), point of view (Green 2005b), and use of probability expressions (Green 2010b). However, it was not a goal of that project to provide a publicly available corpus.

The Araucaria argumentation diagramming tool was developed to aid human analysts and students to visualize and annotate naturally occurring arguments (Reed and Rowe, 2004). Diagrams can be stored as text files with stand-off annotation of premises and conclusions, argumentation schemes, and relationships between arguments. The Araucaria project has created a publicly available corpus of annotated argumentation from newspaper articles, parliamentary records, magazines, and on-line discussion boards (Reed et al., 2010). The corpus has been used in some argumentation mining research (Mochales and Moens, 2011; Feng and Hirst, 2011; Cabrio and Villata, 2012).

2.3 Argumentation Mining

To date, researchers have investigated methods for argumentation mining of non-science content: legal documents (Mochales and Moens, 2011; Bach et al., 2013; Ashley and Walker, 2013; Wyner et al., 2010), on-line debates (Cabrio and Villata, 2012), product reviews (Villalba and Saint-Dizier, 2012; Wyner et al., 2012), and newspaper articles and court–cases (Feng and Hirst, 2011). Here we summarize the work that is most relevant to our project.

Mochales and Moens (2011) experimented with the Araucaria corpus and a legal corpus. They developed a multi-stage approach to argumentation mining. The first stage, *argumentative information detection*, addresses the problem of classifying a sentence (or sentential subunit) as being part of an argument or not. Next, *argument boundary detection*, or segmentation, is the problem of determining the boundaries of each argument. Third, *argumentative proposition classification* labels the sentences in an argument according to their role as a premise or the conclusion. Lastly, *argumentation structure detection* is the problem of detecting the relationships between arguments, i.e., whether two atomic arguments are "chained" (the conclusion of one is a premise of another), whether multiple arguments are provided in support of the same conclusion, and whether one argument attacks another argument in some way. Statistical techniques were used for the first three stages, while manually constructed context-free grammar rules were used for *argumentation structure detection*.

Cabrio and Villata (2012) used an approach to *argumentation structure detection* based on calculating textual entailment (Dagan 2006) to detect support and attack relations between arguments in a corpus of on-line dialogues stating user opinions.

Feng and Hirst (2011) focused on the problem of *argumentation scheme recognition* in the Araucaria corpus. Assuming that the conclusion and premises of an argument have been identified already, classification techniques achieved high accuracy for two argumentation schemes described in (Walton et al., 2008), *argument from example* and *practical reasoning*. Those schemes are less likely to be useful in analysis of scientific texts however.

In fact, since scientific research articles substantially differ from the genres that have been explored for argumentation mining so far, it is an open question what techniques will be successful in the scientific literature.

2.4 Argumentative Zoning and Related Annotation Schemes

Some NLP researchers have studied ways to automatically identify discourse structure in scientific text. The motivation is to provide contextual information that will improve automatic information access without the need to represent or reason about domain knowledge (Teufel, 2010). These researchers have developed several annotation schemes.

The argumentative zoning (AZ) annotation scheme was developed for automatically classifying the sentences of a scientific article in terms of their contribution of new knowledge to a field (Teufel and Moens, 2002; Teufel, 2010). Applied to articles in computational linguistics, AZ labels "zones" or variable-length sequences of sentences with one of seven categories: AIM (the research goal of the article), BASIS (the contribution of existing knowledge to a knowledge claim of the article), CONTRAST (criticizing or negatively contrasting competitors' knowledge claims to a knowledge claim of the article), TEXTUAL (indicating the structure of the article), BACKGROUND (generally accepted background knowledge), OTHER (existing knowledge claims), and OWN (describing any aspect of a new knowledge claim made by the authors).

An extension of AZ (AZ-II) developed for application to chemistry articles, refined AZ's distinctions into fifteen categories (Teufel, 2010). In another extension of AZ developed for genetics articles (Mizuta et al., 2005), the AZ OWN category was replaced by categories distinguishing descriptions of methodology (MTH), experimental results (RSL), insights from experimental results or previous work (INS), and implications (such as conjectures and applications) of experimental results or previous work (IMP).

The CoreSC (Core Scientific Concepts) annotation scheme was developed for automatic classification of sentences in terms of the components of a scientific investigation: Hypothesis, Motivation, Goal, Object, Background, Method, Experiment, Model, Observation, Result and Conclusion (Liakata et al., 2012a). An automatic classifier for CoreSC was developed and evaluated on a corpus of 265 full-text articles in biochemistry and chemistry. A comparison study (Liakata et al., 2012b) in which articles were annotated with both AZ-II and CoreSC "found that CoreSC provides finer granularity ... while the strength of AZ-II lies in detecting the attribution of knowledge claims and identifying the different functions of background information" (Liakata et al. 2012b, p. 45). Liakata et al. (2012b) compared CoreSC to two other scientific discourse annotation schemes (Thompson et al., 2011; De Waard and Pander Maat, 2009). The three schemes were found to be complementary, operating at different levels of granularity.

However, none of the above annotation schemes address argumentation as described in section 2.3. They are not designed to identify the premises and conclusion of each argument (including missing components of enthymemes) and the argumentation scheme, nor relationships between pairs of arguments. Nevertheless, we plan to coordinate our efforts with that research community to benefit from their expertise and to ensure that our corpus will ultimately provide a valuable resource for their research.

3 Examples

In this section we discuss examples of some of the arguments in an article (Schrauwen et al., 2012) that is representative of the articles to be included in the corpus. The main claim of this article is that a c.637+1G>T mutation of the *CABP2* gene in the region 11q12.3-11q13.3 (DFNB93) is a cause of autosomal recessive non-syndromic hearing loss (arNSHL) in humans. The article's body is divided into four sections: Introduction, Material and Methods, Results, and Discussion. The following examples in Table 1 are from the first subsection of the Results section (under the subheading "Next-Generation Sequencing of the DFNB93 Region Identifies a Splice-Site Mutation in *CABP2*"). The excerpt has been manually segmented into regions of text conveying arguments. Adjacent segments not conveying arguments have been omitted to save space; the approximate number of omitted lines is given in square brackets. Also, for readability, alternative identifiers of genetic variants have been replaced by ellipses.

1	¶The DFNB93 region contains more than 300 annotated and hypothetical genes, and several genes are expressed in the mouse and human inner ear. Because there are many strong candidate genes in the region, we sequenced all genes and noncoding genes in this region by using a custom DNA capture array to identify the disease-causing mutation in one affected individual from the family.
	[skip next 5 lines]
2	¶After the identified homozygous variants were filtered through the 1000 Genomes Project November 2010 release and dbSNP131, 47 previously unreported variants remained and included two exonic mutations, one splicing mutation, six nontranslated mutations, 16 intergenic (downstream or upstream) mutations, and 22 intronic mutations.
3	The two exonic variants included one nonsynonymous variant, c.1379A>G ... in PPFIA1 ... and synonymous variant c.174G>A ... in GAL3ST3 ... The splice-site variant, c.637+1G>T ... was located at the 5′ donor site of intron 6 of CABP2 (Figure 1 and Figure S1, available online). ¶The variants in PPFIA1 and CABP2 were subsequently validated by Sanger DNA sequencing, which only confirmed the splicing variant in CABP2.
	[skip next 4 lines]
4	Next, we checked the inheritance of the CABP2 variant in the entire Sh10 family (Figure 1) and screened an additional 100 random Iranian controls to ensure that the variant is not a frequent polymorphism. The mutation was not detected in any of the controls, and inheritance was consistent with hearing loss in the family.

Table 1. Excerpt from (Schrauwen et al., 2012)

In an annotation scheme such as AZ, the first sentence of segment 1 might be classified as BKG (background) and the second as MTH (methodology). In CoreSC, the second sentence might be classified as Hypothesis and Method. However, the following argument is also communicated in (1) to the intended audience of scientists. (A genetics researcher has confirmed our interpretation of the arguments in this paper.) Note that in the following analyses in our paper, square brackets indicate implicit information derivable from the discourse context or domain knowledge. In the following argument, two of the premises are implicit, i.e., this is an example of an enthymeme. Also, premises are distinguished as Data or Warrant, where the former type of premise corresponds to old or new evidence or a conclusion of another argument in the article, and the latter to generally accepted principles or assumptions in genetics. It is understood by the intended audience that warrants may have exceptions and that the conclusions of the following arguments are tentative.

Note that the conclusion of Argument 1 has been recovered from the phrase *there are many strong candidate genes in the region*. The argument can be analyzed in terms of a type of abductive argumentation scheme, i.e., reasoning from effect (arNSHL) to plausible cause (a mutation in the DFNB932 region). For a specification of the argumentation schemes identified in the genetics paper, see (Green and Schug, in preparation).

Argument 1:
Data: Several genes in the DFNB93 region are expressed in the human inner ear.
Data: [arNSHL involves the inner ear]
Warrant: [If a gene is expressed in a tissue related to a genetic condition then a mutation of that gene may be a cause of that condition]
Warrant: [Autosomal recessive genetic conditions are caused by homozygous mutations.]
Conclusion: A [homozygous] mutation of a gene in the DFNB93 region may be a cause of arNSHL in humans.

In an annotation scheme such as AZ, the subordinate clause at the beginning of segment 2 might be classified as MTH, and the main clause as RSL (results). However it has been analyzed in Argument 2 as an instance of an argumentation scheme involving the elimination of candidates. Note that the identity of the arNSHL-affected individual whose DNA was tested (V:14) and the family to which she belonged (Sh 10) was not specified in this section, but was given in the Material and Methods section. Also note that the first premise in Argument 2 is the conclusion of the preceding Argument 1. In our paper, this is indicated by providing the previous argument's identifier in parentheses.

Argument 2:
Data: (Argument 1) [A homozygous mutation of a gene in the DFNB93 region may be a cause of arNSHL in humans]
Data: [In a DNA sample from one arNSHL-affected individual, identified as V:14 of family Sh10] 47 previously unreported [i.e. not frequent polymorphisms] homozygous variant alleles in the DFNB93 region were identified.
Warrant: [If a variant is a frequent polymorphism then it is not a cause of a genetic condition]
Conclusion: [One of the 47 variants may be the cause of arNSHL in individual V:14]

Various clauses in segment 3 might be classified as MTH or RSL in a scheme such as AZ. In an argumentation analysis, however, it conveys an argument that the *CABP2* mutation may be the cause of arNSHL in one individual (:V14), after the elimination of the other candidates.

Argument 3
Data: (Argument 2) [One of the 47 variants may be the cause of arNSHL in individual V:14]
Data: Only splice-site variant c.637+1G>T of *CABP2* was confirmed.
Warrant: [Only confirmed exonic or splice-site variants may be the cause of arNSHL.]
Conclusion: [The c.637+1G>T variant of *CABP2* may be the cause of arNSHL in individual V:14]

Segment 4 uses two different sets of data to argue that the c.637+1G>T variant of *CABP2* may be the cause of arNSHL in the family of V:14, Sh10. In a scheme such as AZ, the first sentence would probably be described as MTH and the second as RSL. However, an argumentation analysis provides two arguments, 4a and 4b. They each support the same conclusion, which is not explicitly stated in the text.

Argument 4a
Data: (Argument 3) [The c.637+1G>T variant of *CABP2* may be the cause of arNSHL in individual V:14]
Data: Inheritance of the variant segregates with arNSHL in family Sh10.
Warrant: [A mutation that is present in one affected family member may be the cause of an autosomal recessive genetic condition in the rest of the family if the mutation segregates with the genetic condition in the family (i.e., the mutation is present in all and only the family members who have the genetic condition, and the occurence of the condition is consistent with autosomal recessive inheritance)]
Conclusion: [The c.637+1G>T variant of *CABP2* may be the cause of arNSHL in family Sh10]

Argument 4b
Data: Inheritance of the variant c.637+1G>T of *CABP2* segregates with arNSHL in family Sh10.
Data: The variant c.637+1G>T of *CABP2* is not found in the DNA of a control group of 100 individuals [who are not in family Sh10 and who are not affected with arNSHL]
Warrant: [If a variant segregates with an autosomal recessive condition in a family but is not found in the DNA of a control group of individuals who are not affected with the condition, then it may be the cause of the condition in that family]
Conclusion: [The c.637+1G>T variant of *CABP2* may be the cause of arNSHL in family Sh10]

In addition to identifying individual arguments, argumentation mining addresses relationships between pairs of arguments. Arguments 1-4a illustrate a chain of arguments, i.e., where the conclusion of Argument *i* is a premise of Argument *i+1*. Also, arguments 4a and 4b illustrate two arguments in support of the same conclusion. Note that, individually, Arguments 1-3 are relatively weak. However, Argument 1 might be useful in answer to a query such as *What regions may carry a mutation leading to arNSHL?* Arguments 2-3 might be useful in answer to a query such as *Have any individual cases of arNSHL been attributed to a mutation of CABP2?* Arguments 1-4a and Argument 4b could be given as the answer to the query *What mutation may be the cause of arNSHL in an affected family?* (Note that in an interactive query facility, instead of presenting the user with a chain of arguments, the system could leave it up to the user to "drill down" to see the subarguments in a chain.)

The above arguments are provided here for purposes of illustration. In the remainder of the genetics article the main claim (that the *CABP2* mutation is a cause of arNSHL in humans) is supported by arguments that the mutation is the cause of arNSHL in two other families. Also, using a different type of argumentation, it provides a biochemical explanation for how the mutation may cause an abnormality in the inner ear that could cause hearing loss. In addition to the main claim, the article contains several other supported claims, e.g., that the c.637+1G>T variant of *CABP2* may be a founder mutation.

4 Challenges

Argumentation mining of this type of discourse will be challenging. A challenge that is shared with BioNLP text mining in general is dealing with the extensive use of biological, chemical, and clinical terminology in the BioNLP domain. A number of challenges specific to argumentation mining are discussed next.

To specify an argument it is necessary to identify the premises (or data and warrant), conclusion, and argumentation scheme. However, as illustrated in the previous examples, arguments with implicit components (enthymemes) are common, e.g., where a conclusion is implicit or used as an implicit premise of another argument. A related challenge is to supply domain knowledge for reconstructing implicit warrants in this genre. Another related challenge is the need to make use of discourse context to supply missing information, e.g., where context is required to supply the identity of individual V:14 in Argument 2. Note that in that case, it was necessary to read the previous Materials and Methods section to supply that information.

Another problem illustrated in the example is that argument boundaries do not coincide with sentential subunit boundaries. For example, segment 4 contains parts of Argument 4a and 4b in the first sentence and parts of those two arguments in the second sentence. Furthermore, identification of argument components does not appear to be systematically associated with discourse markers such as 'therefore'. However, the arguments contain lexical items relating to scientific discovery (e.g., 'confirmed', 'detected', 'consistent with', 'indicate', 'is likely that', 'expected to', 'showed', 'suggests') that may aid in automatic identification of the components.

Our analysis of argumentation in genetic counseling (Green et al., 2011) and in the genetics research literature (Green and Schug, in preparation) has identified other (and more specific) argumentation schemes and critical questions than those listed in (Walton et al., 2008). Since some of the argumentation schemes we have identified are causal, lexical patterns of causality may be useful features for use in argumentation mining.

5 Practical Considerations for Creating the Corpus

In order to ensure that the future corpus can be freely disseminated, we will select articles from journals that are fully open-access, i.e., that are published under the Creative Commons attribution license "which allows articles to be re-used and re-distributed without restriction, as long as the original work is correctly cited" (http://www.biomedcentral. com.about). To date, we have identified the following fully open-access journals that contain biomedical genetics research articles:

- BMC http://www.biomedcentral.com journals: BMC Genetics, BMC Genomics, BMC Medical Genetics, BMC Medical Genomics and BMC Molecular Biology,
- PLoS http://www.plos.org/ journals: Genetics, Biology, Medicine

A number of other journals (e.g. *American Journal of Human Genetics*), indexed by PubMed http://www.pubmedcentral.nih.gov, make a subset of their articles available as open-access.

After selecting articles for the corpus, we will define and evaluate the intercoder reliability (Arstein and Poesio, 2008) of the following types of annotations:

- Data, warrant, and conclusion and argumentation scheme of each argument,
- Multiple arguments for the same conclusion, and
- Chained relationships between arguments, i.e., where the conclusion of an argument is the premise of a subsequent argument.

Note that we plan to employ graduate students with a background in genetics and biochemistry as coders.

Identifying *implicit* components of arguments will be challenging for coders. However, there are a number of constraints that will be given in the instructions to help the coders. First, they will be given a list of commonly accepted principles of genetics as possible warrants, such as Mendel's laws, the concept of segregation in a pedigree, etc. Second, coders will be instructed to look for chained arguments, i.e., where the premises/conclusions of chained arguments can be reconstructed from the relationship between two arguments. Third, coders will be given a description of argumentation schemes, which also constrain the interpretation of argument components.

A pilot annotated corpus and associated documentation of the argumentation coding scheme will be made available to other researchers on a temporary basis for the purpose of publicizing the planned corpus and getting feedback from potential stakeholders.

An important consideration is the selection of corpus annotation tools to facilitate argumentation mining research. On the one hand, the text mining community uses linguistic annotation tools such as GATE (http://gate.ac.uk/), UIMA (http://www.ibm.com/research/uima), and Open-NLP tools http://opennlp.sourceforge.net). It would be advisable to use tools that would allow that community to benefit from the argumentation corpus, as well as to allow argumentation mining researchers to use previously developed tools. For example, argumentation mining researchers may find it useful to automatically preprocess the corpus with linguistic annotations as well as the annotation schemes described in section 2.4. BioNLP researchers may find it useful to consider argumentation annotations as well. Just as modality and negation currently are used for BioNLP tasks, a text segment's participation in argumentation as outlined in this paper may provide useful context at a deeper level of analysis.

On the other hand, the argumentation and educational community uses tools for diagramming argumentation, e.g. Araucaria http://arg.computing.dundee.ac.uk and LASAD http://cscwlab.in.tu-clausthal.de/ lasad). It is important to maintain compatibility between argumentation mining corpora developed with linguistic annotation tools and corpora developed with diagramming tools.

6 Conclusion

This paper described our plan to create a freely available corpus of open-access, full-text scientific articles from the biomedical genetics research literature, annotated to support argumentation mining research. It discussed the argumentation elements to be annotated, theoretical challenges, and practical issues in creating such a corpus. We hope this workshop will provide an opportunity for us to get feedback from potential users (or contributors) to this effort, and possibly even identify synergistic research opportunities.

Acknowledgments

We thank Dr. Malcolm Schug of the Biology Department of the University of North Carolina Greensboro for verifying our interpretation of the arguments in the genetics article.

References

Artstein, R. and Poesio, M. 2008. Inter-Coder Agreement for Computational Linguistics. *Computational Linguistics* 34(4): 555-596.

Ashley, K.D. and Walker, V.R. 2013. Towards Con structing Evidenced-Based Legal Arguments Using Legal Decision Documents and Machine Learning. In *Proc. ICAIL 2013*, June 10-14, Rome.

Bach, N.X., Minh, N.L., Oanh, T.T., and Shimazu, A. 2013. A Two-Phase Framework for Learning Logi cal Structures of Paragraphs in Legal Articles. *ACM Trans. Asian Lang. Inform. Process.* 12, 1, Article 3 (March 2013).

Cabrio, E. and Villata, S. 2012. Generating Abstract Arguments: A Natural Language Approach. In Ver heij, B., Szeider, S., and Woltran, S. (eds.) *Computational Models of Argument: Proceedings of COMMA 2012*. Amsterdam, IOS Press, 454-461.

Dagan, I., Dolan, B., Magnini, B., and Roth, D. 2009. Recognizing textual entailment: Rationale, evalua tion, and approaches. *Natural Language Engineer ing* 15(4): i-xvii.

De Waard, A. and Pander Maat, H. 2012. Knowledge Attribution in Scientific Discourse: A Taxonomy of Types and Overview of Features. In *Proc. of the ACL 2012 Workshop on Detecting Structure in Sci entific Discourse.*

Feng, V.W. and Hirst, G. 2011. Classifying Argu ments by Scheme. In *Proceedings of the 49th Annual Meeting of the Association for Computational Lin guistics,* Portland, OR, 987-996.

Green, N. 2005a. A Bayesian Network Coding Scheme for Annotating Biomedical Information Presented to Genetic Counseling Clients. *Journal of Biomedical Informatics* 38: 130-144.

Green, N. 2005b. Analysis of Linguistic Features As sociated with Point of View for Generating Stylisti cally Appropriate Text. In J. G. Shanahan, James G., Qu, Y., and Wiebe, J. (Eds). *Computing Attitude and Affect in Text: Theory and Applications*, 33-40. Secaucus, NJ: Springer-Verlag.

Green, N. 2010a. Representation of Argumentation in Text with Rhetorical Structure Theory. *Argumenta tion* 24(2): 181-196.

Green, N. 2010b. Analysis of communication of un certainty in genetic counseling patient letters for design of a natural language generation system. *So cial Semiotics*. 20(1):77-86.

Green, N., Dwight, R., Navoraphan, K., and Stadler, B. 2011. Natural Language Generation of Transpar ent Arguments for Lay Audiences. *Argument and Computation* 2(1): 23-50.

Green, N. and Schug, M. In preparation. Modeling Argumentation in Scientific Discourse.

Liakata, M, et al. 2012a. Automatic recognition of conceptualization zones in scientific articles and two life science applications. *Bioinformatics* 28(7).

Liakata, M., et al. 2012b. A Three-Way Perspective on Scientific Discourse Annotation for Knowledge Extraction. In *Proc. of the ACL 2012 Workshop on Detecting Structure in Scientific Discourse,* 37-46.

Mizuta, Y., Korhonen, A., Mullen, T. and Collier, N. 2005. Zone Analysis in Biology Articles as a Basis for Information Extraction. *International Journal of Medical Informatics* 75(6): 468-487.

Mochales, R. and Moens, M. 2011. Argumentation mining. *Artificial Intelligence and Law* 19, 1-22.

Monteserin, A. and Amandi, A. 2010. Building user argumentative models. *Applied Intelligence* 32, 131-145.

Reed, C. and Rowe, G. 2004. Araucaria: Software for argument analysis, diagramming and representation. *International Journal of Artificial Intelligence Tools* 14, 961-980.

Reed, C., Mochales-Palau, R., Moens, M., and Milward, D. 2010. Language resources for studying argument. In *Proceedings of the 6th Conference on Language Resources and Evaluation, LREC2008, ELRA*, 91-100.

Schrauwen et al. 2012. A Mutation in CABP2, Expressed in Cochlear Hair Cells, Causes Autosomal-Recessive Hearing Impairment. *The American Journal of Human Genetics* 91, 636-645, October 5, 2012.

Teufel, S. and Moens, M. 2002. Summarizing Scien tific Articles: Experiments with Relevance and Rhetorical Status. *Computational Linguistics* 28(4), 409-445.

Teufel, S. 2010. *The Structure of Scientific Articles: Applications to Citation Indexing and Summarization*. Stanford, CA, CSLI Publications.

Thompson, P., Nawaz, R., McNaught, J. and Ananiadou, S. 2011. Enriching a biomedical event corpus with meta-knowledge annotation. *BMC Bioinfor matics*, 12: 393.

Toulmin, S. E. 1998. *The Uses of Argument*, Cambridge, UK: Cambridge University Press.

Villalba, M.P.G. and Saint-Dizier, P. 2012. Some Facets of Argument Mining for Opinion Analysis. In *Proc. COMMA 2012*, 23-34.

Walton, D., Reed, C., and Macagno, F. 2008. *Argumentation Schemes.* Cambridge University Press.

Wyner, A., Mochales-Palau, R., Moens, M-F, and Milward, D. 2010. Approaches to Text Mining Arguments from Legal Cases. In *Semantic Pro cessing of Legal Texts*, 60-79.

Wyner, A., Schneider, J., Atkinson, K., and Bench-Capon, T. 2012. Semi-Automated Argumentative Analysis of Online Product Reviews. In *Proc. COMMA 2012*, 43-50.

An automated method to build a corpus of rhetorically-classified sentences in biomedical texts

Hospice Houngbo
Department of Computer Science
The University of Western Ontario
hhoungbo@uwo.ca

Robert E. Mercer
Department of Computer Science
The University of Western Ontario
mercer@csd.uwo.ca

Abstract

The rhetorical classification of sentences in biomedical texts is an important task in the recognition of the components of a scientific argument. Generating supervised machine learned models to do this recognition requires corpora annotated for the rhetorical categories **Introduction** (or Background), **Method**, **Result**, **Discussion** (or Conclusion). Currently, a few, small annotated corpora exist. We use a straightforward feature of co-referring text using the word "this" to build a *self-annotating* corpus extracted from a large biomedical research paper dataset. The corpus is annotated for all of the rhetorical categories except **Introduction** without involving domain experts. In a 10-fold cross-validation, we report an overall F-score of 97% with Naïve Bayes and 98.7% with SVM, far above those previously reported.

1 Introduction

Sentence classification is an important preprocessing task in the recognition of the components of an argument in scientific text. For instance, sentences that are deemed as conclusions of a research paper can be used to validate or refute an hypothesis presented in background or introduction sentences in that paper. Therefore, in order to understand the argumentation flow in scientific publications, we need to understand how different sentences fit into the complete rhetorical structure of scientific writing.

To perform sentence classification using supervised machine learning techniques requires a large training corpus annotated with the appropriate classification tags. In the biomedical domain, some corpora already exist, but many of these corpora are still limited and cannot be generalized to every context. The task of sentence classification in various rhetorical categories is often performed on *ad hoc* corpora derived from a limited number of papers that don't necessarily represent all of the text in the biomedical domain. For instance, the corpus used by Agarwal and Yu (2009) for the task of sentence classification into the IMRaD categories, is composed of only 1131 sentences.

In this study, we hypothesize that using a simple linguistically-based heuristic, we can build a significantly larger corpus comprising sentences that belong to specific categories of the IMRaD rhetorical structure of the biomedical research text, that will not need domain experts to annotate them, and will represent a wider range of publications in the biomedical literature. We have collected pairs of sequential sentences where the second sentence begins with "This method...", "This result...", "This conclusion...". Our hypothesis is that the first sentence in each pair is a sentence that can be categorized respectively as **Method**, **Result** and **Conclusion** sentences.

We have a number of motivations for this work. First, sentences are the basis for most text mining and extraction systems. The second motivation is that biomedical texts are the reports of scientific investigations and their discourse structures should represent the scientific method that drives these investigations. The third and last motivation is that categorizing sentences into the IMRaD categories can help in the task of extracting knowledge discovery elements from scientific papers.

The contribution of our work is twofold. First, we have used a simple linguistic filter to automatically select thousands of sentences that have a high probability of being correctly categorized in the IMRAD scheme, and second, we have used machine learning techniques to classify sentences in order to validate our hypothesis that this linguistic filter works. The rest of this paper is organized as follows. The next section reviews some related

Proceedings of the First Workshop on Argumentation Mining, pages 19–23,
Baltimore, Maryland USA, June 26, 2014.

work. In Section 3, a detailed methodology of corpus construction and sentence classification techniques is presented. In Section 4, the results are described.

2 Related Work

The classification of sentences from scientific research papers into different categories has been investigated in previous works. Many schemes have been used and currently no standard classification scheme has been agreed upon. Teufel et al. (1999) use a classification scheme termed Argumentative Zoning (AZ) to model the rhetorical and argumentative aspects of scientific writing in order to easily detect the different claims that are mentioned in a scientific research paper. AZ has been modified for the annotation of biology articles (Yoko et al., 2006) and chemistry articles (Teufel et al., 2009).

Scientific discourse has also been studied in terms of speculation and modality by Kilicoglu and Bergler (2008) and Medlock and Briscoe (2007). Also, Shatkay et al. (2008) and Wilbur et al. (2006) have proposed an annotation scheme that categorizes sentences according to various dimensions such as focus, polarity and certainty. Many annotation units have also be proposed in previous studies. Sentence level annotation is used in Teufel et al. (1999) whereas de Waard et al. (2009) used a multi-dimensional scheme for the annotation of biomedical events (bio-events) in texts.

Liakata et al. (2012) attempt to classify sentences into the Core Scientific Concept (CoreSC) scheme. This classification scheme consists of a number of categories distributed into hierarchical layers. The first layer consists of 11 categories, which describe the main components of a scientific investigation, the second layer consists of properties of those categories (e.g. Novelty, Advantage), and the third layer provides identifiers that link together instances of the same concept.

Some other recent works have focussed on the classification of sentences from biomedical articles into the IMRaD (Introduction, Methods, Research, and, Discussion) categories. Agarwal and Yu (2009) use a corpus of 1131 sentences to classify sentences from biomedical research papers into these categories. In this study, sentence level annotation is used and multinomial Naïve Bayes machine learning has proved to perform better than simple Naïve Bayes. The authors report an overall F-measure score of 91.55% with a mutual information feature selection technique. The present study provides an alternative way to build a larger IMRaD annotated corpus, which combined with existing corpora achieves a better performance.

Methods for training supervised machine-learning systems on non-annotated data, were presented in (Yu and Hatzivassiloglou, 2003), which assumed that in a full-text, IMRaD-structured article, the majority of sentences in each section will be classified into their respective IMRaD category. Also, Agarwal and Yu (2009) used the same method to build a baseline classifier that achieved about 77.81% accuracy on their corpus.

3 Methodology

3.1 Constructing a self-annotating corpus from a biomedical dataset

The goal of this study is to show that the classification of sentences from scientific research papers to match the IMRaD rhetorical structure with supervised machine learning can be enhanced using a self-annotating corpus. The first task consists of the curation of a corpus that contains sentences representative of the defined categorization scheme. We have chosen to build the corpus by extracting sentences from a large repository of full-text scientific research papers, a publicly available full-text subset of the PubMed repository.

Since most demonstrative pronouns are co-referential, a sentence that begins with the demonstrative noun phrase "This method..." or "This result..." or "This conclusion..." is co-referential and its antecedents are likely to be found in previous sentences. Torii and Vijay-Shanker (2005) reported that nearly all antecedents of such demonstrative phrases can be found within two sentences. As well, Hunston (2008) reported that interpreting recurring phrases in a large corpus enables us to capture the consistency in meaning as well as the role of specific words in such phrases. So, the recurring semantic sequences "This method..." or "This result..." or "This conclusion..." in the Pubmed corpus can help us to capture valuable information in the context of their usage. A similar technique was used in (Houngbo and Mercer, 2012), to build a corpus for method mention extraction from biomedical research papers.

Our assumption is that a sentence that appears

in the co-referential context of the co-referencing phrase "This method...", will likely talk about a methodology used in a research experiment or analysis. Similarly, a sentence that starts with the expression "This result..." is likely to refer to a result. And, similarly, for sentences that begin with "This conclusion...". The **Introduction** (Background) rhetorical category does not have a similar co-referential structure. We have chosen to only consider the immediately preceding sentence to the "This" referencing sentence. Some examples are shown below.

Category	# of Sentences	Proportion
Method	3163	31.9%
Result	6288	62.7%
Conclusion	534	5.4%
Total	9985	100%

Table 1: Initial Self-annotated Corpus Statistics

1. *We have developed a DNA microarray-based method for measuring transcript length ...* **This method**, called the Virtual Northern, is a complementary approach ...

2. *Interestingly, Drice the downstream caspase activated ... was not affected by inhibition of Dronc and Dredd.* **This result**, ... suggests that some other mechanism activates Drice.

3. *We obtained a long-range PCR product from the latter interval, that appeared to encompass the breakpoint on chromosome 2 ...* **This conclusion**, however , was regarded with caution , since ...

Table 1 shows the number of sentences per category in this initial self-annotated corpus.

3.1.1 Feature Extraction

We have used the set of features extracted from the Agarwal and Yu (2009) IMRaD corpus. The reason for this choice is to be able to validate our claim against this previous work. Agarwal and Yu (2009) experimented with mutual information and chi-squared for feature selection and obtained their best performance using the top 2500 features comprised of a combination of individual words as well as bigrams and trigrams. A feature that indicates the presence of a citation in a sentence is also used as it can be an important feature for distinguishing some categories; for example, citations are more frequently used in **Introduction** than in **Results**. All numbers were replaced by a unique symbol #NuMBeR. Stop words were not removed since certain stop words are also more likely to be associated with certain IMRaD categories. Words that refer to a figure or table are not removed, since such references are more likely to occur in sentences indicating the outcome of the study. We also used verb tense features as some categories may be associated with the presence of the present tense or the past tense in the sentence. We used the Stanford parser (Klein and Manning, 2003) to identify these tenses.

(a) Classification with Multinomial Naïve Bayes.

Class	Precision	Recall	F-Measure
Method	0.923	0.661	0.77
Result	0.627	0.813	0.708
Conclusion	0.68	0.821	0.744
Average	0.779	0.74	0.744

(b) Classification with Support Vector Machine

Class	Precision	Recall	F-Measure
Method	0.818	0.521	0.636
Result	0.511	0.908	0.654
Conclusion	0.923	0.226	0.364
Average	0.72	0.621	0.604

Table 2: Precision, Recall, F-measure : Classifier trained with the initial self-annotated corpus and tested on a reduced Agarwal and Yu (2009) corpus (Method, Result, Conclusion)

3.1.2 Self-annotation

In our first experiment we trained a model on the initial self-annotated corpus discussed above and tested the model on the Agarwal and Yu (2009) corpus. Table 2 shows F-measures that are below the baseline classifier levels. We suggest that there are two causes: many of the important n-grams in the larger corpus are not present in the 2500 n-gram feature set; and there is noise in the initial self-annotated corpus. To reduce the noise in the initial self-annotated corpus and to maintain the 2500 n-gram feature set we pruned our initial self-annotated corpus using a semi-supervised learning step using an initial model based on the Agarwal and Yu feature set and learned from the Agarwal and Yu corpus. We describe below the semi-supervised method to do this pruning of the initial self-annotated corpus.

Our method for categorizing sentences into the IMRaD categories does not work for the **Introduction** category, so from the Agarwal and Yu (2009) IMRaD corpus, we have extracted instances belonging to the **Method**, **Result** and **Conclusion** categories and have used this corpus to build a model with a supervised multinomial Naïve Bayes method. This model is then used to classify sentences in the initial self-annotated corpus. When the model matches the initial self-annotated corpus category with a confidence level greater than 98%, this instance is added to what we will now call the model-validated self-annotated corpus. The composition of this model-validated corpus is presented in Table 3.

Category	# of Sentences	Proportion
Method	878	23.6%
Result	2399	64.5%
Conclusion	443	11.9%
Total	3719	100%

Table 3: Model-validated Self-annotated Corpus Statistics

3.2 Automatic text classification

For all supervised learning, we have used two popular supervised machine-learning algorithms, multinomial Naïve Bayes (NB) and Support Vector Machine (SVM), provided by the open-source Java-based machine-learning library Weka 3.7 (Witten and Frank, 2005).

4 Results and Discussion

In the first classification task a classifier is trained with the model-validated self-annotated corpus using 10-fold cross-validation. The model achieves an F-measure score of 97% with NB and 98.7% with SVM. See Table 4. The average F-measure that Agarwal and Yu (2009) report for their 10-fold cross-validation (which includes **Introduction**) is 91.55. The category F-measures that Agarwal and Yu (2009) report for their 10-fold cross-validation with the features that we use are: **Method**: 91.4 (95.04) (their best scores, in parentheses, require inclusion of the IMRaD section as a feature), **Result**: 88.3 (92.24), and **Conclusion**: 69.03 (73.77).

In the last classification task, a classifier is trained with the model-validated self-annotated corpus and tested on the Agarwal and Yu (2009) corpus. The F-measures in Table 5 are a substantial improvement over those in Table 2.

(a) Classification with Multinomial Naïve Bayes.

Class	Precision	Recall	F-Measure
Method	0.981	0.957	0.969
Result	0.966	0.992	0.979
Conclusion	0.98	0.885	0.93
Average	0.971	0.971	0.971

(b) Classification with Support Vector Machine

Class	Precision	Recall	F-Measure
Method	0.986	0.984	0.985
Result	0.988	0.995	0.992
Conclusion	0.986	0.95	0.968
Average	0.987	0.987	0.987

Table 4: Precision, Recall, F-measure : Classifier trained with the model-validated self-annotated corpus (Method, Result, Conclusion) using 10-fold cross-validation

(a) Classification with Multinomial Naïve Bayes.

Class	Precision	Recall	F-Measure
Method	0.937	0.806	0.866
Result	0.763	0.873	0.814
Conclusion	0.836	0.911	0.872
Average	0.858	0.847	0.848

(b) Classification with Support Vector Machine

Class	Precision	Recall	F-Measure
Method	0.893	0.824	0.857
Result	0.763	0.85	0.804
Conclusion	0.835	0.811	0.823
Average	0.837	0.832	0.833

Table 5: Precision, Recall, F-measure : Classifier trained with the model-validated self-annotated corpus and tested on a reduced Agarwal and Yu (2009) corpus (Method, Result, Conclusion)

Sentence classification is important in determining the different components of argumentation. We have suggested a method to annotate sentences from scientific research papers into their IMRaD categories, excluding **Introduction**. Our results show that it is possible to extract a large self-annotated corpus automatically from a large repository of scientific research papers that generates very good supervised machine learned models.

Acknowledgments

This work was partially funded through a Natural Sciences and Engineering Research Council of Canada (NSERC) Discovery Grant to R. Mercer.

References

Shashank Agarwal and Hong Yu. 2009. Automatically classifying sentences in full-text biomedical articles into introduction, methods, results and discussion. *Bioinformatics*, 25(23):3174–3180.

Anita de Waard, Paul Buitelaar, and Thomas Eigner. 2009. Identifying the epistemic value of discourse segments in biology texts. In *Proceedings of the Eighth International Conference on Computational Semantics*, IWCS-8 '09, pages 351–354. Association for Computational Linguistics.

Hospice Houngbo and Robert E. Mercer. 2012. Method mention extraction from scientific research papers. In *Proceedings of COLING 2012*, pages 1211–1222, Mumbai, India.

Susan Hunston. 2008. Starting with the small words. Patterns, lexis and semantic sequences. *International Journal of Corpus Linguistics*, 13:271–295.

Halil Kilicoglu and Sabine Bergler. 2008. Recognizing speculative language in biomedical research articles: A linguistically motivated perspective. *BMC Bioinformatics*, 9(S-11):S10.

Dan Klein and Christopher D. Manning. 2003. Accurate unlexicalized parsing. In *Proceedings of the 41st Annual Meeting on Association for Computational Linguistics*, ACL '03, pages 423–430. Association for Computational Linguistics.

Maria Liakata, Shyamasree Saha, Simon Dobnik, Colin R. Batchelor, and Dietrich Rebholz-Schuhmann. 2012. Automatic recognition of conceptualization zones in scientific articles and two life science applications. *Bioinformatics*, 28(7):991–1000.

Ben Medlock and Ted Briscoe. 2007. Weakly supervised learning for hedge classification in scientific literature. In *Proceedings of the 45th Annual Meeting of the Association of Computational Linguistics*, ACL '07, pages 992–999. Association for Computational Linguistics.

Hagit Shatkay, Fengxia Pan, Andrey Rzhetsky, and W. John Wilbur. 2008. Multi-dimensional classification of biomedical text: Toward automated, practical provision of high-utility text to diverse users. *Bioinformatics*, 24(18):2086–2093.

Simone Teufel, Jean Carletta, and Marc Moens. 1999. An annotation scheme for discourse-level argumentation in research articles. In *Proceedings of the Ninth Conference of the European Chapter of the Association for Computational Linguistics*, pages 110–117. Association for Computational Linguistics.

Simone Teufel, Advaith Siddharthan, and Colin Batchelor. 2009. Towards discipline-independent argumentative zoning: Evidence from chemistry and computational linguistics. In *Proceedings of the 2009 Conference on Empirical Methods in Natural Language Processing: Volume 3*, EMNLP '09, pages 1493–1502. Association for Computational Linguistics.

Manabu Torii and K. Vijay-Shanker. 2005. Anaphora resolution of demonstrative noun phrases in Medline abstracts. In *Proceedings of PACLING 2005*, pages 332–339.

W. John Wilbur, Andrey Rzhetsky, and Hagit Shatkay. 2006. New directions in biomedical text annotation: definitions, guidelines and corpus construction. *BMC Bioinformatics*, 7:356.

Ian H. Witten and Eibe Frank. 2005. *Data Mining: Practical Machine Learning Tools and Techniques*. Morgan Kaufmann Series in Data Management Systems. Morgan Kaufmann Publishers Inc., San Francisco, CA, USA, 2nd edition.

Mizuta Yoko, Anna Korhonen, Tony Mullen, and Nigel Collier. 2006. Zone analysis in biology articles as a basis for information extraction. *International Journal of Medical Informatics*, 75:468–487.

Hong Yu and Vasileios Hatzivassiloglou. 2003. Towards answering opinion questions: Separating facts from opinions and identifying the polarity of opinion sentences. In *Proceedings of the 2003 Conference on Empirical Methods in Natural Language Processing*, EMNLP '03, pages 129–136. Association for Computational Linguistics.

Ontology-Based Argument Mining and Automatic Essay Scoring

Nathan Ong, Diane Litman, and Alexandra Brusilovsky
Department of Computer Science, University of Pittsburgh
Pittsburgh, PA 15260 USA
nro5,dlitman,apb27@pitt.edu

Abstract

Essays are frequently used as a medium for teaching and evaluating argumentation skills. Recently, there has been interest in diagrammatic outlining as a replacement to the written outline that often precedes essay writing. This paper presents a preliminary approach for automatically identifying diagram ontology elements in essays, and demonstrates its positive correlation with expert scores of essay quality.

1 Introduction

Educators tend to favor students providing a minimal-writing structure, or an outline, before writing a paper. This allows teachers to give early feedback to students to reduce the amount of structural editing that might be needed later on. However, there is evidence to suggest that standard text-based outlines do not necessarily improve writing quality (Torrance et al., 2000). Recently, there has been growing interest in graphical outline representations, especially for argumentative essays in various domains (Scheuer et al., 2009; Scheuer et al., 2010; Peldszus and Stede, 2013; Reed and Rowe, 2004; Reed et al., 2007). Not only do they provide a different outlining format, but they also allow students to concretely visualize their argumentation structure. Our work is part of the ArgumentPeer project (Falakmassir et al., 2013), which combines computer-supported argument diagramming and peer-review with the goal of improving students' writing skills.

In this paper, we follow the lead of others in discourse parsing for essay scoring (Burstein et al., 2001), and we preliminarily attempt to answer two questions: Q1) Can an argument mining system be developed to automatically recognize the argument ontology used during diagramming, when processing a student's later written essay? Q2) If so, is the number of ontological elements that can be recognized in a student's essay correlated with the essay's argumentation quality? Potentially, answering these questions in the affirmative would allow us to assist students with their writing by allowing computer tutors to label sentences with the ontology, determine which elements are missing, and suggest adding these missing elements to improve essay quality.

2 Corpus

Our corpus for argument mining consists of 52 essays written in two University of Pittsburgh undergraduate psychology courses. In both courses, students were asked to write an argumentative essay supporting two separate hypotheses that they created based on data they were given. The average essay contains 5.2 paragraphs, 28.6 sentences, and 592.1 words.

Before writing the essay, students were first required to generate an argument diagram justifying their hypotheses using the LASAD argumentation system[1]. LASAD argument diagrams consist of nodes and arcs from an instructor-defined ontology, as shown in Figure 1. Next, students were required to turn their diagrams into written argumentative essays. Automatically tagging these essays according to the 4 node types (**Current Study, Hypothesis, Claim, Citation**) and 2 arc types (**Supports, Opposes**) common to both courses is the argument mining goal of this paper. The tagged essay corresponding to Figure 1 is shown in Table 1.[2] While the diagram is required to be completed by students, this work does not utilize the student diagrams.

[1] http://lasad.dfki.de

[2] Both diagrams and papers were distributed to other students in the class for peer review. While the diagrams were not required to be revised, students needed to revise their essays to address peer feedback. To maximize diagram and essay similarity, here we work with only the first drafts.

Proceedings of the First Workshop on Argumentation Mining, pages 24–28,
Baltimore, Maryland USA, June 26, 2014.

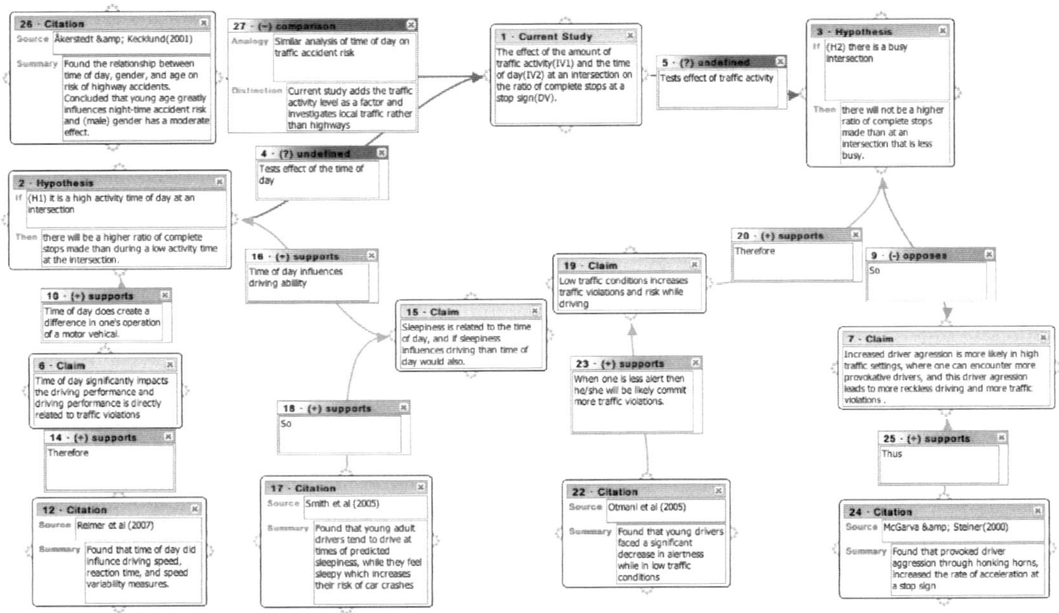

Figure 1: An argument diagram from a research methods course.

After the courses, expert graders were asked to score all essays on a 5-point Likert scale (with 1 being the lowest and 5 being the highest) without the diagrams, using a rubric with multiple criteria. For the essay as a whole, graders not only checked for correct grammar usage, but also for flow and organization. In addition, essays were graded based on the logic behind their argumentation of their hypotheses, as well as addressing claims that both supported and opposed their hypotheses. While not an explicit category, many of the criteria required students to present multiple citations backing their hypotheses. The average expert score for the 52 essays is 3.03, and the median is 3, with the scores distributed as shown in column four of Table 2.

3 Methodology

Essay Discourse Processing. Firstly, raw essays are parsed for discourse connectives. Explicit discourse connectives are then tagged with their sense (i.e. *Expansion, Contingency, Comparison*, or *Temporal*) using the Discourse Connectives Tagger[3], as shown in Table 1.

Mining the Argument Ontology. We developed a rule-based algorithm to label each sentence in an essay with at most one label from our target argument ontology. Our rules were developed using our intuition and informal examination of 9 essays from the corpus of 52. The algorithm consists of the following ordered[4] rules:

Rule 1: If the sentence begins with a *Comparison* discourse connective, or if the sentence contains any string prefixes from {conflict, oppose} and a four-digit number (intended as a year for a citation), then tag with **Opposes**.

Rule 2: If the sentence begins with a *Contingency* connective and does not contain a four-digit number, then tag with **Supports**.

Rule 3: If the sentence contains a four-digit number, then tag with **Citation**.

Rule 4: If the sentence contains string prefixes from {suggest, evidence, shows, Essentially, indicate} (case-sensitive), then tag with **Claim**.

Rule 5: If the sentence is in the first, second, or last paragraph, and contains string prefixes from {hypothes, predict}, or if the sentence contains the word "should" and contains no *Contingency* connectives, and does not contain a four-digit number and does not contain string prefixes from {conflict, oppose}, then tag with **Hypothesis**.

Rule 6: If the previous sentence was tagged with Hypothesis, and this sentence begins with an *Expansion* connective and does not contain a four-

[3] http://www.cis.upenn.edu/~epitler/discourse.html

[4] When multiple rules apply, the tag of the earliest is used.

#	Essay Sentence	Label	Rule
1	The ultimate goal of this study is to investigate the relationship between stop-sign violations and traffic activity.	Current Study	7
2	To do this we analyzed two different variables on traffic activity: time of day and location.	None	8
...	...	...	...
6	Stop-signs indicate that the driver must come to a complete stop before the sign and check for oncoming and opposing traffic before[-*Temporal*] proceeding on.	Claim	4
7	For a stop to be considered complete the car must completely stop moving.	None	8
...	...	...	...
16	The first hypothesis was: If[-*Contingency*] it is a high activity time of day at an intersection then[-Contingency], there will be a higher ratio of complete stops made than during a low activity time at the intersection.	Hypothesis	5
17	The second hypothesis was: If[-*Contingency*] there is a busy intersection then[-*Contingency*], there will be a higher ratio of complete stops made than at an intersection that is less busy.	Hypothesis	5
18	So[-*Contingency*] essentially, it was expected that when[-*Temporal*] there was a higher traffic activity level, either due to location or time of day, there were to be less stop-sign violations.	Supports	2
19	There have been many studies which indicate that people do drive differently at different times of day and[-*Expansion*] that it does have an impact on driving risk.	Claim	4
20	Reimer et al (2007) found that time of day did influence driving speed, reaction time, and speed variability measures.	Citation	3
...	...	...	...
24	However[-*Comparison*], McGarva & Steiner (2000) oppose the second hypothesis because[-*Contingency*] they found that provoked driver aggression through honking horns, increased the rate of acceleration at a stop sign.	Opposes	1
...	...	...	...

Table 1: Essay sentences, their mined ontological labels, and rules used to determine the labels, for the essay associated with Figure 1. Inferred discourse connective senses are *italicized* in square brackets.

digit number, then tag with **Hypothesis**.

Rule 7: If the sentence is in the first or last paragraph and contains at least one word from {study, research} and does not contain the words {past, previous, prior} (first letter case-insensitive) and does not contain string prefixes from {hypothes, predict} and does not contain a four-digit number, then tag with **Current Study**.

Rule 8: Do not assign a tag to the sentence.

Some sample output can be found on Table 1. Note that sentence 24 could have been tagged as **Citation** using Rule 3, but because it fits the criteria for Rule 1, it is tagged as **Opposes**.

Ontology-Based Essay Scoring. We also developed a rule-based algorithm to score each essay in the corpus. These rules were developed using our intuition in conjunction with the examination of the expert grading rubric. These rules take a labeled essay from the argument mining algorithm and outputs a score in the continuous range [0,5] using the following procedure:[5]

1: Assign one point to essays that have at least one sentence tagged with **Current Study** (**CS**).

2: Assign one point to essays that have at least one sentence tagged with **Hypothesis** (**H**).

3: Assign one point to essays that have at least one sentence tagged with **Opposes** (**O**).

4: Assign points based on the sum of the number of sentences tagged with **Claim** (**Cl**) and the number of sentences tagged with **Supports** (**S**), all divided by the number of paragraphs (**#¶**). If this

[5]Score 0 occurs when no labels are assigned to the essay.

value exceeds 1, assign only one point.

5: Assign points based on the number of sentences tagged with **Citation (Ci)** divided by the number of paragraphs (**#¶**). If this value exceeds 1, assign only one point.

6: Sum all of the previously computed points.

For the three paragraph essay excerpted in Table 1 (assigned expert score 3), there were three sentences tagged with **Current Study**, three with **Hypothesis,** one with **Opposes**, one with **Supports**, two with **Claim** and three with **Citation**. The score is computed as follows:

$$1_{CS} + 1_H + 1_O + \frac{2_{Cl} + 1_S}{3_{\#\P}} + \frac{3_{Ci}}{3_{\#\P}} = 5$$

4 Results

Since our essays do not have gold-standard ontology labels yet, we cannot intrinsically evaluate the argument mining algorithm. We instead performed an extrinsic evaluation via our use of the mined argument labels for essay scoring.

The average automatic score for the corpus is 3.42 and the median is 3.5, while the corresponding expert values are 3.03 and 3, respectively. A paired t-test of the means has a significance of $p < 0.01$, suggesting that our algorithm over-scores the essays. We also ran a one-sample t-test on each expert score value to see if the automatic scores were similar to the expert scores. We hypothesized that within each expert score category predicted accurately, we should not see a significant difference ($p \geq 0.05$). Table 2 shows that while the automatic score is not significantly different for expert score 4, the scores are significantly different for scores 2 and 3.

We also examined the Spearman's rank correlation between the computed and expert scores.[6] We see that the Spearman's rank correlation shows significance of $p < 0.0001$ with a rho value of 0.997. Together these metrics suggest that our automated scores are currently useful for ranking but not for rating.

5 Conclusion and Future Work

We have presented simple rule-based algorithms for argumentation mining in student essays and essay scoring using argument mining. Based on preliminary extrinsic evaluation, our pattern-based recognition of a basic argumentation ontology seems to provide some insight into essay scores across two courses. While the automatic scores did not necessarily reflect the expert scores, the ranking correlation demonstrated that more argumentative elements were related to higher scores. Even with the limitations of this study (e.g. no intrinsic evaluation, a small essay corpus, a limited argument ontology, a scoring algorithm using only ontology features, application of discourse connector for a different genre), our results suggest the promise of using argument mining to trigger feedback in a writing tutoring system.

To develop a more linguistically sophisticated and accurate argument mining algorithm, our future plans include exploiting discourse information beyond connectives, e.g., by parsing our essays in terms of PDTB (Lin et al., 2011) or RST relations (Feng and Hirst, 2012). We also plan to look at the helpfulness of argumentation schemes (Feng and Hirst, 2011), and other linguistic and essay features for automatic evaluation (Crossley and McNamara, 2010). In addition, our essays are being annotated with diagram ontology labels, which will enable us to use machine learning to conduct intrinsic argument mining evaluations and to learn the weights for each rule or determine new rules. Finally, we plan to explore using the diagrams to bootstrap the essay annotation process. While some sentences in an essay can easily be mapped to the corresponding diagram (e.g. sentence 1 in Table 1 to node 1 in Figure 1), the complication is that essays tend to be more fleshed-out than diagrams, and at least in our corpus, also contain argument changes motivated by diagram peer-review. While sentence 6 in Table 1 is correctly tagged as a **Claim**, this content is not in Figure 1.

expert score	avg. auto score	t	n	p
1	4.33	–	1	–
2	3.23	3.21	8	0.013
3	3.30	2.10	31	0.044
4	3.80	-1.00	12	0.337

Table 2: One-sample t-test results for scores.

Acknowledgments

This work is supported by NSF Award 1122504. We thank Huy Nguyen, Wenting Xiong, and Michael Lipschultz.

[6] A Pearson correlation did not give significant results.

References

[Burstein et al.2001] Jill Burstein, Karen Kukich, Susanne Wolff, Ji Lu, and Martin Chodorow. 2001. *Enriching automated essay scoring using discourse marking*. ERIC Clearinghouse.

[Crossley and McNamara2010] Scott A Crossley and Danielle S McNamara. 2010. Cohesion, coherence, and expert evaluations of writing proficiency. In *Proceedings of the 32nd annual conference of the Cognitive Science Society*, pages 984–989. Austin, TX: Cognitive ScienceSociety.

[Falakmassir et al.2013] Mohammad Falakmassir, Kevin Ashley, and Christian Schunn. 2013. Using argument diagramming to improve peer grading of writing assignments. In *Proceedings of the 1st Workshop on Massive Open Online Courses at the 16th Annual Conference on Artificial Intelligence in Education*, Memphis, TN.

[Feng and Hirst2011] Vanessa Wei Feng and Graeme Hirst. 2011. Classifying arguments by scheme. In *Proceedings of the 49th Annual Meeting of the Association for Computational Linguistics: Human Language Technologies-Volume 1*, pages 987–996. Association for Computational Linguistics.

[Feng and Hirst2012] Vanessa Wei Feng and Graeme Hirst. 2012. Text-level discourse parsing with rich linguistic features. In *Proceedings of the 50th Annual Meeting of the Association for Computational Linguistics: Long Papers-Volume 1*, pages 60–68. Association for Computational Linguistics.

[Lin et al.2011] Ziheng Lin, Hwee Tou Ng, and Min-Yen Kan. 2011. Automatically evaluating text coherence using discourse relations. In *Proceedings of the 49th Annual Meeting of the Association for Computational Linguistics: Human Language Technologies-Volume 1*, pages 997–1006. Association for Computational Linguistics.

[Peldszus and Stede2013] Andreas Peldszus and Manfred Stede. 2013. From argument diagrams to argumentation mining in texts: A survey. *International Journal of Cognitive Informatics and Natural Intelligence (IJCINI)*, 7(1):1–31.

[Reed and Rowe2004] Chris Reed and Glenn Rowe. 2004. Araucaria: Software for argument analysis, diagramming and representation. *International Journal on Artificial Intelligence Tools*, 13(04):961–979.

[Reed et al.2007] Chris Reed, Douglas Walton, and Fabrizio Macagno. 2007. Argument diagramming in logic, law and artificial intelligence. *The Knowledge Engineering Review*, 22(01):87–109.

[Scheuer et al.2009] Oliver Scheuer, Bruce M. McLaren, Frank Loll, and Niels Pinkwart. 2009. An analysis and feedback infrastructure for argumentation learning systems. In *Proceedings of the 2009 Conference on Artificial Intelligence in Education: Building Learning Systems That Care: From Knowledge Representation to Affective Modelling*, pages 629–631, Amsterdam, The Netherlands, The Netherlands. IOS Press.

[Scheuer et al.2010] Oliver Scheuer, Frank Loll, Niels Pinkwart, and Bruce M. McLaren. 2010. Computer-supported argumentation: A review of the state of the art. *International Journal of Computer-Supported Collaborative Learning*, 5(1):43–102.

[Torrance et al.2000] Mark Torrance, Glyn V. Thomas, and Elizabeth J. Robinson. 2000. Individual differences in undergraduate essay-writing strategies: A longitudinal study. *Higher Education*, 39(2):181–200.

Identifying Appropriate Support for Propositions in Online User Comments

Joonsuk Park
Department of Computer Science
Cornell University
Ithaca, NY, USA
jpark@cs.cornell.edu

Claire Cardie
Department of Computer Science
Cornell University
Ithaca, NY, USA
cardie@cs.cornell.edu

Abstract

The ability to analyze the adequacy of supporting information is necessary for determining the strength of an argument.[1] This is especially the case for online user comments, which often consist of arguments lacking proper substantiation and reasoning. Thus, we develop a framework for automatically classifying each proposition as UNVERIFIABLE, VERIFIABLE NON-EXPERIENTIAL, or VERIFIABLE EXPERIENTIAL[2], where the appropriate type of support is *reason*, *evidence*, and *optional evidence*, respectively[3]. Once the existing support for propositions are identified, this classification can provide an estimate of how adequately the arguments have been supported. We build a gold-standard dataset of 9,476 sentences and clauses from 1,047 comments submitted to an eRulemaking platform and find that Support Vector Machine (SVM) classifiers trained with n-grams and additional features capturing the verifiability and experientiality exhibit statistically significant improvement over the unigram baseline, achieving a macro-averaged F_1 of 68.99%.

1 Introduction

Argumentation mining is a relatively new field focusing on identifying and extracting argumentative structures in documents. An *argument* is typically defined as a conclusion with supporting premises, which can be conclusions of other arguments themselves (Toulmin, 1958; Toulmin et al., 1979; Pollock, 1987). To date, much of the argumentation mining research has been conducted on domains like news articles, parliamentary records and legal documents, where the documents contain well-formed explicit arguments, i.e. propositions with supporting reasons and evidence present in the text (Moens et al., 2007; Palau and Moens, 2009; Wyner et al., 2010; Feng and Hirst, 2011; Ashley and Walker, 2013).

Unlike documents written by professionals, online user comments often contain arguments with inappropriate or missing justification. One way to deal with such implicit arguments is to simply disregard them and focus on extracting arguments containing proper support (Villalba and Saint-Dizier, 2012; Cabrio and Villata, 2012). However, recognizing such propositions as part of an argument,[4] and determining the appropriate types of support can be useful for assessing the adequacy of the supporting information, and in turn, the strength of the whole argument. Consider the following examples:

> *How much does a small carton of milk cost?$_1$ More children should drink milk$_2$, because children who drink milk everyday are taller than those who don't$_3$. Children would want to drink milk, anyway$_4$.*

Firstly, **Sentence 1** does not need any support, nor is it part of an argument. Next, **Proposition 2** is an *unverifiable* proposition because it cannot be proved with objective evidence, due to the value judgement. Instead, it can be supported by a reason explaining why it may be true. If the reason, **Proposition 3**, were not true, the whole ar-

[1] In this work, even unsupported propositions are consider part of an argument. Not disregarding such implicit arguments allows us to discuss the types of support that can further be provided to strengthen the argument, as a form of assessment.

[2] Verifiable Experiential propositions are verifiable propositions about personal state or experience. See Table 1 for examples.

[3] We are assuming that there is no background knowledge that eliminates the need of support.

[4] Not all sentences in user comments are part of an argument, e.g. questions and greetings. We address this in Section 4.1

Proceedings of the First Workshop on Argumentation Mining, pages 29–38,
Baltimore, Maryland USA, June 26, 2014.

gument would fall apart, giving little weight to **Proposition 2**. Thus, an objective evidence supporting **Proposition 3**, which is a *verifiable* proposition, could be provided to strengthen the argument. Lastly, as **Proposition 4** is *unverifiable*, we cannot expect an objective evidence that proves it, but a reason as its support. Note that providing a reason why **Proposition 3** might be true is not as effective as substantiating it with a proof, but is still better than having no support. This shows that not only the presence, but also the type of supporting information affects the strength of the argument.

Examining each proposition in this way, i.e. with respect to its verifiability, provides a means to determine the desirable types of support, if any, and enables the analysis of the arguments in terms of the adequacy of their support. Thus, we propose the task of classifying each proposition (the elementary unit of argumentation in this work) in an argument as UNVERIFIABLE, VERIFIABLE PUBLIC, or VERIFIABLE PRIVATE, where the appropriate type of support is *reason*, *evidence*, and *optional evidence*, respectively. To perform the experiments, we annotate 9,476 sentences and clauses from 1,047 comments extracted from an eRulemaking platform.

In the remainder of the paper, we describe the annotation scheme and a newly created dataset (Section 2), propose a supervised learning approach to the task (Section 3), evaluate the approach (Section 4), and survey related work (Section 5). We find that Support Vector Machines (SVM) classifiers trained with n-grams and other features to capture the verifiability and experientiality exhibit statistically significant improvement over the unigram baseline, achieving a macro-averaged F_1 score of 68.99%.

2 Data

We have collected and manually annotated sentences and (independent) clauses from user comments extracted from an eRulemaking website, *Regulation Room*[5]. Rulemaking is the process by which U.S. government agencies make new regulations and enact public policy; its digital counterpart — *eRulemaking* — moves the process to online platforms (see, e.g. (Park et al., 2012)). By providing platforms in which the public can discuss regulations that interest them, government agencies hope to enlist the expertise and experience of participants to create better regulations. In many rulemaking scenarios, agencies are, in fact, required to obtain feedback from the public on the proposed regulation as well as to address all substantive questions, criticisms or suggestions that are raised (Lubbers, 2006). In this way, public comments can produce changes in the final rule (Hochschild and Danielson, 1998) that, in turn, can affect millions of lives. It is crucial, therefore, for rule makers to be able to identify credible comments from those submitted.

Regulation Room is an experimental website operated by Cornell eRulemaking Initiative (CeRI)[6] to promote public participation in the rulemaking process, help users write more informative comments and build collective knowledge via active discussions guided by human moderators. *Regulation Room* hosts actual regulations from government agencies, such as the U.S. Department of Transportation.

For our research, we collected and manually annotated 9,476 propositions from 1,047 user comments from two recent rules: Airline Passenger Rights (serving peanuts on the plane, tarmac delay contingency plan, oversales of tickets, baggage fees and other airline traveller rights) and Home Mortgage Consumer Protection (loss mitigation, accounting error resolution, etc.).

2.1 Annotation Scheme

To start, we collected 1,147 comments and randomly selected 100 of them to devise an annotation scheme for identifying appropriate types of support for propositions and to train annotators. Initially, we allowed the annotators to define the span for a propositions, leading to various complications and a low inter-annotator reliability. Thus, we introduced an additional step in which comments were manually sliced into propositions (or non-propositional sentences) before being given to the annotators. A proposition or sentence found this way was split further if it consisted of two or more independent clauses. The sliced comments were then coded by two annotators into the following four disjoint classes (See Figure 1 for an overview):

Verifiable Proposition [Experiential(VERIF_{EXP}) and Non-experiential(VERIF_{NON})]. A proposition is verifiable if it contains an objective asser-

[5]http://www.regulationroom.org

[6]http://www.lawschool.cornell.edu/ceri/

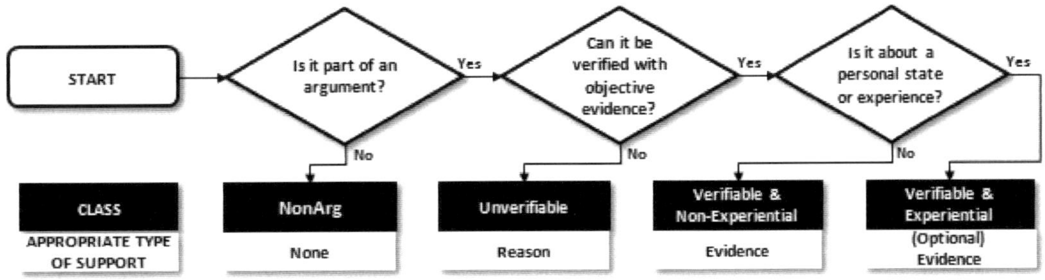

Figure 1: Flow chart for annotation (*It* refers to the sentence (or clause) being annotated)

	#	proposition
VERIF$_{EXP}$	1	I've been a physician for 20 years.
	2	My son has hypolycemia.
	3	They flew me to NY in February.
	4	The flight attendant yelled at the passengers.
VERIF$_{NON}$	5	*They can have inhalation reactions.*
	6	since *they serve them to the whole plane.*
	7	*Peanuts do not kill people.*
	8	Clearly, *peanuts do not kill people.*
	9	I believe *peanuts do not kill people.*
	10	*The governor said* that he enjoyed it.
	11	*food allergies are rare*
	12	*food allergies are seen in less than 20% of the population*
UNVERIF	13	Again, keep it simple.
	14	Banning peanuts will reduce deaths.
	15	I enjoy having peanuts on the plane.
	16	others are of uncertain significance
	17	banning peanuts is a slippery slope
NONARG	18	Who is in charge of this?
	19	I have two comments
	20	http://www.someurl.com
	21	Thanks for allowing me to comment.
	22	- Mike

Table 1: Example Sentences.

* Italics is used to illustrate *core clause* (Section 3.2).

tion, where *objective* means "expressing or dealing with facts or conditions as perceived without distortion by personal feelings, prejudices, or interpretations."[7] Such assertions have truth values that can be proved or disproved with objective evidence[8]:

Consider the examples from Table 1. propositions 1 through 7 are clearly verifiable because they only contain objective assertions. propositions 8 and 9 show that adding subjective expressions such as "Clearly" (e.g. sentence 8) or "I believe that" (e.g. sentence 9) to an objectively verifiable proposition (e.g. sentence 7) does not affect the verifiability of the proposition. Sentence 10 is considered verifiable because whether or not the governor *said* "he enjoyed the peanuts" can be verified with objective evidence, even though whether he really does or not cannot be verified.

For the purpose of identifying an appropriate type of support, we employ a rather lenient notion of objectivity: an assertion is objectively verifiable if the *domain of comparison* is free of interpretation. For instance, sentence 11 is regarded as objectively verifiable, because it is clear, i.e. it is not open for interpretation, that *percentage of the population* is the metric under comparison even though the *threshold* is purely subjective[9]. The rationale is that this type of proposition can be sufficiently substantiated with objective evidence (e.g. published statistics showing the percentage of people suffering from food allergies). Another way to think about it is that sentence 11 is a loose way of saying a (more obviously) verifiable sentence 12, where the commenter neglected to mention the threshold. This is fundamentally different from propositions 13 through 16 for which objective evidence cannot exist[10].

A verifiable proposition can further be distinguished as experiential or not, depending on whether the proposition is about the writer's personal state or experience (VERIF$_{EXP}$) or something non-experiential (VERIF$_{NON}$). This difference determines whether objective evidence is mandatory or optional with respect to the credibility of the comment. Evidence is optional when the evidence contains private information or is practically impossible to be provided: While propositions 1 through 3 can be proved with pictures of official documents, for instance, the commenters may not want to provide them for privacy reasons. Also, the website interface may not al-

[7] http://www.merriam-webster.com/

[8] The correctness of the assertion or the availability of the objective evidence does not matter.

[9] One may think anything less frequent than the average is rare and another may have more stricter notion.

[10] Objective evidence may exist for propositions that provide *reasons* for propositions 13 through 16.

Regulation	VERIF$_{NON}$	VERIF$_{EXP}$	UNVERIF	Subtotal	NONARG	Total	# of Comments
APR	1106	851	4413	6370	522	6892	820
HMCP	251	416	1733	2400	186	2586	227
Total	1357	1267	6146	8770	708	9476	1047

Table 2: Class Distribution Over Sentences and Clauses

low pictures to be uploaded in comment section, which is the case with most websites. sentence 4 is practically impossible to prove unless the commenter happened to have recorded the conversation, and the website interface allows multimedia files to be uploaded. This is different from propositions 5 through 12, which should be (if valid, that is) based on non-experiential knowledge the commenter acquired through objective evidence available to the public.

In certain domains, VERIF$_{EXP}$ propositions—sometimes referred to as *anectotal evidence*—provide the novel knowledge that readers are seeking. In eRulemaking, for instance, agencies accept a wide variety of comments from the public, including accounts of personal experience with the problems or conditions the new regulation proposes to address. If these accounts are relevant and plausible, the agencies may use them, even if they include no independent substantiation. Taking it to an extreme, even if the "experience" is fake, the "experience" and opinions based on them are valuable to the agencies as long as the "experience" is realistic.

Unverifiable Proposition (UNVERIF). A proposition is unverifiable if it cannot be proved with objective evidence. UNVERIF propositions are typically opinions, suggestions, judgements, or assertions about what will happen in the future. (See propositions 13 through 17.) Assertions about the future are typically unverifiable, because there is no direct evidence that something will happen. A very prominent exception is a prediction based on a policy of organizations, i.e. "The store will be open this Sunday." where the policy serves as a direct evidence.

Non-Argumentative (NONARG). A sentence or clause is in this category if it is not a proposition, i.e. it cannot be verified with objective evidence and no supporting reason is required for the purpose of improving the comment quality. Examples include question, greeting, citation, and URL. (See sentences 18 through 21.)

2.2 Annotation Results

The resulting distribution of classes is shown in Table 2. Note that even though we employed a rather lenient definition of objective propositions, the distribution is highly skewed towards UNVERIF propositions. This is expected because the comments are written by people who want to express their opinions about a regulation. Also, NONARG sentences comprise about 7% of the data, suggesting that most comment propositions need to be supported with a reason or evidence for maximal credibility.

The inter-coder reliability checked on 30% of the data is moderate, yielding an *Unweighted Cohen's* κ of 0.73. Most of the disagreement occurred in propositions like "Airlines have to provide compensation for both fees and lost bags" in which it is not clear from the context whether it is an opinion (UNVERIF) or a law (VERIF$_{NON}$). Also, opinions that may be verifiable (e.g. "The problems with passenger experience are not dependant on aircraft size!") seem to cause disagreement among annotators.

3 Proposition Type Classification

3.1 Learning Algorithm

To classify each proposition in an argument as VERIF$_{NON}$, VERIF$_{EXP}$, or UNVERIF, we train multiclass Support Vector Machines (SVM) as formulated by Crammer and Singer (2002), and later extended by Keerthi et al.(2008). We use the LibLinear (Fan et al., 2008) implementation. We experimented with other multiclass SVM approaches such as 1-vs-all and 1-vs-1 (all-vs-all), but the differences were statistically insignificant, consistent with Hsu and Lin's (2002) empirical comparison of these methods. Thus, we only report the performance of the Crammer and Singer version of Multiclass SVM.

3.2 Features

The features are binary-valued, and the feature vector for each data point is normalized to have the unit length: "Presence" features are binary features indicating whether the given feature is present in the proposition or not; "Count" features are numeric counts of the occurrence of each feature is converted to a set of three binary features each denoting 0, 1 and 2 or more occurrences. We first tried a *binning* method with each digit as its own interval, resulting in binary features of the form $featCnt_n$, but the three-interval approach proved to be better empirically, and is consistent with the approach by Riloff and Shoen (1995).

The features can be grouped into three categories by purpose: Verifiability-specific (VER), Experientiality-specific (EXP) and Basic Features, each designed to capture the given proposition's verifiability, experientiality, and both, respectively. Now we discuss the features in more detail.

3.2.1 Basic Features

N-gram Presence A set of binary features denote whether a given unigram or bigram occurs in the proposition. The intuition is that by examining the occurrence of words or phrases in VERIF$_{NON}$, VERIF$_{EXP}$, and UNVERIF propositions, the classes that have close ties to certain words and phrases can be identified. For instance, when a proposition contains the word *happy*, the proposition tends to be UNVERIF. From this observation, we can speculate that *happy* is highly associated with UNVERIF, and *went*, VERIF$_{EXP}$. n-gram presence, rather than the raw or normalized frequency is chosen for its superior performance (O'Keefe and Koprinska, 2009).

Core Clause Tag (CCT) To correctly classify propositions with main or subordinate clauses that do not affect the verifiability of the proposition (e.g. propositions 8 through 10 in Table 1, respectively), it is necessary to distinguish features that appear in the main clause from those that appear in the subordinate clause. Thus, we employ an auxiliary feature that adds clausal information to other features by tagging them as either *core* or *accessory* clause.

Let's consider propositions 7, 9 and 10 in Table 1: In all three examples, the *core clause* is italicized. In single clause cases like proposition 7, the entire proposition is the core clause. However, for proposition 9, the core clause is the subordinate clause introduced by the main clause, i.e. "I believe" should be ignored, since the verifiability of "peanuts do not kill people" is not dependent on it. It is the opposite for proposition 10: the main clause "The governor said" is the core clause, and the rest need not be considered. The reason is that "said" is a speech event, and it is possible to objectively verify whether or not the governor verbally expressed his appreciation of peanuts.

To realize this intuition, we use syntactic parse trees generated by the Stanford Parser (De Marneffe et al., 2006). In particular, Penn Treebank 2 Tags contain a clause-level tag *SBAR* denoting a "clause introduced by a subordinating conjunction" (Marcus et al., 1993). The "that" clause in proposition 10 spans a subtree rooted by *SBAR*, whose left-most child has a lexical value "that." Similarly, the subordinate (non-italicized) clause in proposition 9 falls in a subtree rooted by *SBAR*, whose only child is *S*. Once the main clause of a given proposition is identified, all features set off by the clause are tagged as "core" and the rest are tagged as "accessory." If a speech event is present, the tags are flipped.

3.2.2 Verifiability-specific Features (*VER*)

Parts-of-Speech (POS) Count Rayson et al. (2001) have shown that the POS distribution is distinct in imaginative vs. informative writing. We expect this feature to distinguish UNVERIF propositions from the rest.

Sentiment Clue Count Wilson et al. (2005) provides a subjectivity clue lexicon, which is a list of words with sentiment strength tags, either strong or weak, along with additional information, such as the sentiment polarity, *Part-of-Speech Count* (POS), etc. We suspect that propositions containing more sentiment words is more likely to be UNVERIF.

Speech Event Count We use the 50 most frequent *Objective-speech-event* text anchors crawled from the *MPQA 2.0* corpus (Wilson and Wiebe, 2005) as a speech event lexicon. The speech event text anchors refer to words like "stated" and "wrote" that introduce written or spoken propositions attributed to a source. propositions containing speech events such as proposition 10 in Table 1 are generally VERIF$_{NON}$ or VERIF$_{EXP}$, since whether the attributed source has indeed made the proposition he allegedly made is objectively verifiable regardless of the subjectivity of the proposition itself.

Imperative Expression Count Imperatives, i.e. commands, are generally UNVERIF (e.g. "Do the homework now!" that is, we expect there to be no objective evidence proving that the homework should be done right away.), unless the sentence is a law or general procedure (e.g. "The library should allow you to check out books." where the context makes it clear that the writer is claiming that the library lends out books.) This feature denotes whether the proposition begins with a verb or contains the following: *must, should, need to, have to, ought to*.

Emotion Expression Count These features target specific tokens "!", and "..." as well as fully capitalized word tokens to capture the emotion in text. The rationale is that expression of emotion is likely to be more prevalent in UNVERIF propositions.

3.2.3 Experientiality-specific Features (*EXP*)

Tense Count propositions written in past tense are rarely VERIF_{NON}, because even in the case that the statment is verifiable, they are likely to be the commenter's past experience, i.e. VERIF_{EXP}. Future tense are typically UNVERIF because propositions about what will happen in the future are often unverifiable with objective evidence, with exception being propositions like predictions based on policy of organizations, i.e. "Fedex will deliver on Sunday." To take advantage of these observations, three binary features capture each of three tenses: *past, present,* and *future*.

Person Count First person narratives can suggest that the proposition is UNVERIF or VERIF_{EXP}, except for rare cases like "We, the passengers,..." in which the first person pronoun refers to a large body of individuals. This intuition is captured by having binary features for: *1st, 2nd* and *3rd person*.

4 Experiments

4.1 Methodology

A Note on Argument Detection A natural first step in argumentation mining is to determine which portions of the given document comprise an argument. It can also be framed as a binary classification task in which each proposition in the document needs to be classified as either argumentative or not. Some authors choose to skip this step (Feng and Hirst, 2011), while others make use of various classifiers to achieve high level of accuracy, as Palau and Moens achieved over 70% accuracy on Araucaria and ECHR corpus (Reed and Moens, 2008; Palau and Moens, 2009).

As we have discussed in Section 1, our setup is a bit unique in that we also consider implicit arguments, where propositions are not supported with explicit reason or evidence, as argumentative. As a result, only about 7%($\frac{\text{NONARG}}{\text{TOTAL}}$ in Table 2) of our entire dataset is marked as non-argumentative, most of which consists of questions and greetings. By simply searching for specific unigrams, such as "?" and "thank", we achieve over 99% F_1 score in determining which propositions are part of an argument.

The remaining experiments were done without non-argumentative propositions, i.e. NONARG in Table 2.

Experimental Setup We first randomly selected 292 comments as held-out test set, resulting in the distribution shown in Table 4. Then, VERIF_{NON} and VERIF_{EXP} in the training set were oversampled so that the classes are equally distributed. During training, five fold cross-validation was done on the training set to tune the *C* parameter to *32*. Because the micro-averaged F_1 score can be easily boosted on datasets with highly skewed class distribution, we optimize for the macro-averaged F_1 score.

Preprocessing was kept at a minimal level: capital letters were lowercased after counting fully capitalized words, and numbers were converted to a *NUM* token.

	VERIF_{NON}	VERIF_{EXP}	UNVERIF	Total
Train	987	900	4459	6346
Test	370	367	1687	2424
Total	1357	1267	6146	8770

Table 4: # of propositions in Train and Test Set

4.2 Results & Analysis

Table 3 shows a summary of the classification results. The best overall performance is achieved by combining all features (*UNI+BI+VER+EXP*), yielding 68.99% macro-averaged F_1, where the gain over the baseline is statistically significant according to the bootstrap method with 10,000 samples (Efron and Tibshirani, 1994; Berg-Kirkpatrick et al., 2012).

Core Clause Tag (CCT) We do not report the performance of employing feature sets with *Core Clause Tag (CCT)* in Table 3, because the effect of *CCT* on each of the six sets of features is statistically insignificant. This is surprising at first, given the strong motivation for distinguishing the core clause from auxiliary clause, as addressed in the previous section: Subordinate clauses like "I believe" should not cause the entire proposition to be classified as UNVERIF, and clauses like "He said" should serve as a queue for VERIF_{NON} or VERIF_{EXP}, even if an unverifiable clause follows

Feature Set	UNVERIF vs All			VERIF$_{NON}$ vs All			VERIF$_{EXP}$ vs All			Average F_1	
	Pre.	Rec.	F_1	Pre.	Rec.	F_1	Pre.	Rec.	F_1	Macro	Micro
UNI(base)	85.24	79.43	82.23	42.57	51.89	46.77	61.10	66.76	63.80	64.27	73.31
UNI+BI	82.14	89.69*	85.75*	51.67*	37.57	43.51	73.48*	62.67	67.65*	65.63	77.64*
VER	88.52*	52.10	65.60	28.41	61.35*	38.84	42.41	73.02*	53.65	52.70	56.68
EXP	82.42	4.45	8.44	20.92	76.49*	32.85	31.02	82.83*	45.14	28.81	27.31
VER+EXP	89.40*	49.50	63.72	29.25	71.62*	41.54	50.00	79.56*	61.41	55.55	57.43
UNI+BI+ VER+EXP	86.86*	83.05*	84.91*	49.88*	55.14	52.37*	66.67*	73.02*	69.70*	**68.99***	77.27*

Table 3: Three class classification results in % (Crammer & Singer's Multiclass SVMs)

Precision, recall, and F_1 scores are computed with respect to each one-vs-all classification problem for evaluation purposes, though a single machine is built for the multi-class classification problem, instead of 3 one-vs-all classifiers. The star (*) indicates that the given result is statistically significantly better than the unigram baseline.

Fts		*UNI*	*UNI$_{CCT}$*
UNVERIF	+	should, whatever, responsibility	should$_C$, should$_A$, understand$_C$
	-	previous, solve, florida, exposed, reacted, reply, kinds	exposed$_C$, solve$_C$, NUM$_C$, florida$_C$, reacted$_C$, pool$_C$, owed$_C$
VERIF$_{NON}$	+	impacted, NUM, solve, cars, pull, kinds, congress	impacted$_C$, solve$_C$, cars$_C$, NUM$_C$, pool$_C$, writing$_C$, death$_C$, link$_C$
	-	should, seems, comments	should$_C$, comments$_C$
VERIF$_{EXP}$	+	owed, consumed, saw, expert, interesting, him, reacted, refinance	owed$_C$, consumed$_C$, expert$_C$, reacted$_C$, happened$_C$, interesting$_C$
	-	impacted, wo	impacted$_C$, wo$_C$, concern$_C$, died$_C$

Table 5: Most Informative Features for *UNI* and *UNI$_{CCT}$*

10 Unigrams with the largest weight (magnitude) with respect to each class (+ : positive weight / - : negative weight).

it. Our conjecture turned out to be wrong, mainly because such distinction can be made for only a small subset of the data: For instance, over 83% of the unigrams are tagged as *core* in the *UNI* feature set. Thus, most of the important features for feature sets with *CCT* end up being features with *core* tag, and the important features for feature sets with and without *CCT* are practically the same, as shown in Table 5, resulting in statistically insignificant performance differences.

Informative Features The most informative features reported in Table 6 exhibit interesting differences among the three classes: Sentiment bearing words, i.e. "should" and strong sentiment clues, are good indicators of UNVERIF, whereas person and tense information is crucial for VERIF$_{EXP}$. As expected, the strong indicators of UNVERIF and VERIF$_{EXP}$, namely "should" and PER$_{1st}$ are negatively associated with VERIF$_{NON}$. It is intriguing to see that the heavily weighted features of VERIF$_{NON}$ are non-verb content words, unlike those of the other classes. One explanation for this is that VERIF$_{NON}$ are rarely indicated by specific cues; instead, a good sign of VERIF$_{NON}$ is the absences of cues for the other classes, which are often function words and verbs. What is remaining, then, are non-verb content words. Also, certain content words seem to be more likely to bring about factual discussions. For instance, technical terms like"allergen" and "airborne," appear in verifiable non-experiential propositions as "The FDA requires labeling for the following 8 allergens."

Feature Set		*UNI+BI+VER+EXP*
UNVERIF	+	should,StrSentClue$_{>2}$, VB$_{>2}$
	-	StrSentClue$_0$, VBD$_{>2}$, air, since, no_one, allergic, not_an
VERIF$_{NON}$	+	die, death, reaction, person, allergen, airborne, no_one, allergies
	-	PER$_{1st}$, should
VERIF$_{EXP}$	+	VBD$_{>2}$, PER$_{1st}$, i_have, his, he, him, time_!
	-	VBZ$_{>2}$, PER$_{2nd}$

Table 6: Most Informative Features for *UNI+BI+VER+EXP*

10 Features with the largest weight (magnitude) with respect to each class (+ : positive weight / - : negative weight).

Non-n-gram Features Table 3 clearly shows that the three non-n-gram features, *VER*, *EXP*, and *VER+EXP*, do not perform as well as the n-gram features. But still, the performance is impressive, given the drastic difference in the dimensionality of the features: Even the combined feature set, *VER+EXP*, consists of only about 100 features, when there are over 8,000 unigrams and close to 70,000 bigrams. In other words, the non-n-gram features are effectively capturing characteristics of each class. This is very promising, since this shows that a better understanding of the types of proposition can potentially lead to a more concise set of features with equal, or even better, performance.

Also notice that *VER* outperforms *EXP* for the most part, even with respect to VERIF$_{NON}$ *vs All* and VERIF$_{EXP}$ *vs All*, except for recall. This is intriguing, because *VER* are mostly from subjectivity detection domain, intended to capture the subjectivity of words in the propositions leveraging on pre-built lexia. Simply considering subjectivity of words should provide no means of distinguishing VERIF_{NON} from VERIF_{EXP}. One of the reasons for *VER*'s superior performance over *EXP* is that *EXP* by itself is inadequate for the classification task: *EXP* consists of only 6 (or 12 with CCT) features denoting the person and tense information. Another reason is that *VER*, in a limited fashion, does encode experientiality: For instance, past tense propositions can be identified with the existence of *VBD*(verb, past tense) and *VBN*(verb, past participle).

5 Related Work

Argumentation Mining The primary goal of argumentation mining has been to identify and extract argumentative structures present in documents, which are often written by professionals (Moens et al., 2007; Wyner et al., 2010; Feng and Hirst, 2011; Ashley and Walker, 2013). In certain cases, the specific document structure allows additional means of identify arguments (Mochales and Moens, 2008). Even the work on online text data, which are less rigid in structure and often contain insufficiently supported propositions, focus on the extraction of arguments (Villalba and Saint-Dizier, 2012; Cabrio and Villata, 2012). We, however, are interested in the assessment of the argumentative structure, potentially providing recommendations to readers and feedback to the writers. Thus it is crucial that we also process unsubstantiated propositions, which we consider as implicit arguments. Our approach should be valuable for processing documents like online user comment where arguments may not have adequate support and an automatic means of analysis can be useful.

Subjectivity Detection Work to distinguish subjective from objective propositions (e.g.(Wiebe and Riloff, 2005)), often a subtask for sentiment analysis (Pang and Lee, 2008), is relevant to our work since we are concerned with the objective verifiability of propositions. In particular, previous work attempts to detect certain types of subjective proposition: Conrad et al. (2012) identify *arguing subjectivity* propositions and tag them with argument labels in order to cluster argument paraphrases. Others incorporate this task as a component for solving related problems, such as answering opinion-based questions and determining the writer's political stance (Somasundaran et al., 2007; Somasundaran and Wiebe, 2010). Similarly, Rosenthal and McKeown (2012) identify *opinionated* propositions expressing beliefs, leveraging from previous work in sentiment analysis and belief tagging. While the class of *subjective* propositions in subjectivity detection strictly contains UNVERIF propositions, it also partially overlaps with the VERIF_{EXP} and VERIF_{NON} classes of our work: We want to identify verifiable assertions within propositions, rather than determine the subjectivity of the proposition as a whole (e.g. proposition 8 in Table 1 is classified as a VERIF_{NON}, though "Clearly" is subjective.). We also distinguish two types of verifiable propositions, which is necessary for the purpose of identifying appropriate types of support.

6 Conclusions and Future Work

We have proposed a novel task of automatically classifying each proposition as UNVERIFIABLE, VERIFIABLE NONEXPERIENTIAL, or VERIFIABLE EXPERIENTIAL, where the appropriate type of support is *reason*, *evidence*, and *optional evidence*, respectively. This classification, once the existing support relations among propositions are identified, can provide an estimate of how well the arguments are supported. We find that Support Vector Machines (SVM) classifiers trained with n-grams and other features to capture the verifiability and experientiality exhibit statistically significant improvement over the unigram baseline, achieving a macro-averaged F_1 score of 68.99%. In the process, we have built a gold-standard dataset of 9,476 propositions from 1,047 comments submitted to an eRulemaking platform.

One immediate avenue for future work is to incorporate the identification of relations among the propositions in an argument to the system to analyze the adequacy of the supporting information in the argument. This, in turn, can be used to recommend comments to readers and provide feedback to writers so that they can construct better arguments.

Acknowledgments

This work was supported in part by NSF grants IIS-1111176 and IIS–1314778. We thank our annotators, Pamela Ijeoma Amaechi and Simon Boehme, as well as the Cornell NLP Group and the reviewers for helpful comments.

References

Kevin D. Ashley and Vern R. Walker. 2013. From information retrieval (ir) to argument retrieval (ar) for legal cases: Report on a baseline study. In *JURIX*, pages 29–38.

Taylor Berg-Kirkpatrick, David Burkett, and Dan Klein. 2012. An empirical investigation of statistical significance in nlp. In *Proceedings of the 2012 Joint Conference on Empirical Methods in Natural Language Processing and Computational Natural Language Learning*, EMNLP-CoNLL '12, pages 995–1005, Stroudsburg, PA, USA. Association for Computational Linguistics.

Elena Cabrio and Serena Villata. 2012. Combining textual entailment and argumentation theory for supporting online debates interactions. In *Proceedings of the 50th Annual Meeting of the Association for Computational Linguistics (Volume 2: Short Papers)*, pages 208–212, Jeju Island, Korea, July. Association for Computational Linguistics.

Alexander Conrad, Janyce Wiebe, Hwa, and Rebecca. 2012. Recognizing arguing subjectivity and argument tags. In *Proceedings of the Workshop on Extra-Propositional Aspects of Meaning in Computational Linguistics*, ExProM '12, pages 80–88, Stroudsburg, PA, USA. Association for Computational Linguistics.

Koby Crammer and Yoram Singer. 2002. On the algorithmic implementation of multiclass kernel-based vector machines. *J. Mach. Learn. Res.*, 2:265–292, March.

Marie-Catherine De Marneffe, Bill Maccartney, and Christopher D. Manning. 2006. Generating typed dependency parses from phrase structure parses. In *In Proc. Intl Conf. on Language Resources and Evaluation (LREC*, pages 449–454.

B. Efron and R.J. Tibshirani. 1994. *An Introduction to the Bootstrap*. Chapman & Hall/CRC Monographs on Statistics & Applied Probability. Taylor & Francis.

Rong-En Fan, Kai-Wei Chang, Cho-Jui Hsieh, Xiang-Rui Wang, and Chih-Jen Lin. 2008. Liblinear: A library for large linear classification. *J. Mach. Learn. Res.*, 9:1871–1874, June.

Vanessa Wei Feng and Graeme Hirst. 2011. Classifying arguments by scheme. In *Proceedings of the 49th Annual Meeting of the Association for Computational Linguistics: Human Language Technologies - Volume 1*, HLT '11, pages 987–996, Stroudsburg, PA, USA. Association for Computational Linguistics.

Jennifer L. Hochschild and Michael Danielson, 1998. *Can We Desegregate Public Schools and Subsidized Housing? Lessons from the Sorry History of Yonkers, New York*, chapter 2, pages 23–44. University Press of Kansas, Lawrence KS, edited by clarence stone edition.

Chih-Wei Hsu and Chih-Jen Lin. 2002. A comparison of methods for multiclass support vector machines. *Trans. Neur. Netw.*, 13(2):415–425, March.

S. Sathiya Keerthi, S. Sundararajan, Kai-Wei Chang, Cho-Jui Hsieh, and Chih-Jen Lin. 2008. A sequential dual method for large scale multi-class linear svms. In *Proceedings of the 14th ACM SIGKDD international conference on Knowledge discovery and data mining*, KDD '08, pages 408–416, New York, NY, USA. ACM.

Jeffrey S. Lubbers. 2006. *A Guide to Federal Agency Rulemaking*. American Bar Association Chicago, 4th ed. edition.

Mitchell P. Marcus, Beatrice Santorini, and Mary Ann Marcinkiewicz. 1993. Building a large annotated corpus of english: The penn treebank. *COMPUTATIONAL LINGUISTICS*, 19(2):313–330.

Raquel Mochales and Marie-Francine Moens. 2008. Study on the structure of argumentation in case law. In *Proceedings of the 2008 Conference on Legal Knowledge and Information Systems: JURIX 2008: The Twenty-First Annual Conference*, pages 11–20, Amsterdam, The Netherlands, The Netherlands. IOS Press.

Marie-Francine Moens, Erik Boiy, Raquel Mochales Palau, and Chris Reed. 2007. Automatic detection of arguments in legal texts. In *Proceedings of the 11th International Conference on Artificial Intelligence and Law*, ICAIL '07, pages 225–230, New York, NY, USA. ACM.

Tim O'Keefe and Irena Koprinska. 2009. Feature selection and weighting methods in sentiment analysis. In *Proceedings of the 14th Australasian Document Computing Symposium*.

Raquel Mochales Palau and Marie-Francine Moens. 2009. Argumentation mining: The detection, classification and structure of arguments in text. In *Proceedings of the 12th International Conference on Artificial Intelligence and Law*, ICAIL '09, pages 98–107, New York, NY, USA. ACM.

Bo Pang and Lillian Lee. 2008. Opinion mining and sentiment analysis. *Found. Trends Inf. Retr.*, 2(1-2):1–135, January.

Joonsuk Park, Sally Klingel, Claire Cardie, Mary Newhart, Cynthia Farina, and Joan-Josep Vallbé. 2012. Facilitative moderation for online participation in erulemaking. In *Proceedings of the 13th Annual International Conference on Digital Government Research*, dg.o '12, pages 173–182, New York, NY, USA. ACM.

John L. Pollock. 1987. Defeasible reasoning. *Cognitive Science*, 11:481–518.

Paul Rayson, Andrew Wilson, and Geoffrey Leech. 2001. Grammatical word class variation within the british national corpus sampler. Language and Computers.

Raquel Mochales Palau Rowe Glenn Reed, Chris and Marie-Francine Moens. 2008. Language resources for studying argument. In *Proceedings of the 6th conference on language resources and evaluation - LREC 2008*, pages 91–100. ELRA.

Ellen Riloff and Jay Shoen. 1995. Automatically acquiring conceptual patterns without an annotated corpus. In *In Proceedings of the Third Workshop on Very Large Corpora*, pages 148–161.

Sara Rosenthal and Kathleen McKeown. 2012. Detecting opinionated claims in online discussions. In *ICSC*, pages 30–37.

Swapna Somasundaran and Janyce Wiebe. 2010. Recognizing stances in ideological on-line debates. In *Proceedings of the NAACL HLT 2010 Workshop on Computational Approaches to Analysis and Generation of Emotion in Text*, CAAGET '10, pages 116–124, Stroudsburg, PA, USA. Association for Computational Linguistics.

Swapna Somasundaran, Josef Ruppenhofer, and Janyce Wiebe. 2007. Detecting arguing and sentiment in meetings. In *Proceedings of the SIGdial Workshop on Discourse and Dialogue*.

Stephen E. Toulmin, Richard Rieke, and Allan Janik. 1979. *An Introduction to Reasoning*. Macmillan Publishing Company.

S.E. Toulmin. 1958. *The Uses of Argument*. Cambridge University Press.

Maria Paz Garcia Villalba and Patrick Saint-Dizier. 2012. Some facets of argument mining for opinion analysis. In *COMMA*, pages 23–34.

Janyce Wiebe and Ellen Riloff. 2005. Creating subjective and objective sentence classifiers from unannotated texts. In *In CICLing2005*, pages 486–497.

Theresa Wilson and Janyce Wiebe. 2005. Annotating attributions and private states. In *Proceedings of ACL Workshop on Frontiers in Corpus Annotation II: Pie in the Sky*.

Theresa Wilson. 2005. Recognizing contextual polarity in phrase-level sentiment analysis. In *In Proceedings of HLT-EMNLP*, pages 347–354.

Adam Wyner, Raquel Mochales-Palau, Marie-Francine Moens, and David Milward. 2010. Semantic processing of legal texts. chapter Approaches to Text Mining Arguments from Legal Cases, pages 60–79. Springer-Verlag, Berlin, Heidelberg.

Analyzing Argumentative Discourse Units in Online Interactions

Debanjan Ghosh* Smaranda Muresan† Nina Wacholder* Mark Aakhus* Matthew Mitsui**
*School of Communication and Information, Rutgers University
†Center of Computational Learning Systems, Columbia University
**Department of Computer Science, Rutgers University
debanjan.ghosh|ninwac|aakhus|mmitsui@rutgers.edu, smara@ccls.columbia.edu

Abstract

Argument mining of online interactions is in its infancy. One reason is the lack of annotated corpora in this genre. To make progress, we need to develop a principled and scalable way of determining which portions of texts are argumentative and what is the nature of argumentation. We propose a two-tiered approach to achieve this goal and report on several initial studies to assess its potential.

1 Introduction

An increasing portion of information and opinion exchange occurs in online interactions such as discussion forums, blogs, and webpage comments. This type of user-generated conversational data provides a wealth of naturally occurring arguments. Argument mining of online interactions, however, is still in its infancy (Abbott et al., 2011; Biran and Rambow, 2011; Yin et al., 2012; Andreas et al., 2012; Misra and Walker, 2013). One reason is the lack of annotated corpora in this genre. To make progress, we need to develop a principled and scalable way of determining which portions of texts are argumentative and what is the nature of argumentation.

We propose a multi-step coding approach grounded in findings from argumentation research on managing the difficulties of coding arguments (Meyers and Brashers, 2010). In the first step, trained expert annotators identify basic argumentative features (coarse-grained analysis) in full-length threads. In the second step, we explore the feasibility of using crowdsourcing and novice annotators to identify finer details and nuances of the basic argumentative units focusing on limited thread context. Our coarse-grained scheme for argumentation is based on Pragmatic Argumentation Theory (PAT) (Van Eemeren et al., 1993; Hutchby,

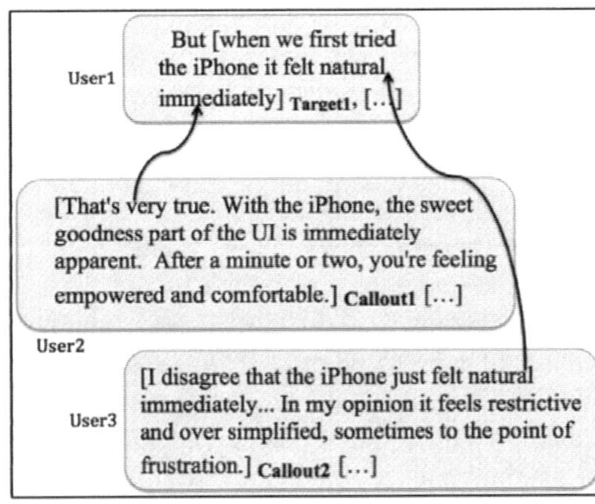

Figure 1: Argumentative annotation of an Online Thread

2013; Maynard, 1985). PAT states that an argument can arise at any point when two or more actors engage in *calling out* and making problematic some aspect of another actor's *prior contribution* for what it (could have) said or meant (Van Eemeren et al., 1993). The argumentative relationships among contributions to a discussion are indicated through links between what is *targeted* and how it is *called-out*. Figure 1 shows an example of two Callouts that refer back to the same Target.

The annotation task performed by the trained annotators includes three subtasks that Peldszus and Stede (2013a) identify as part of the argument mining problem: 1) Segmentation, 2) Segment classification, and 3) Relationship identification. In the language of Peldszus and Stede (2013a), Callouts and Targets are the basic Argument Discourse Units (ADUs) that are segmented, classified, and linked. There are two key advantages of our coarse-grained annotation scheme: 1) It does not initially prescribe what constitutes an argumentative text; 2) It makes it possible for Expert Annotators (EAs) to find ADUs in long

Proceedings of the First Workshop on Argumentation Mining, pages 39–48,
Baltimore, Maryland USA, June 26, 2014.

threads. Assigning finer grained (more complex) labels would have unduly increased the already heavy cognitive load for the EAs. In Section 2 we present the corpus, describe the annotation scheme and task, calculate Inter Annotator Agreement (IAA), and propose a hierarchical clustering approach to identify text segments that the EAs found easier or harder to annotate.

In Section 3, we report on two Amazon Mechanical Turk (MTurk) experiments, which demonstrate that crowdsourcing is a feasible way to obtain finer grained annotations of basic ADUs, especially on the text segments that were easier for the EAs to code. In the first crowd sourcing study, the Turkers (the workers at MTurk, who we consider novice annotators) assigned labels (Agree/Disagree/Other) to the relations between Callout and Target identified by the EAs. In the second study, Turkers labeled segments of Callouts as Stance or Rationale. Turkers saw only a limited context of the threaded discussion, i.e. a particular Callout-Target pair identified by the EA(s) who had analyzed the entire thread. In addition we report on initial classification experiments to detect agreement/disagreement, with the best F1 of 66.9% for the Agree class and 62.6% for the Disagree class.

2 Expert Annotation for Coarse-Grained Argumentation

Within Pragmatic Argumentation Theory, argumentation refers to the ways in which people (seek to) make some prior action or antecedent event disputable by performing challenges, contradictions, negations, accusations, resistance, and other behaviors that *call out* a *'Target'*, a prior action or event. In this section, we present the corpus, the annotation scheme based on PAT and the annotation task, the inter-annotator agreement, and a method to identify which pieces of text are easier or harder to annotate using a hierarchical clustering approach.

2.1 Corpus

Our corpus consists of blog comments posted as responses to four blog postings selected from a dataset crawled from Technorati between 2008-2010 [1]. We selected blog postings in the general topic of technology and considered only postings that had more than 200 comments. For the annotation we selected the first one hundred comments on each blog together with the original posting. Each blog together with its comments constitutes a thread. The topics of each thread are: *Android* (comparison of features of iPhone and Android phones), *iPad* (the usefulness of iPads), *Twitter* (the usefulness of Twitter as a microblogging platform), and *Layoffs* (downsizing and outsourcing efforts of technology companies). We refer to these threads as the *argumentative corpus*. We plan to make the corpus available to the research community.

2.2 Annotation Scheme and Expert Annotation Task

The coarse-grained annotation scheme for argumentation is based on the concept of Callout and Target of Pragmatic Argumentation Theory. The experts' annotation task was to identify expressions of Callout and their Targets while also indicating the links between them. We prepared a set of guidelines with careful definitions of all technical terms. The following is an abbreviated excerpt from the guidelines:

- **Callout**: A *Callout* is a subsequent action that selects (i.e., refers back to) all or some part of a prior action (i.e., Target) and comments on it in some way. In addition to referring back to the Target, a Callout explicitly includes either one or both of the following: Stance (indication of attitude or position relative to the Target) and Rationale (argument/justification/explanation of the Stance taken).
- **Target**: A *Target* is a part of a prior action that has been called out by a subsequent action.

Fig. 1 shows two examples of Callouts from two comments referring back to the same Target. Annotators were instructed to mark any text segment (from words to entire comments) that satisfied the definitions above. A single text segment could be a Target and a Callout. To per-form the expert annotation, we hired five graduate students who had a strong background in humanities and who received extensive training for the task. The EAs performed three annotation subtasks mentioned by Peldszus and Stede (2013a): Segmentation (identify the Argumentative Dis-course

[1] http://technorati.com/blogs/directory/

Thread	A1	A2	A3	A4	A5
Android	73	99	97	118	110
iPad	68	86	85	109	118
Layoffs	71	83	74	109	117
Twitter	76	102	70	113	119
Avg.	72	92.5	81.5	112.3	116

Table 1: Number of Callouts by threads and EA

Thread	F1_EM	F1_OM	α
Android	54.4	87.8	0.64
iPad	51.2	86.0	0.73
Layoffs	51.9	87.5	0.87
Twitter	53.8	88.5	0.82

Table 2: IAA for 5 EA: F1 and alpha values per thread

Units (ADUs) including their boundaries), Segment classification (label the roles of the ADUs, in this case Callout and Target) and relation identification (indicate the link between a Callout and the most recent Target to which is a response).

The segmentation task, which Artstein and Poesio (2008) refer to as the unitization problem, is particularly challenging. Table 1 shows extensive variation in the number of ADUs (Callout in this case) identified by the EAs for each of the four threads. Annotator A1 identified the fewest Callouts (72) while A4 and A5 identified the most (112.3 and 116, respectively). Although these differences could be due to the issues with training, we interpret the consistent variation among coders as an indication that judges can be characterized as "lumpers" or "splitters". What lumpers considered a single long unit was treated as two (or more) shorter units by splitters. This is an example of the problem of annotator variability discussed in (Peldszus and Stede, 2013b). Similar behavior was noticed for Targets. [2]

2.3 Inter Annotator Agreement

Since the annotation task includes the segmentation step, to measure the IAA we have to account for fuzzy boundaries. Thus, we con-sider two IAA metrics usually used in literature for such cases: the information retrieval (IR) in-spired precision-recall (P/R/F1) measure (Wiebe et al., 2005) and Krippendorff's α (Krippendorff, 2004). We present here the main results; a detailed discussion of the IAA is left for a different paper. Following Wiebe et al. (2005), to calculate P/R/F1 for two annotators, one annotator's ADUs are selected as the gold standard. If more than two annotators are employed, the IAA is the average of the pairwise P/R/F1. To determine if two annotators have selected the same text span to represent an ADU, we use the two methods of Somasundaran et al. (2008): exact match (EM) - text spans that vary at the start or end point by five characters or less, and overlap match (OM) - text spans that have at least 10% of same overlapping characters. Table 2 shows the F1 measure for EM and OM for the five EAs on each of the four threads. As expected, the F1 measures are much lower for EM than for OM.

For the second IAA metric, we implement Krippendorff's α (Krippendorff, 2004), where the character overlap between any two annotations and the gap between them are utilized to measure the expected disagreement and the observed disagreement. Table 2 shows α values for each thread, which means significant agreement.

While the above metrics show reasonable agreement across annotators, they do not tell us what pieces of text are easier or harder to annotate. In the next section we report on a hierarchical clustering technique that makes it possible to assess how difficult it is to identify individual text segments as Callouts.

2.4 Clustering of Callout ADUs

We use a hierarchical clustering technique (Hastie et al., 2009) to cluster ADUs that are variants of the same Callout. Each ADU starts in its own cluster. The start and end points of each ADU are utilized to identify overlapping characters in pairs of ADUs. Then, using a "bottom up" clustering approach, two ADUs (in this case, pairs of Callouts) that share overlapping characters are merged into a cluster. This process continues until no more text segments can be merged. Clusters with five overlapping ADUs include a text segment that all five annotators have labeled as a Callout, while clusters with one ADU indicates that only one annotator classified the text segment as a Callout (see Table 3). These numbers provide information about what segments of text are easier or harder to code. For instance, when a cluster contains only two ADUs, it means that three of the five annotators did not label the text segment as a Callout. Our MTurk study of Stance/Rationale (Sec. 3.2) could highlight one reason for the variation – some coders consider a segment of text as Callout when an implicit Stance is present, while others do not.

[2]Due to space limitations, here and in the rest of this paper we report only on Callouts.

# Of EAs	Callout	Target
5	I disagree too. some things they get right, some things they do not.	the iPhone is a truly great design.
	I disagree too … they do not.	That happened because the iPhone is a truly great design.
	I disagree too.	But when we first tried the iPhone it felt natural immediately … iPhone is a truly great design.
	Hi there, I disagree too … they do not. Same as OSX.	–Same as above-
	I disagree too… Same as OSX … no problem.	–Same as above-
2	Like the reviewer said … (Apple) the industry leader… . Good luck with that (iPhone clones).	Many of these iPhone … griping about issues that will only affect them once in a blue moon
	Like the reviewer said… (Apple) the industry leader.	Many of these iPhone…
1	Do you know why the Pre … various handset/builds/resolution issues?	Except for games?? iPhone is clearly dominant there.

Table 3: Examples of Callouts lusters and their corresponding Targets

Thread	# of Clusters	# of EA ADUs per cluster				
		5	4	3	2	1
Android	91	52	16	11	7	5
Ipad	88	41	17	7	13	10
Layoffs	86	41	18	11	6	10
Twitter	84	44	17	14	4	5

Table 4: Number of clusters for each cluster type

Table 4 shows the number of Callout clusters in each thread. The number of clusters with five and four annotators shows that in each thread there are Callouts that are plausibly easier to identify. On the other hand, the clusters selected by only one or two annotators are harder to identify.

3 Crowdsourcing for Fine-grained Argumentation

To understand better the nature of the ADUs, we conducted two studies asking Turkers to perform finer grained analysis of Callouts and Targets. Our first study asked five Turkers to label the relation between a Callout and its corresponding Target as Agree, Disagree, or Other. The Other relation may be selected in a situation where the Callout has no relationship with the Target (e.g., a possible digression) or is in a type of argumentative relationship that is difficult to classify as either Agreement or Disagreement. The second study asked five Turkers to identify Stance and Rationale in Callouts identified by EAs. As discussed in Section 2, by definition, a Callout contains an explicit instance of Stance, Rationale or both. In both of these crowdsourcing studies the Turkers were shown only a limited portion of the threaded discussion, i.e. the Callout-Target pairs that the EAs had linked.

Crowdsourcing is becoming a popular mechanism to collect annotations and other type of data for natural language processing research (Wang and Callison-Burch, 2010; Snow et al., 2008; Chen and Dolan, 2011; Post et al., 2012). Crowdsourcing platforms such as Amazon Mechanical Turk (MTurk) provide a flexible framework to submit various types of NLP tasks where novice annotators (Turkers) can generate content (e.g., translations, paraphrases) or annotations (labeling) in an inexpensive way and with limited training. MTurk also provides researchers with the ability to control the quality of the Turkers, based on their past performances. Section 3.1 and 3.2 describe our two crowdsourcing studies for fine grain argumentation annotation.

3.1 Crowdsourcing Study 1: Labeling the Relation between Callout and Target

In this study, the Turkers' task was to assign a relation type between a Callout and its associated Target. The choices were Agree, Disagree, or Other. Turkers were provided with detailed instructions, including multiple examples of Callout and Target pairs and their relation type. Each HIT (Human Intelligence Task, in the language of MTurk) contained one Callout-Target pair and Turkers were paid 2 cents per HIT. To assure a level of quality control, only qualified Turkers were allowed to perform the task (i.e., Master level with more than 95% approval rate and at least 500 approved HITs).

For this experiment, we randomly selected a Callout from each cluster, along with its corresponding Target. Our assumption is that all Callout ADUs in a given cluster have the same relation type to their Targets (see Table 3). While this assumption is logical, we plan to fully investigate it in future work by running an MTurk experiment on all the Callout ADUs and their corresponding Targets.

We utilized Fleiss' kappa (Fleiss, 1971) to compute IAA between the Turkers (every HIT was completed by five Turkers). Kappa is between 0.45-0.55 for each thread showing moderate agreement between the Turkers (Landis et al., 1977). These agreement results are in line with the agreement noticed in previous studies on agreement/disagreement annotations in online interactions (Bender et al., 2011; Abbott et al., 2011). To select a gold standard for the relation type, we used majority voting. That is, if three or more Turkers agreed on a label, we selected that label as the gold standard. In cases where there was no majority, we assigned the label Other. The total number of Callouts that are in agreement and in disagreement with Targets are 143 and 153, respectively.

Table 5 shows the percentage of each type of relation identified by Turkers (Agree/Disagree/Other) for clusters annotated by different number of EAs. The results suggest that there is a correlation between text segments that are easier or harder to annotate by EAs with the ability of novice annotators to identify an Agree/Disagree relation type between Callout and Target. For example, Turkers generally discovered Agree/Disagree relations between Callouts and their Targets when the Callouts are part of those clusters that are annotated by a higher number of EAs. Turkers identified 57% as showing a disagreement relation between Callout and Target, and 39% as showing an agreement relation (clusters with 5 EAs). For those clusters, only 4% of the Callouts are labeled as having an Other relation with the Target. For clusters selected by fewer EAs, however, the number of Callouts having a relation with the Target labeled as Other is much higher (39% for clusters with two EAs and 32% for clusters with one EA). These results show that those Callouts that are easier to discover (i.e., identified by all five EAs) mostly have a relation with the Target (Agree or Disagree) that is clearly expressed and thus recognizable to the Turkers. Table 5 also shows that in some cases even if some EAs agreed on a piece of text to be considered as a Callout, the novice annotators assigned the Other relation to the Callout and Target ADUs. There are two possible explanations:

Relation label	# of EA ADUs per cluster				
	5	4	3	2	1
Agree	39.36	43.33	42.50	35.48	48.39
Disagree	56.91	31.67	32.50	25.81	19.35
Other	3.72	25.00	25.00	38.71	32.26

Table 5: Percentage of Relation labels per EA cluster type

either the novice annotators could not detect an implicit agreement or disagreement and thus they selected Other, or there are other types of relations besides Agreement and Disagreement between Callouts and their corresponding Targets. We plan to extend this study to other fine grained relation types in future work. In the next section we discuss the results of building a supervised classifier to predict the Agree or Disagree relation type between Callout/Target pairs.

3.1.1 Predicting the Agree/Disagree Relation Label

We propose a supervised learning setup to classify the relation types of Callout-Target pairs. The classification categories are the labels collected from the MTurk experiment. We only consider the Agree and Disagree categories since the Other category has a very small number of instances (53). Based on the annotations from the Turkers, we have 143 Agree and 153 Disagree training instances.

We first conducted a simple baseline experiment to check whether participants use words or phrases to express explicit agreement or disagreement such as 'I agree', 'I disagree'. We collected two small lists (twenty words each) of words from Merriam-Webster dictionary that explicitly represent agreement and disagreement Stances. The agreement list contains the word 'agree' and its synonyms such as 'accept', 'concur', and 'accede'. The disagreement list contains the word 'disagree' and synonyms such as 'differ' and 'dissent'. We then checked whether the text of the Callouts contains these explicit agreement/disagreement markers. Note, that these markers are utilized as rules and no statistical learning is involved in this stage of experiment.

The first row of the Table 6 represents the baseline results. Though the precision is high for agreement category, the recall is quite low and that results in a poor overall F1 measure. This shows that even though markers like 'agree' or 'disagree'

Features	Category	P	R	F1
Baseline	Agree	83.3	6.9	12.9
	Disagree	50.0	5.2	9.5
Unigrams	Agree	57.9	61.5	59.7
	Disagree	61.8	58.2	59.9
MI-based unigram	Agree	60.1	66.4	63.1
	Disagree	65.2	58.8	61.9
LexF	Agree	61.4	73.4	66.9
	Disagree	69.6	56.9	62.63

Table 6: Classification of Agree/Disagree

Features	Category	P	R	F1
LexF	Agree	61.4	73.4	66.9
	Disagree	69.6	56.9	62.6
LexF-SL	Agree	60.6	74.1	66.7
	Disagree	69.4	54.9	61.3
LexF-IU	Agree	58.1	69.9	63.5
	Disagree	65.3	52.9	58.5
LexF-LO	Agree	57.2	74.8	64.8
	Disagree	67.0	47.7	55.7

Table 7: Importance of Lexical Features

are very precise, they occur in less than 15% of all the Callouts expressing agreement or disagreement.

For the next set of experiments we used a supervised machine learning approach for the two-way classification (Agree/Disagree). We use Support Vector Machines (SVM) as our machine-learning algorithm for classification as implemented in Weka (Hall et al., 2009) and ran 10-fold cross validation. As a SVM baseline, we first use all unigrams in Callout and Target as features (Table 6, Row 2). We notice that the recall improves significantly when compared with the rule-based method. To further improve the classification accuracy, we use Mutual Information (MI) to select the words in the Callouts and Targets that are likely to be associated with the categories Agree and Disagree, respectively. Specifically, we sort each word based on its MI value and then select the first 180 words in each of the two categories to represent our new vocabulary set of 360 words. The feature vector includes only words present in the MI list. Compared to the all unigrams baseline, the MI-based unigrams improve the F1 by 4% (Agree) and 2% (Disagree) (Table 6). The MI approach discovers the words that are highly associated with Agree/Disagree categories and these words turn to be useful features for classification. In addition, we consider several types of lexical features (LexF) inspired by previous work on agreement and disagreement (Galley et al., 2004; Misra and Walker, 2013).

- **Sentiment Lexicon (SL)**: Two features are designed using a sentiment lexicon (Hu and Liu, 2004) where the first feature represents the number of times the Callout and the Target contain a positive emotional word and the second feature represents the number of the negative emotional words.

- **Initial unigrams in Callout (IU)**: Instead of using all unigrams in the Callout and Target, we only select the first words from the Callout (maximum ten). The assumption is that the stance is generally expressed at the beginning of a Callout. We used the same MI-based technique to filter any sparse words.

- **Lexical Overlap and Length (LO)**: This set of features represents the lexical overlap between the Callout and the Target and the length of each ADU.

Table 6 shows that using all these types of lexical features improves the F1 score for both categories as compared to the MI-based unigram features. Table 7 shows the impact of removing each type of lexical features. From these results it seems that initial unigrams of Callout (IU) and lexical overlap (LO) are useful features: removing each of them lowers the results for both Agree/Disagree categories. In future work, we plan to explore context-based features such as the thread structure, and semantic features such as WordNet-based semantic similarity. We also hypothesize that with additional training instances the ML approaches will achieve better results.

3.2 Crowdsourcing Study 2: Analysis of Stance and Rationale

In the second study aimed at identifying the argumentative nature of the Callouts identified by the expert annotators, we focus on identifying the Stance and Rationale segments of a Callout. Since the presence of at least an explicit Stance or Rationale was part of the definition of a Callout, we selected these two argumentation categories as our finer-grained scheme for this experiment.

Given a pair of Callout and Target ADUs, five Turkers were asked to identify the Stance and Rationale segments in the Callout, including the exact boundaries of the text segments. Identifying Stance and Rationale is a difficult task and thus, we also asked Turkers to mark the level of difficulty in the identification task. We provided the

Diff	Number of EAs per cluster				
	5	4	3	2	1
VE	22.11	22.38	20.25	16.67	10.71
E	28.55	24.00	24.02	28.23	20.00
M	19.69	17.87	20.72	19.39	23.57
D	11.50	10.34	11.46	9.52	12.86
VD	7.02	5.61	4.55	4.42	6.43
TD	11.13	19.79	19.00	21.77	26.33

Table 8: Difficulty judgments by Turkers compared to number of EAs who selected a cluster

Turkers with a scale of difficulty (similar to a Likert scale), where the Turkers have to choose one of the following: *very easy* (VE), *easy* (E), *moderate* (M), *difficult* (D), *very difficult* (VD), *too difficult to code* (TD). Turkers were instructed to select the too difficult to code choice only in cases where they felt it was impossible to detect a Stance or Rationale in the Callout.

The Turkers were provided with detailed instructions including examples of Stance and Rationale annotations for multiple Callouts and only highly qualified Turkers were allowed to perform the task. Unlike the previous study, we also ran a pre-screening testing phase and only Turkers that passed the screening were allowed to complete the tasks. Because of the difficult nature of the annotation task, we paid ten cents per HIT.

For the Stance/Rationale study, we considered all the Callouts in each cluster along with the associated Targets. We selected all the Callouts from each cluster because of variability in the boundaries of ADUs, i.e., in the segmentation process. One benefit of this crowdsourcing experiment is that it helps us understand better what the variability means in terms of argumentative structure. For example, one EA might mark a text segment as a Callout only when it expresses a Stance, while another EA might mark as Callout a larger piece of text expressing both the Stance and Rationale (See examples of Clusters in Table 3). We leave this deeper analysis as future work.

Table 8 shows there is a correlation between the number of EAs who selected a cluster and the difficulty level Turkers assigned to identifying the Stance and Rationale elements of a Callout. This table shows that for more than 50% of the Callouts that are identified by 5 EAs, the Stance and Rationale can be easily identified (refer to the 'VE' and 'E' rows), where as in the case of Callouts that are identified by only 1 EA, the number is just 31%. Similarly, more than 26% of the Callouts in that same category (1 EA) were labeled as 'Too difficult to code', indicating that the Turkers could not identify either a Stance or Rationale in the Callout. These numbers are comparable to what our first crowdsourcing study showed for the Agree/Disagree/Other relation identification (Table 5). Table 9 shows results where we selected overall difficulty level by majority voting. We combined the *easy* and *very easy* categories to the category *easy (E)* and the *difficult* and *very difficult* categories to the category *difficult (D)* for a simpler presentation.

Diff	Number of EAs per cluster				
	5	4	3	2	1
E	81.04	70.76	60.98	63.64	25.00
M	7.65	7.02	17.07	6.06	25.00
D	5.91	5.85	7.32	9.09	12.50
TD	5.39	16.37	14.63	21.21	37.50

Table 9: Difficulty judgment (majority voting)

Table 9 also shows that more than 80% of the time, Turkers could easily identify Stance and/or Rationale in Callouts identified by 5 EAs, while they could perform the finer grained analysis easily only 25% of time for Callouts identified by a single EA. Only 5% of Callouts identified by all 5 EAs were considered *too difficult to code* by the Turkers (i.e., the novice annotators could not identify a Stance or a Rationale). In contrast, more than 37% of Callouts annotated only by 1 EA were considered *too difficult to code* by the novice annotators. Table 10 presents some of the examples of Stance and Rationale pairs as selected by the Turkers along with the difficulty labels.

4 Related Work

Primary tasks for argument analysis are to segment the text to identify ADUs, detect the roles of each ADUs, and to establish the relationship between the ADUs (Peldszus and Stede, 2013a). Similarly, Cohen (1987) presented a computational model of argument analysis where the structure of each argument is restricted to the claim and evidence relation. Teufel et al. (2009) introduce the argumentative zoning (AZ) idea that identifies important sections of scientific articles and later Hachey and Grover (2005) applied similar idea of AZ to summarize legal documents. Wyner et al. (2012) propose a rule-based tool that can highlight potential argumentative sections of text according to discourse cues like 'suppose' or 'therefore'. They tested their system on product reviews

Target	Callout	Stance	Rationale	Difficulty
the iPhone is a truly great design.	I disagree too. some things they get right, some things they do not.	I...too	Some things ... do not	Easy
the dedicated 'Back' button	that back button is key. navigation is actually much easier on the android.	That back button is key	Navigation is... android	Moderate
It's more about the features and apps and Android seriously lacks on latter.	Just because the iPhone has a huge amount of apps, doesn't mean they're all worth having.	—	Just because the iPhone has a huge amount of apps, doesn't mean they're all worth having.	Difficult
I feel like your comments about Nexus One is too positive ...	I feel like your poor grammar are to obvious to be self thought...	—	—	Too difficult to code

Table 10: Examples of Callout/Target pairs with difficulty level (majority voting)

(Canon Camera) from Amazon e-commerce site.

Relatively little attention has so far been devoted to the issue of building argumentative corpora from naturally occurring texts (Peldszus and Stede, 2013a; Feng and Hirst, 2011). However, (Reed et al., 2008; Reed and Rowe, 2004) have developed the Araucaria project that maintains an online repository of arguments (AraucariaDB), which recently has been used as research corpus for several automatic argumentation analyses (Palau and Moens, 2009; Wyner et al., 2010; Feng and Hirst, 2011). Our work contributes a new principled method for building annotated corpora for online interactions. The corpus and guidelines will also be shared with the research community.

Another line of research that is correlated with ours is recognition of agreement/disagreement (Misra and Walker, 2013; Yin et al., 2012; Abbott et al., 2011; Andreas et al., 2012; Galley et al., 2004; Hillard et al., 2003) and classification of stances (Walker et al., 2012; Somasundaran and Wiebe, 2010) in online forums. For future work, we can utilize textual features (contextual, dependency, discourse markers), relevant multiword expressions and topic modeling (Mukherjee and Liu, 2013), and thread structure (Murakami and Raymond, 2010; Agrawal et al., 2003) to improve the Agree/Disagree classification accuracy.

Recently, Cabrio and Villata (2013) proposed a new direction of argumentative analysis where the authors show how arguments are associated with Recognizing Textual Entailment (RTE) research. They utilized RTE approach to detect the relation of support/attack among arguments (entailment expresses a 'support' and contradiction expresses an 'attack') on a dataset of arguments collected from online debates (e.g., Debatepedia).

5 Conclusion and Future Work

To make progress in argument mining for online interactions, we need to develop a principled and scalable way to determine which portions of texts are argumentative and what is the nature of argumentation. We have proposed a two-tiered approach to achieve this goal. As a first step we adopted a coarse-grained annotation scheme based on Pragmatic Argumentation Theory and asked expert annotators to label entire threads using this scheme. Using a clustering technique we identified which pieces of text were easier or harder for the Expert Annotators to annotate. Then we showed that crowdsourcing is a feasible approach to obtain annotations based on a finer grained argumentation scheme, especially on text segments that were easier for the Expert Annotators to label as being argumentative. While more qualitative analysis of these results is still needed, these results are an example of the potential benefits of our multi-step coding approach.

Avenues for future research include but are not limited to: 1) analyzing the differences between the stance and rationale annotations among the novice annotators; 2) improving the classification accuracies of the Agree/Disagree classifier using more training data; 3) using syntax and semantics inspired textual features and thread structure; and 4) developing computational models to detect Stance and Rationale.

Acknowledgements

Part of this paper is based on work supported by the DARPA-DEFT program for the first two authors. The views expressed are those of the authors and do not reflect the official policy or position of the Department of Defense or the U.S. Government.

References

Rob Abbott, Marilyn Walker, Pranav Anand, Jean E Fox Tree, Robeson Bowmani, and Joseph King. 2011. How can you say such things?!?: Recognizing disagreement in informal political argument. In *Proceedings of the Workshop on Languages in Social Media*, pages 2–11. Association for Computational Linguistics.

Rakesh Agrawal, Sridhar Rajagopalan, Ramakrishnan Srikant, and Yirong Xu. 2003. Mining newsgroups using networks arising from social behavior. In *Proceedings of the 12th international conference on World Wide Web*, pages 529–535. ACM.

Jacob Andreas, Sara Rosenthal, and Kathleen McKeown. 2012. Annotating agreement and disagreement in threaded discussion. In *LREC*, pages 818–822.

Ron Artstein and Massimo Poesio. 2008. Inter-coder agreement for computational linguistics. *Computational Linguistics*, 34(4):555–596.

Emily M Bender, Jonathan T Morgan, Meghan Oxley, Mark Zachry, Brian Hutchinson, Alex Marin, Bin Zhang, and Mari Ostendorf. 2011. Annotating social acts: Authority claims and alignment moves in wikipedia talk pages. In *Proceedings of the Workshop on Languages in Social Media*, pages 48–57. Association for Computational Linguistics.

Or Biran and Owen Rambow. 2011. Identifying justifications in written dialogs by classifying text as argumentative. *International Journal of Semantic Computing*, 5(04):363–381.

Elena Cabrio and Serena Villata. 2013. A natural language bipolar argumentation approach to support users in online debate interactions. *Argument & Computation*, 4(3):209–230.

David L Chen and William B Dolan. 2011. Collecting highly parallel data for paraphrase evaluation. In *Proceedings of the 49th Annual Meeting of the Association for Computational Linguistics: Human Language Technologies-Volume 1*, pages 190–200. Association for Computational Linguistics.

Robin Cohen. 1987. Analyzing the structure of argumentative discourse. *Computational linguistics*, 13(1-2):11–24.

Vanessa Wei Feng and Graeme Hirst. 2011. Classifying arguments by scheme. In *Proceedings of the 49th Annual Meeting of the Association for Computational Linguistics: Human Language Technologies-Volume 1*, pages 987–996. Association for Computational Linguistics.

Joseph L Fleiss. 1971. Measuring nominal scale agreement among many raters. *Psychological bulletin*, 76(5):378.

Michel Galley, Kathleen McKeown, Julia Hirschberg, and Elizabeth Shriberg. 2004. Identifying agreement and disagreement in conversational speech: Use of bayesian networks to model pragmatic dependencies. In *Proceedings of the 42nd Annual Meeting on Association for Computational Linguistics*, page 669. Association for Computational Linguistics.

Ben Hachey and Claire Grover. 2005. Automatic legal text summarisation: experiments with summary structuring. In *Proceedings of the 10th international conference on Artificial intelligence and law*, pages 75–84. ACM.

Mark Hall, Eibe Frank, Geoffrey Holmes, Bernhard Pfahringer, Peter Reutemann, and Ian H Witten. 2009. The weka data mining software: an update. *ACM SIGKDD explorations newsletter*, 11(1):10–18.

Trevor Hastie, Robert Tibshirani, Jerome Friedman, T Hastie, J Friedman, and R Tibshirani. 2009. *The elements of statistical learning*, volume 2. Springer.

Dustin Hillard, Mari Ostendorf, and Elizabeth Shriberg. 2003. Detection of agreement vs. disagreement in meetings: Training with unlabeled data. In *Proceedings of the 2003 Conference of the North American Chapter of the Association for Computational Linguistics on Human Language Technology: companion volume of the Proceedings of HLT-NAACL 2003–short papers-Volume 2*, pages 34–36. Association for Computational Linguistics.

Minqing Hu and Bing Liu. 2004. Mining and summarizing customer reviews. In *Proceedings of the tenth ACM SIGKDD international conference on Knowledge discovery and data mining*, pages 168–177. ACM.

Ian Hutchby. 2013. *Confrontation talk: Arguments, asymmetries, and power on talk radio*. Routledge.

Klaus Krippendorff. 2004. Measuring the reliability of qualitative text analysis data. *Quality & quantity*, 38:787–800.

J Richard Landis, Gary G Koch, et al. 1977. The measurement of observer agreement for categorical data. *biometrics*, 33(1):159–174.

Douglas W Maynard. 1985. How children start arguments. *Language in society*, 14(01):1–29.

Renee A Meyers and Dale Brashers. 2010. Extending the conversational argument coding scheme: Argument categories, units, and coding procedures. *Communication Methods and Measures*, 4(1-2):27–45.

Amita Misra and Marilyn A Walker. 2013. Topic independent identification of agreement and disagreement in social media dialogue. In *Proceedings of the SIGDIAL 2013 Conference*, pages 41–50. Association for Computational Linguistics.

Arjun Mukherjee and Bing Liu. 2013. Discovering user interactions in ideological discussions. In *Proceedings of the 51st Annual Meeting on Association for Computational Linguistics*, pages 671–681. Citeseer.

Akiko Murakami and Rudy Raymond. 2010. Support or oppose?: classifying positions in online debates from reply activities and opinion expressions. In *Proceedings of the 23rd International Conference on Computational Linguistics: Posters*, pages 869–875. Association for Computational Linguistics.

Raquel Mochales Palau and Marie-Francine Moens. 2009. Argumentation mining: the detection, classification and structure of arguments in text. In *Proceedings of the 12th international conference on artificial intelligence and law*, pages 98–107. ACM.

Andreas Peldszus and Manfred Stede. 2013a. From argument diagrams to argumentation mining in texts: A survey. *International Journal of Cognitive Informatics and Natural Intelligence (IJCINI)*, 7(1):1–31.

Andreas Peldszus and Manfred Stede. 2013b. Ranking the annotators: An agreement study on argumentation structure. In *Proceedings of the 7th linguistic annotation workshop and interoperability with discourse*, pages 196–204.

Matt Post, Chris Callison-Burch, and Miles Osborne. 2012. Constructing parallel corpora for six indian languages via crowdsourcing. In *Proceedings of the Seventh Workshop on Statistical Machine Translation*, pages 401–409. Association for Computational Linguistics.

Chris Reed and Glenn Rowe. 2004. Araucaria: Software for argument analysis, diagramming and representation. *International Journal on Artificial Intelligence Tools*, 13(04):961–979.

Chris Reed, Raquel Mochales Palau, Glenn Rowe, and Marie-Francine Moens. 2008. Language resources for studying argument. In *Proceedings of the 6th conference on language resources and evaluation-LREC 2008*, pages 91–100.

Rion Snow, Brendan O'Connor, Daniel Jurafsky, and Andrew Y Ng. 2008. Cheap and fast—but is it good?: evaluating non-expert annotations for natural language tasks. In *Proceedings of the conference on empirical methods in natural language processing*, pages 254–263. Association for Computational Linguistics.

Swapna Somasundaran and Janyce Wiebe. 2010. Recognizing stances in ideological on-line debates. In *Proceedings of the NAACL HLT 2010 Workshop on Computational Approaches to Analysis and Generation of Emotion in Text*, pages 116–124. Association for Computational Linguistics.

Swapna Somasundaran, Josef Ruppenhofer, and Janyce Wiebe. 2008. Discourse level opinion relations: An annotation study. In *Proceedings of the 9th SIGdial Workshop on Discourse and Dialogue*, pages 129–137. Association for Computational Linguistics.

Simone Teufel, Advaith Siddharthan, and Colin Batchelor. 2009. Towards discipline-independent argumentative zoning: evidence from chemistry and computational linguistics. In *Proceedings of the 2009 Conference on Empirical Methods in Natural Language Processing: Volume 3-Volume 3*, pages 1493–1502. Association for Computational Linguistics.

Frans H Van Eemeren, Rob Grootendorst, Sally Jackson, and Scott Jacobs. 1993. *Reconstructing argumentative discourse.* University of Alabama Press.

Marilyn A Walker, Pranav Anand, Rob Abbott, Jean E Fox Tree, Craig Martell, and Joseph King. 2012. That is your evidence?: Classifying stance in online political debate. *Decision Support Systems*, 53(4):719–729.

Rui Wang and Chris Callison-Burch. 2010. Cheap facts and counter-facts. In *Proceedings of the NAACL HLT 2010 Workshop on Creating Speech and Language Data with Amazon's Mechanical Turk*, pages 163–167. Association for Computational Linguistics.

Janyce Wiebe, Theresa Wilson, and Claire Cardie. 2005. Annotating expressions of opinions and emotions in language. *Language resources and evaluation*, 39(2-3):165–210.

Adam Wyner, Raquel Mochales-Palau, Marie-Francine Moens, and David Milward. 2010. Approaches to text mining arguments from legal cases. In *Semantic processing of legal texts*, pages 60–79. Springer.

Adam Wyner, Jodi Schneider, Katie Atkinson, and Trevor JM Bench-Capon. 2012. Semi-automated argumentative analysis of online product reviews. In *COMMA*, pages 43–50.

Jie Yin, Paul Thomas, Nalin Narang, and Cecile Paris. 2012. Unifying local and global agreement and disagreement classification in online debates. In *Proceedings of the 3rd Workshop in Computational Approaches to Subjectivity and Sentiment Analysis*, pages 61–69. Association for Computational Linguistics.

Back up your Stance: Recognizing Arguments in Online Discussions

Filip Boltužić and **Jan Šnajder**
University of Zagreb
Faculty of Electrical Engineering and Computing
Text Analysis and Knowledge Engineering Lab
Unska 3, 10000 Zagreb, Croatia
{filip.boltuzic, jan.snajder}@fer.hr

Abstract

In online discussions, users often back up their stance with arguments. Their arguments are often vague, implicit, and poorly worded, yet they provide valuable insights into reasons underpinning users' opinions. In this paper, we make a first step towards *argument-based opinion mining* from online discussions and introduce a new task of *argument recognition*. We match user-created comments to a set of predefined topic-based arguments, which can be either attacked or supported in the comment. We present a manually-annotated corpus for argument recognition in online discussions. We describe a supervised model based on comment-argument similarity and entailment features. Depending on problem formulation, model performance ranges from 70.5% to 81.8% F1-score, and decreases only marginally when applied to an unseen topic.

1 Introduction

Whether about coffee preparation, music taste, or legal cases in courtrooms, arguing has always been the dominant way of rationalizing opinions. An argument consists of one or more premises leading to exactly one conclusion, while argumentation connects together several arguments (Van Eemeren et al., 2013). Across domains, argumentation differs in vocabulary, style, and purpose, ranging from legal (Walton, 2005) and scientific argumentation (Jiménez-Aleixandre and Erduran, 2007) to media (Walton, 2007) and social argumentation (Shum, 2008). When argumentation involves interactive argument exchange with elements of persuasion, we talk about debating. In the increasingly popular online debates, such as VBATES,[1] users can engage in debates over controversial topics, introduce new arguments or use existing ones.

Early computational approaches to argumentation have developed in two branches: logic-based approaches (Bos and Gabsdil, 2000; Lauriar et al., 2001) and argumentative zoning (Teufel and others, 2000). The latter aims to recognize argumentative sections of specific purpose in scientific papers, such as goals, related work, or conclusion. Moens et al. (2007) introduced argumentation mining as a research area involved with the automatic extraction of argumentation structure from free text, residing between NLP, argumentation theory, and information retrieval.

Prior work in argumentation mining has focused on official documents, such as legal cases (Palau and Moens, 2009), or moderated sources, such as debates (Cabrio and Villata, 2012). However, by far the largest source of opinions are online user discussions: comments on newspaper articles, social networks, blogs, and discussion forums – all argumentation arenas without strict rules. Despite the fact that the user-generated content is not moderated nor structured, one can often find an abundance of opinions, most of them backed up with arguments. By analyzing such arguments, we can gain valuable insight into the reasons underpinning users' opinions. Understanding the reasons has obvious benefits in social opinion mining, with applications ranging from brand analysis to political opinion mining.

Inspired by this idea, in this paper we take on the task of *argument-based opinion mining*. Instead of merely determining the general opinion or stance of users towards a given topic, in argument-based opinion mining we wish to determine the arguments on which the users base their stance. Unlike in argumentation mining, we are not ultimately interested in recovering the argumentation structure. Instead, we wish to recognize what arguments the user has used to back up her opinion.

[1] http://vbate.idebate.org/

Proceedings of the First Workshop on Argumentation Mining, pages 49–58,
Baltimore, Maryland USA, June 26, 2014.

As an example, consider a discussion on the topic *"Should gay marriage be legal?"* and the following comment:

> *Gay marriages must be legal in all 50 states. A marriage is covenant between 2 people regardless of their genders. Discrimination against gay marriage is unconstitutional and biased. Tolerance, education and social justice make our world a better place.*

This comment supports the argument *"It is discriminatory to refuse gay couples the right to marry"* and denies the argument *"Marriage should be between a man and a woman"*. The technical challenge here lies in the fact that, unlike in debates or other more formal argumentation sources, the arguments provided by the users, if any, are less formal, ambiguous, vague, implicit, or often simply poorly worded.

In this paper, we make a first step towards argument-based opinion mining from online discussions and introduce the task of *argument recognition*. We define this task as identifying what arguments, from a predefined set of arguments, have been used in users' comments, and how. We assume that a topic-dependent set of arguments has been prepared in advance. Each argument is described with a single phrase or a sentence. To back up her stance, the user will typically use one or more of the predefined arguments, but in their own wording and with varying degree of explicitness. The task of argument recognition amounts to matching these arguments to the predefined arguments, which can be either attacked or supported by the comment. Note that the user's comment may by itself be a single argument. However, we refer to it as *comment* to emphasize the fact that in general it may contain several arguments as well as non-argumentative text.

The contribution of our work is twofold. First, we present COMARG, a manually-annotated corpus for argument recognition from online discussions, which we make freely available. Secondly, we describe a supervised model for argument recognition based on comment-argument comparison. To address the fact that the arguments expressed in user comments are mostly vague and implicit, we use a series of semantic comment-argument comparison features based on semantic textual similarity (STS) and textual entailment (TE). To this end, we rely on state-of-the-art off-the-shelf STS and TE systems. We consider different feature subsets and argument recognition tasks of varying difficulty. Depending on task formulation, their performance ranges from 70.5% to 81.8% micro-averaged F1-score. Taking into account the difficulty of the task, we believe these results are promising. In particular, we show that TE features work best when also taking into account the stance of the argument, and that a classifier trained to recognize arguments in one topic can be applied to another one with a decrease in performance of less than 3% F1-score.

The rest of the paper is structured as follows. In the next section we review the related work. In Section 3 we describe the construction and annotation of the COMARG corpus. Section 4 describes the argument recognition model. In Section 5 we discuss the experimental results. Section 6 concludes the paper and outlines future work.

2 Related Work

Argument-based opinion mining is closely related to argumentation mining, stance classification, and opinion mining.

Palau and Moens (2009) approach argumentation mining in three steps: (1) argument identification (determining whether a sentence is argumentative), (2) argument proposition classification (categorize argumentative sentences as premises or conclusions), and (3) detection of argumentation structure or "argumentative parsing" (determining the relations between the arguments). The focus of their work is on legal text: the Araucaria corpus (Reed et al., 2008) and documents from the European Court of Human Rights.

More recently, Cabrio and Villata (2012) explored the use of textual entailment for building argumentation networks and determining the acceptability of arguments. Textual entailment (TE) is a generic NLP framework for recognizing inference relations between two natural language texts (Dagan et al., 2006). Cabrio and Villata base their approach on Dung's argumentation theory (Dung, 1995) and apply it to arguments from online debates. After linking the arguments with support/attack relations using TE, they are able to compute a set of acceptable arguments. Their system helps the participants to get an overview of a debate and the accepted arguments.

Our work differs from the above-described work in that we do not aim to extract the argumentation structure. Similarly to Cabrio and Villata (2012), we use TE as one of the features of our system to recognize the well-established arguments in user generated comments. However, aiming at argument-based opinion mining from noisy comments, we address a more general problem in which each comment may contain several arguments as well as non-argumentative text. Thus, in contrast to Cabrio and Villata (2012) who framed the problem as a binary yes/no entailment task, we tackle a more difficult five-class classification problem. We believe this is a more realistic task from the perspective of opinion mining.

A task similar to argument recognition is that of *stance classification*, which involves identifying a subjective disposition towards a particular topic (Lin et al., 2006; Malouf and Mullen, 2008; Somasundaran and Wiebe, 2010; Anand et al., 2011; Hasan and Ng, 2013). Anand et al. (2011) classified stance on a corpus of posts across a wide range of topics. They analyzed the usefulness of meta-post features, contextual features, dependency features, and word-based features for signaling disagreement. Their results range from 54% to 69% accuracy. Murakami and Raymond (2010) identify general user opinions in online debates. They distinguish between global positions (opinions on the topic) and local positions (opinions on previous remarks). By calculating user pairwise rates of agreement and disagreement, users are grouped into "support" and "oppose" sets.

In contrast to stance classification, argument recognition aims to uncover the reasons underlying an opinion. This relates to the well-established area of opinion mining. The main goal of opinion mining or sentiment analysis (Pang and Lee, 2008) is to analyze the opinions and emotions from (most often user-created) text. Opinions are often associated with user reviews (Kobayashi et al., 2007), unlike stances, which are more common for debates. Hasan and Ng (2013) characterize stance recognition as a more difficult task than opinion mining. Recently, however, there has been interesting work on combining argumentation mining and opinion mining (Chesñevar et al., 2013; Grosse et al., 2012; Hogenboom et al., 2010).

3 ComArg Corpus

For training and evaluating argument recognition models, we have compiled a corpus of user comments, manually annotated with arguments, to which we refer as ComArg. The ComArg corpus is freely available for research purposes.[2]

3.1 Data Description

As a source of data, we use two web sites: *Procon.org*[3] and *Idebate.org*.[4] The former is a discussion site covering ideological, social, political, and other topics. Users express their personal opinions on a selected topic, taking either the pro or con side. *Idebate.org* is a debating website containing online debates and an archive of past debates. Each archived topic contains a set of prominent arguments presented in the debate. Each argument is labeled as either for or against the topic. The arguments are moderated and edited to provide the best quality of information.

The two data sources are complementary to each other: *Procon.org* contains user comments, while *Idebate.org* contains the arguments. We manually identified near-identical topics covered by both web sites. From this set, we chose two topics: *"Under God in Pledge"* (UGIP) and *"Gay Marriage"* (GM). We chose these two topics because they have a larger-than-average number of comments (above 300) and are well-balanced between pro and con stances. For these two topics, we then took the corresponding comments and arguments from *Procon.org* and *Idebate.org*, respectively. As the users can post comments not relevant for the topic, we skim-read the comments and removed the spam. We end up with a set of 175 comments and 6 arguments for the UGIP topic, and 198 comments and 7 arguments for the GM topic. The comments are often verbose: the average number of words per comment is 116. This is in contrast to the less noisy dataset from Cabrio and Villata (2012), where the average comment length is 50 words.

Each comment has an associated stance (pro or con), depending on how it was classified in *Procon.org*. Similarly, each argument either attacks or supports the claim of the topic, depending on how it was classified in *Idebate.org*. To simplify the exposition, we will refer to them as "pro arguments" and "con arguments". Table 1 shows the arguments for UGIP and GM topics.

Users may attack or support both pro and con arguments. We will refer to the way how the argument is *used* (attacked or supported) as *argument*

[2] Freely available under the CC BY-SA-NC license from http://takelab.fer.hr/data/comarg

[3] http://www.procon.org

[4] http://idebate.org

"Under God in Pledge" (UGIP): *Should the words "under God" be in the U.S. Pledge of Allegiance?*		
(A1.1)	*Likely to be seen as a state sanctioned condemnation of religion*	Pro
(A1.2)	*The principles of democracy regulate that the wishes of American Christians, who are a majority are honored*	Pro
(A1.3)	*Under God is part of American tradition and history*	Pro
(A1.4)	*Implies ultimate power on the part of the state*	Con
(A1.5)	*Removing under god would promote religious tolerance*	Con
(A1.6)	*Separation of state and religion*	Con
"Gay Marriage" (GM): *Should gay marriage be legal?*		
(A2.1)	*It is discriminatory to refuse gay couples the right to marry*	Pro
(A2.2)	*Gay couples should be able to take advantage of the fiscal and legal benefits of marriage*	Pro
(A2.3)	*Marriage is about more than procreation, therefore gay couples should not be denied the right to marry due to their biology*	Pro
(A2.4)	*Gay couples can declare their union without resort to marriage*	Con
(A2.5)	*Gay marriage undermines the institution of marriage, leading to an increase in out of wedlock births and divorce rates*	Con
(A2.6)	*Major world religions are against gay marriages*	Con
(A2.7)	*Marriage should be between a man and a woman*	Con

Table 1: Predefined arguments for the two topics in the COMARG corpus

Label	Description: Comment...
A	...explicitly **attacks** the argument
a	...vaguely/implicitly **attacks** the argument
N	...makes **no use** of the argument
s	...vaguely/implicitly **supports** the argument
S	...explicitly **supports** the argument

Table 2: Labels for comment-argument pairs in the COMARG corpus

No, of course not. The original one was good enough. The insertion of Under God" between "Our nation" and "indivisible" is symbolic of how religion divides this country."
The Pledge of Allegiance reflects our morals and values. Therefore, it should reflect the ideas of all Americans not 80%. This country has no national religion, so why should we promote a god. Also, Thomas Jefferson, a founding father, was athiest.
I believe that since this country was founded under God why should we take that out of the pledge? Men and women have fought and gave their lives for this country, so that way we can have freedom and be able to have God in our lives. And since this country was founded under God and the Ten Commandments in mind, it needs to stay in. If it offends you well I am sorry but get out of this country!

Table 3: Example comments with low IAA from UGIP

polarity. Typically, but not necessarily, users who take the pro stance do so by supporting one of the pro arguments, and perhaps attacking some of the con arguments, while for users who take the con stance it is the other way around.

3.2 Annotation

The next step was to annotate, for each comment, the arguments used in the comment as well as their polarity. For each topic we paired all comments with all possible arguments for that topic, resulting in 1,050 and 1,386 comment-argument pairs for the UGIP and GM topics, respectively. We then asked the annotators (not the authors) to annotate each pair. The alternative would have been to ask the annotators to assign arguments to comments, but we believe annotating pairs reduces the annotation efforts and improves annotation quality.[5]

[5] We initially attempted to crowdsource the annotation, but the task turned out to be too complex for the workers, resulting in unacceptably low interannotator agreement.

Acknowledging the fact that user-provided arguments are often vague or implicit, we decided to annotate each comment-argument pair using a five-point scale. The labels are shown in Table 2. The labels encode the presence/absence of an argument in a comment, its polarity, as well as the degree of explicitness.

The annotation was carried out by three trained annotators, in two steps. In the first step, each annotator independently annotated the complete dataset of 2,436 comment-argument pairs. To improve the annotation quality, we singled out the problematic comment-argument pairs. We considered as problematic all comment-argument pairs for which (1) there is no agreement among the three annotators or (2) the ordinal distance between any of the labels assigned by the annotators is greater than one. Table 3 shows some examples of problematic comments. As for the arguments, the most problematic ones are A1.3 and A1.5 for the UGIP topic and arguments A2.1 and A2.7 for the GM topic (cf. Table 1).

In the second step, we asked the annotators to independently revise their decisions for the problematic comment-argument pairs. Each annotator re-annotated 515 pairs, of which for 86 the annotations were revised. In total, the annotation and

IAA	UGIP	GM	UGIP+GM
Fleiss' Kappa	0.46	0.51	0.49
Cohen's Kappa	0.46	0.51	0.49
Weighted Kappa	0.45	0.51	0.50
Pearson's r	0.68	0.74	0.71

Table 4: Interannotator agreement on the ComArg corpus

	Labels					
Topic	A	a	N	s	S	Total
UGIP	48	86	691	58	130	1,013
GM	89	73	849	98	176	1,285
UGIP+GM	137	159	1,540	156	306	2,298

Table 5: Distribution of labels in the ComArg corpus

subsequent revision took about 30 person-hours.

Table 4 shows the interannotator agreement (IAA). We compute Fleiss' multirater kappa, Cohen's kappa (averaged over three annotator pairs), Cohen's linearly weighted kappa (also averaged), and Pearson's r. The latter two reflect the fact that the five labels constitute an ordinal scale. According to standard interpretation (Landis and Koch, 1977), these values indicate moderate agreement, proving that argument recognition is a difficult task.

Finally, to obtain the the gold standard annotation, we took the majority label for each comment-argument pair, discarding the pairs for which there are ties. We ended up with a dataset of 2,249 comment-argument pairs. Table 6 shows examples of annotated comment-argument pairs.

3.3 Annotation Analysis

Table 5 shows the distribution of comment-argument pairs across labels. Expectedly, the majority (67.0%) of comment-argument pairs are cases in which the argument is not used (label **N**). Attacked arguments (labels **A** or **a**) make up 12.9%, while supported arguments (labels **S** or **s**) make up 20.1% of cases. Among the cases not labeled as **N**, arguments are used explicitly in 58.4% (labels **A** and **S**) and vague/implicit (labels **a** and **s**) in 41.5% of cases. There is a marked difference between the two topics in this regard: in UGIP, arguments are explicit in 55.3%, while in GM in 60.7% of cases. Note that this might be affected by the choice of the predefined arguments as well as how they are worded.

The average number of arguments per comment is 1.9 (1.8 for UGIP and 2.0 for GM). In GM, 62.8% of arguments used are pro arguments, while in UGIP pro arguments make up 52.2% of cases.

4 Argument Recognition Model

We cast the argument recognition task as a multi-class classification problem. Given a comment-argument pair as input, the classifier should predict the correct label from the set of five possible labels (cf. Table 2). The main idea is for the classifier to rely on comment-argument comparison features, which in principle makes the model less domain dependent than if we were to use features extracted directly from the comment or the arguments.

We use three kinds of features: textual entailment (TE) features, semantic text similarity (STS) features, and one "stance alignment" (SA) feature. The latter is a binary feature whose value is set to one if a pro comment is paired with a pro argument or if a con comment is paired with a con argument. This SA feature presupposes that comment stance is known a priori. The TE and STS features are described bellow.

4.1 Textual Entailment

Following the work of Cabrio and Villata (2012), we use textual entailment (TE) to determine whether the comment (the text) entails the argument phrase (the hypothesis). To this end we use the Excitement Open Platform (EOP), a rich suite of textual entailment tools designed for modular use (Padó et al., 2014). From EOP we used seven pre-trained *entailment decision algorithms* (EDAs). Some EDAs contain only syntactical features, whereas others rely on resources such as WordNet (Fellbaum, 1998) and VerbOcean (Chklovski and Pantel, 2004). Each EDA outputs a binary decision (*Entailment* or *NonEntailment*) along with the degree of confidence. We use the outputs (decisions and confidences) of all seven EDAs as the features of our classifier (14 features in total). We also experimented with using additional features (the disjunction of all classifier decisions, the maximum confidence value, and the mean confidence value), but using these did not improve the performance.

In principle, we expect the comment text (which is usually longer) to entail the argument phrase (which is usually shorter). This is also confirmed by the ratio of positive entailment decision across labels (averaged over seven EDAs), shown in

Id	Comment	Argument	Label
2.23.4	*All these arguments on my left are and have always been FALSE. Marriage is between a MAN and a WOMAN by divine definition. Sorry but, end of story.*	*It is discriminatory to refuse gay couples the right to marry.*	s
2.111.4	*Marriage isn't the joining of two people who have intentions of raising and nurturing children. It never has been. There have been many married couples whos have not had children. (...) If straight couples can attempt to work out a marriage, why can't homosexual couple have this same privilege? (...)*	*It is discriminatory to refuse gay couples the right to marry*	s
2.114.2	*(...) I truly believe that the powers behind the cause to re-define marriage stem from a stronger desire to attack a religious institution that does not support homosexuality, rather than a desire to achieve the same benefits as marriage for same sex couples. (...)"*	*Gay couples should be able to take advantage of the fiscal and legal benefits of marriage.*	S
2.101.2	*(...) One part of marriage is getting benefits from the other. Many married couples never have children but still get the benefits of marriage, should we take those benefits away because they don't have children? Another is the promise to be with each other for an eternity" etc. Marriage is also about being able to celebrate having each other. And last, marriage is about being there for each other. (...)"*	*Gay couples should be able to take advantage of the fiscal and legal benefits of marriage.*	S
2.157.2	*(...) There are no legal reasons why two homosexual people should not be allowed to marry, only religious ones (...)*	*Gay couples should be able to take advantage of the fiscal and legal benefits of marriage.*	N
1.45.2	*I am not bothered by under God but by the highfalutin christians that do not realize that phrase was never in the original pledge - it was not added until 1954. So stop being so pompous and do not offend my parents and grandparents who never used "under God" when they said the pledge. Let it stay, but know the history of the Cold War and fear of communism.*	*"Under God" is part of American tradition and history.*	a

Table 6: Example of comment-argument annotations from the COMARG corpus

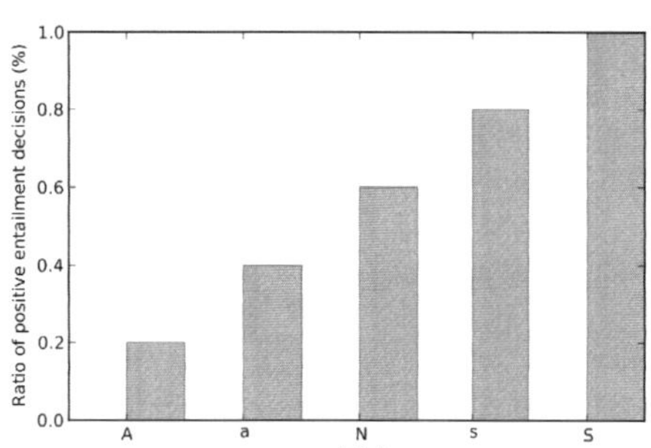

Figure 1: Ratio of positive entailment decisions across labels, scaled to a $[0, 1]$ interval

Fig. 1. Pro arguments have a higher ratio of positive entailment decisions than con arguments. Also, vaguely/implicitly supported arguments have a lower rate of entailment decisions than explicitly supported arguments.

4.2 Semantic Textual Similarity

Formally speaking, the argument should either be entailed or not entailed from the comment. The former case also includes a simple argument paraphrase. In the latter case, the argument may be contradicted or it may simply be a *non sequitur*. While we might expect these relations to be recognizable in texts from more formal genres, such as legal documents and parliamentary debates, it is questionable to what extent these relations can be detected in user-generated content, where the arguments are stated vaguely and implicitly.

To account for this, we use a series of argument-comment comparison features based on semantic textual similarity (STS). STS measures "the degree of semantic equivalence between two texts" (Agirre et al., 2012). It is a looser notion than TE and, unlike TE, it is a non-directional (symmetric) relation. We rely on the freely available TakeLab STS system by Šarić et al. (2012). Given a comment and an argument, the STS system outputs a continuous similarity score. We also compute the similarity between the argument and each sentence from the comment, which gives us a vector of similarities. The vector length equals the largest number of sentences in a comment, which in COMARG is 29. Additionally, we compute the maximum and the

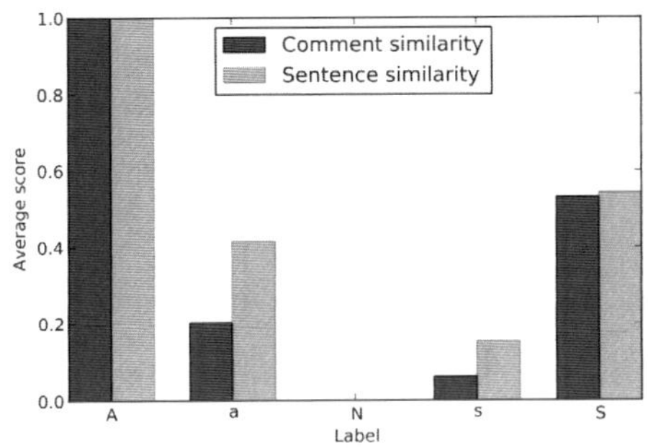

Figure 2: Average similarity score on sentence and comment level across labels, scaled to a [0, 1] interval

mean of sentence-level similarities. In total, we use 31 STS features.

Fig. 2 shows the average comment- and sentence-level similarity scores across labels on ComArg, scaled to a [0, 1] interval. Interestingly, attacked arguments on average receive a larger score than supported arguments.

5 Experimental Evaluation

5.1 Experimental Setup

We consider three formulations of the argument detection task. In the first setting (**A-a-N-s-S**), we consider the classification of a comment-argument into one of the five labels, i.e., we wish to determine whether an argument has been used, its polarity, as well as the degree of explicitness. In the second setting (**As-N-sS**), we conflate the two labels of equal polarity, thus we only consider whether an argument has been used and with what polarity. In the third setting (**A-N-S**), we only consider the comment-argument pairs in which arguments are either not used or used explicitly. This setting is not practically relevant, but we include it for purposes of comparison.

We compare to two baselines: (1) a majority class classifier (MCC), which assigns label **N** to every instance, and (2) a bag-of-words overlap classifier (BoWO), which uses the word overlap between the comment and the argument as the only feature.

For classification, we use the Support Vector Machine (SVM) algorithm with a Radial Basis Function kernel. In each setting, we train and evaluate the model using nested 5×3 cross-validation. The hyperparameters C and γ of the SVM are optimized using grid search. We rely on the well-known LibSVM implementation (Chang and Lin, 2011).

	A-a-N-s-S		Aa-N-sS		A-N-S	
Model	UGIP	GM	UGIP	GM	UGIP	GM
MCC baseline	68.2	69.4	68.2	69.4	79.5	76.6
BoWO baseline	68.2	69.4	67.8	69.5	79.6	76.9
TE	69.1	**81.1**	69.6	72.3	80.1	73.4
STS	67.8	68.7	67.3	69.9	79.2	75.8
SA	68.2	69.4	68.2	69.4	79.5	76.6
STS+SA	68.2	69.5	67.5	68.7	79.6	76.1
TE+SA	68.9	72.4	**71.0**	**73.7**	**81.8**	**80.3**
TE+STS+SA	**70.5**	72.5	68.9	73.4	81.4	79.7

Table 7: Argument recognition F1-score (separate models for UGIP and GM topics)

	UGIP → GM		GM → UGIP	
Model	A-a-N-s-S	Aa-N-sS	A-a-N-s-S	Aa-N-sS
STS+SA	69.4	69.4	68.2	68.2
TE+SA	**72.6**	**73.5**	**70.2**	**71.2**
STS+TE+SA	71.5	72.2	68.2	69.6

Table 8: Argument recognition F1-score on UGIP and GM topics (cross-topic setting)

5.2 Results

Table 7 shows the micro-averaged F1-score for the three problem formulations, for models trained separately on UGIP and GM topics. The two baselines perform similarly. The models that use only the STS or the SA features perform similar to the baseline. The TE model outperforms the baselines in all but one setting and on both topics: the difference ranges from 0.6 to 11.7 percentage points, depending on problem formulation, while the variation between the two topics is negligible. The STS model does not benefit from adding the SA feature, while the TE model does so in simpler settings (**Aa-N-sS** and **A-N-S**), where the average F1-scores increases by about 3 percentage points. This can be explained by referring to Fig. 1, which shows that even for the attacked arguments (labels **A** and **a**) entailment decisions are sometimes positive. In such cases, the stance alignment feature helps to distinguish between entailment (supported argument) and contradiction (attacked argument). Combining all three feature types gives the best results for the **A-a-N-s-S** setting and the UGIP topic.

The above evaluation was carried out in a within-topic setting. To test how the models perform when applied to comments and arguments from unseen topics, we trained each model on one topic and

	A-a-N-s-S				Aa-N-sS				A-N-S			
Model	P	R	F1	micro-F1	P	R	F1	micro-F1	P	R	F1	micro-F1
MCC baseline	13.8	20.0	16.3	68.9	23.0	33.3	27.2	68.9	26.0	33.3	29.2	77.9
TE+SA	**47.6**	26.6	27.9	71.1	**68.8**	**46.6**	**49.4**	**73.3**	**66.1**	**47.3**	**51.1**	**81.6**
STS+TE+SA	46.3	**27.2**	**28.6**	**71.6**	61.6	43.5	45.5	71.4	63.7	44.9	48.2	80.4

Table 9: Argument recognition F1-score for TE+SA and STS+TE+SA models on UGIP+GM topics

evaluated on the other. The results are shown in Table 8 (we show results only for the two problem formulations of practical interest). The difference in performance is small (0.7 on average). The best-performing model (TE+SA) does not suffer a decrease in performance. This suggests that the models are quite topic independent, but a more detailed study is required to verify this finding.

Finally, we trained and tested the TE+SA and STS+TE+SA models on the complete ComArg dataset. The results are shown in Table 9. We report macro-averaged precision, recall, and F1-score, as well as micro-averaged F1-score.[6] Generally, our models perform less well on smaller classes (**A**, **a**, **s**, and **S**), hence the macro-averaged F1-scores are much lower than the micro-averaged F1-scores. The recall is lower than the precision: the false negatives are mostly due to our models wrongly classifying comment-argument pairs as **N**. The STS+TE+SA model slightly outperforms the TE+SA model on the **A-a-N-s-S** problem, while on the other problem formulations the TE+SA model performs best.

5.3 Error Analysis

The vague/implicit arguments posed the greatest challenge for all models. A case in point is the comment-argument pair 2.23.4 from Table 6. Judging solely from the comment text, it is unclear what the user actually meant. Perhaps the user is attacking the argument, but there are certain additional assumptions that would need to be met for the argument to be entailed.

The second major problem is distinguishing between arguments that are mentioned and those that are not. Consider the comment-argument pairs 2.111.4 and 2.114.2 from Table 6. In the former case, classifier mistakenly predicts **S** instead of **s**. The decision is likely due to the low difference in argument-comment similarities for these two classes. In the latter example the classifier wrongly predicts that the argument is used in the comment.

The TE model in the majority of cases outperforms the STS model. Nonetheless, in case of the comment-argument pair 2.157.2 from Table 6, the STS-based model outperformed the entailment model. In this case, the word overlap between the argument and the comment in quite high, although they completely differ in meaning. Conversely, argument-comment 2.101.2 is a good example of when entailment was correctly recognized, whereas the STS model has failed.

6 Conclusion

In this paper we addressed the argument recognition task as a first step towards argument-based opinion mining from online discussions. We have presented the ComArg corpus, which consists of manually annotated comment-argument pairs. On this corpus we have trained a supervised model for three argument recognition tasks of varying difficulty. The model uses textual entailment and semantic textual similarity features. The experiments as well as the inter-annotator agreement show that argument recognition is a difficult task. Our best models outperform the baselines and perform in a 70.5% to 81.8% micro-averaged F1-score range, depending on problem formulation. The outputs of several entailment decision algorithms, combined with a stance alignment feature, proved to be the best features. Additional semantic textual similarity features seem to be useful in when we distinguish between vague/implicit and explicit arguments. The model performance is marginally affected when applied to an unseen topic.

This paper has only touched the surface of argument recognition. We plan to extend the ComArg corpus with more topics and additional annotation, such as argument segments. Besides experimenting with different models and feature sets, we intend to investigate how argument interactions can be exploited to improve argument recognition, as well as how argument recognition can be used for stance classification.

[6]We replace undefined values with zeros when computing the macro-averages.

References

Eneko Agirre, Mona Diab, Daniel Cer, and Aitor Gonzalez-Agirre. 2012. Semeval-2012 task 6: A pilot on semantic textual similarity. In *Proceedings of the First Joint Conference on Lexical and Computational Semantics-Volume 1: Proceedings of the main conference and the shared task, and Volume 2: Proceedings of the Sixth International Workshop on Semantic Evaluation*, pages 385–393. Association for Computational Linguistics.

Pranav Anand, Marilyn Walker, Rob Abbott, Jean E Fox Tree, Robeson Bowmani, and Michael Minor. 2011. Cats rule and dogs drool!: Classifying stance in online debate. In *Proceedings of the 2nd Workshop on Computational Approaches to Subjectivity and Sentiment Analysis*, pages 1–9. Association for Computational Linguistics.

Johan Bos and Malte Gabsdil. 2000. First-order inference and the interpretation of questions and answers. *Proceedings of Gotelog*, pages 43–50.

Elena Cabrio and Serena Villata. 2012. Combining textual entailment and argumentation theory for supporting online debates interactions. In *Proceedings of the 50th Annual Meeting of the Association for Computational Linguistics: Short Papers-Volume 2*, pages 208–212. Association for Computational Linguistics.

Chih-Chung Chang and Chih-Jen Lin. 2011. Libsvm: a library for support vector machines. *ACM Transactions on Intelligent Systems and Technology (TIST)*, 2(3):27.

Carlos I Chesñevar, María Paula González, Kathrin Grosse, and Ana Gabriela Maguitman. 2013. A first approach to mining opinions as multisets through argumentation. In *Agreement Technologies*, pages 195–209. Springer.

Timothy Chklovski and Patrick Pantel. 2004. Verbocean: Mining the web for fine-grained semantic verb relations. In *EMNLP*, volume 2004, pages 33–40.

Ido Dagan, Oren Glickman, and Bernardo Magnini. 2006. The PASCAL recognising textual entailment challenge. In *Machine Learning Challenges. Evaluating Predictive Uncertainty, Visual Object Classification, and Recognising Tectual Entailment*, pages 177–190. Springer.

Phan Minh Dung. 1995. On the acceptability of arguments and its fundamental role in nonmonotonic reasoning, logic programming and n-person games. *Artificial Intelligence*, 77(2):321–357.

Christiane Fellbaum. 1998. *WordNet: An Electronic Lexical Database*. MIT Press.

Kathrin Grosse, Carlos Iván Chesñevar, and Ana Gabriela Maguitman. 2012. An argument-based approach to mining opinions from Twitter. In *AT*, pages 408–422.

Kazi Saidul Hasan and Vincent Ng. 2013. Extra-linguistic constraints on stance recognition in ideological debates. In *Proceedings of the 51st Annual Meeting of the Association for Computational Linguistics*, pages 816–821.

Alexander Hogenboom, Frederik Hogenboom, Uzay Kaymak, Paul Wouters, and Franciska De Jong. 2010. Mining economic sentiment using argumentation structures. In *Advances in Conceptual Modeling – Applications and Challenges*, pages 200–209. Springer.

María Pilar Jiménez-Aleixandre and Sibel Erduran. 2007. Argumentation in science education: An overview. In *Argumentation in Science Education*, pages 3–27. Springer.

Nozomi Kobayashi, Kentaro Inui, and Yuji Matsumoto. 2007. Extracting aspect-evaluation and aspect-of relations in opinion mining. In *EMNLP-CoNLL*, pages 1065–1074.

J. Richard Landis and Gary G. Koch. 1977. The measurement of observer agreement for categorical data. *Biometrics*, 33(1):159–174.

Stanislao Lauriar, Johan Bos, Ewan Klein, Guido Bugmann, and Theocharis Kyriacou. 2001. Training personal robots using natural language instruction. *IEEE Intelligent Systems*, 16(5):38–45.

Wei-Hao Lin, Theresa Wilson, Janyce Wiebe, and Alexander Hauptmann. 2006. Which side are you on?: Identifying perspectives at the document and sentence levels. In *Proceedings of the Tenth Conference on Computational Natural Language Learning*, pages 109–116. Association for Computational Linguistics.

Robert Malouf and Tony Mullen. 2008. Taking sides: User classification for informal online political discourse. *Internet Research*, 18(2):177–190.

Marie-Francine Moens, Erik Boiy, Raquel Mochales Palau, and Chris Reed. 2007. Automatic detection of arguments in legal texts. In *Proceedings of the 11th International Conference on Artificial Intelligence and Law*, pages 225–230. ACM.

Akiko Murakami and Rudy Raymond. 2010. Support or oppose?: Classifying positions in online debates from reply activities and opinion expressions. In *Proceedings of the 23rd International Conference on Computational Linguistics: Posters*, pages 869–875. Association for Computational Linguistics.

Sebastian Padó, Tae-Gil Noh, Asher Stern, Rui Wang, and Roberto Zanoli. 2014. Design and realization of a modular architecture for textual entailment. *Natural Language Engineering*, FirstView:1–34, 2.

Raquel Mochales Palau and Marie-Francine Moens. 2009. Argumentation mining: The detection, classification and structure of arguments in text. In *Proceedings of the 12th International Conference on Artificial Intelligence and Law*, pages 98–107. ACM.

Bo Pang and Lillian Lee. 2008. Opinion mining and sentiment analysis. *Foundations and trends in information retrieval*, 2(1-2):1–135.

Chris Reed, Raquel Mochales Palau, Glenn Rowe, and Marie-Francine Moens. 2008. Language resources for studying argument. In *Proceedings of the 6th Conference on Language Resources and Evaluation (LREC 2008)*, pages 91–100.

Frane Šarić, Goran Glavaš, Mladen Karan, Jan Šnajder, and Bojana Dalbelo Bašić. 2012. Takelab: Systems for measuring semantic text similarity. In *Proceedings of the Sixth International Workshop on Semantic Evaluation (SemEval 2012)*, pages 441–448, Montréal, Canada, 7-8 June. Association for Computational Linguistics.

Simon Buckingham Shum. 2008. Cohere: Towards web 2.0 argumentation. volume 8, pages 97–108.

Swapna Somasundaran and Janyce Wiebe. 2010. Recognizing stances in ideological on-line debates. In *Proceedings of the NAACL HLT 2010 Workshop on Computational Approaches to Analysis and Generation of Emotion in Text*, pages 116–124. Association for Computational Linguistics.

Simone Teufel et al. 2000. *Argumentative zoning: Information extraction from scientific text*. Ph.D. thesis, University of Edinburgh.

Frans H. Van Eemeren, Rob Grootendorst, Ralph H. Johnson, Christian Plantin, and Charles A. Willard. 2013. *Fundamentals of argumentation theory: A handbook of historical backgrounds and contemporary developments*. Routledge.

Douglas Walton. 2005. *Argumentation methods for artificial intelligence in law*. Springer.

Douglas Walton. 2007. *Media argumentation: dialectic, persuasion and rhetoric*. Cambridge University Press.

Automated argumentation mining to the rescue? Envisioning argumentation and decision-making support for debates in open online collaboration communities

Jodi Schneider*
INRIA Sophia Antipolis, France
jodi.schneider@inria.fr

Abstract

Argumentation mining, a relatively new area of discourse analysis, involves automatically identifying and structuring arguments. Following a basic introduction to argumentation, we describe a new possible domain for argumentation mining: debates in open online collaboration communities. Based on our experience with manual annotation of arguments in debates, we envision argumentation mining as the basis for three kinds of support tools, for authoring more persuasive arguments, finding weaknesses in others' arguments, and summarizing a debate's overall conclusions.

1 Introduction

Argumentation mining, a relatively new area of discourse analysis, involves automatically identifying and structuring arguments. Following a basic introduction to argumentation, we describe online debates as a future application area for argumentation mining, describing how we have manually identified and structured argumentation, and how we envision argumentation mining being applied to support these debates in the future.

1.1 What is an argument

Informally, an argument is a communication presenting reasons for accepting a conclusion. Unlike proofs that lead step-by-step from premises with logical justifications for a conclusion, arguments are non-monotonic and can be disproven. Arguments may use various approaches including generalization, analogy, inference, and prediction.

This work was carried out during the tenure of an ERCIM "Alain Bensoussan" Fellowship Programme. The research leading to these results has received funding from the European Union Seventh Framework Programme (FP7/2007-2013) under grant agreement n° 246016.

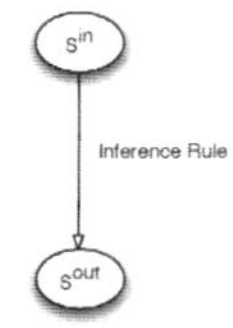

Figure 1: The simplest possible argument.

The simplest possible argument connects two Statements by means of an Inference Rule (Figure 1). Inference Rules are functions that input one or more Statements (the premises) and return one or more Statements (the conclusions).

1.2 More complex arguments

Far more complex arguments can be formed. Arbitrary numbers of arguments can be joined into a larger and more complex argument. Useful terminology is introduced by (Wyner et al., 2008), who reserve the term *argument* to refer to the simplest kind: non-decomposable arguments. They distinguish *cases* which support a single conclusion (see Figure 2) from *debates* which argue for and against a single conclusion.

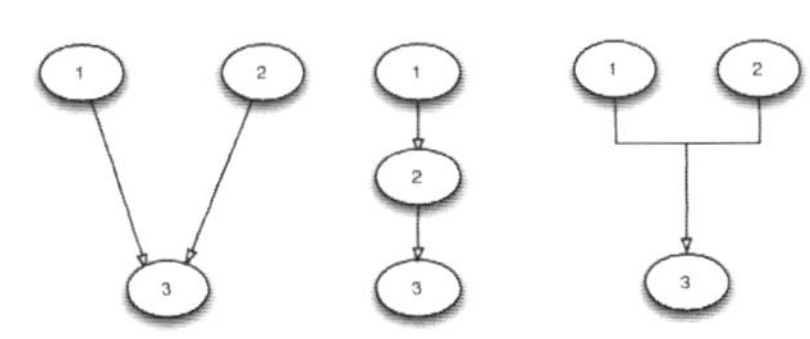

Figure 2: Cases support a single conclusion. Cases may (a) use multiple, independent premises to support a single conclusion; (b) draw an intermediate conclusion, and use it as an additional premise in order to support a final conclusion; or (c) require two linked premises (both required as input to the inference rule) to support a conclusion.

Figure 3 shows a simple debate, where two arguments *attack* one another. There are three ways

Proceedings of the First Workshop on Argumentation Mining, pages 59–63,
Baltimore, Maryland USA, June 26, 2014. ©2014 Association for Computational Linguistics

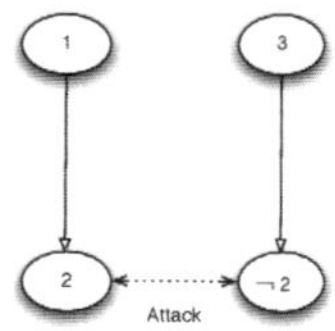

Figure 3: *Debates* argue for and against a single conclusion. This kind of attack is called a *rebuttal*.

of attacking an argument: attacking a premise (known as *undermining*), attacking a conclusion (known as *rebutting*), and attacking an inference (known as *undercutting*), following (Prakken, 2010).[1]

1.3 Inference Rules

Argumentation schemes, e.g. (Walton et al., 2008) are one way of expressing Inference Rules. These are *patterns* for arguing which are stated abstractly: to use an argumentation scheme, it must be instantiated with details. To indicate possible flaws in reasoning, associated with each scheme there are critical questions pointing to the possible counterarguments.

We next introduce an example from our own work, where automated argumentation mining could be used.

2 Rationale-based debate in open online communities

One place where argumentation mining could be applied is in rationale-based debate in open online communities. The Web has enabled large-scale collaboration, even among people who may never meet face-to-face. A large number of participants present their views and reasoning to make decisions for open, online collaborative software and knowledge development in Mozilla, Wikipedia, OpenStreetMap, etc. In these groups, asynchronous textual debates are the basis for decision making. Participants argue for decisions based on rationales, since the *reasons* for opinions, rather than majority votes or aggregate sentiment, justify decisions. Thus large-scale decision support in these communities should make evident not just the overall tendency of the group (as in opinion mining) but rather the arguments made, focusing especially on the rationales, or reasons given for a preferred outcome.

In our work, we have analyzed a corpus of debates, to understand how the English-language version of Wikipedia makes decisions about which articles to include and exclude from the encyclopedia. We used two approaches to argumentation theory to annotate asynchronous messages in each debate, in iterative multiparty annotation experiments (Schneider, 2014).

2.1 Analysis using argumentation schemes

First, we used Walton's argumentation schemes (outlined in Ch. 9 of (Walton et al., 2008)) in order to annotate the arguments, focusing on the internal reasoning of each message. First one person (this author) annotated all the arguments found in the corpus against Walton's 60 schemes, finding 1213 arguments in 741 messages (Schneider et al., 2013). Then, we focused on the subset of 14 argumentation schemes that appeared more than 2% of the time, with iterative, multiparty annotation. There was a sharp divide between the two most prevalent argument types–*Argument from Evidence to Hypothesis* (19%) and *Argument from Rules* (17%)–and the remaining 12 types that appeared from 2-4% of the time.

Besides these patterns, we found statistically significant differences between how experts and novices in the community argued in our corpus of debates. Experts were more likely to use *Argument from Precedent*, while novices (who had little experience in the debates and in the wider Wikipedia community) were more likely to use several argumentation schemes that the community viewed as less sound bases for decision making.[2] These included *Argumentation from Values*, *Argumentation from Cause to Effect*, and *Argument from Analogy*.

2.2 Analysis using factors analysis

Second, we used a very different approach, based on factors analysis (Ashley, 1991) and dimensions theory (Bench-Capon and Rissland, 2001), which

[1]Rebut and undercut are drawn from the well-known work of (Pollock, 1994); Prakken credits undermining to (Vreeswijk, 1993) and (Elvang-Gøransson et al., 1993).

[2]Our analysis of acceptability of arguments drew from community documentation and took community responses to messages into account. For instance, *Argumentation from Values* might be countered by a messages saying "Whether you personally like an article or its subject, is totally irrelevant." (This exchange appeared in our corpus in fact `http://en.wikipedia.org/wiki/Wikipedia:Articles_for_deletion/Log/2011_January_29`.)

have most commonly been used in case-based reasoning. We iteratively derived four factors important in the discussions: Notability, Sources, Maintenance, and Bias (Schneider et al., 2012). This was an easier annotation task, with stronger inter-annotator agreement than for Walton's argumentation schemes: factors analysis had Cohen's kappa (Cohen, 1960) of .64-.82 depending on the factor (Schneider et al., 2012), versus .48 for Walton's argumentation schemes (Schneider et al., 2013)). Factors provide a good way to organize the debate; filtering discussions based on each factor can show the rationale topic by topic, which supported decision making in a pilot user-based evaluation (Schneider, 2014).

We can also identify the misunderstandings that newcomers have about which factors are important, and about what kind of support is necessary to justify claims about whether a factor holds. When an article is unacceptable because it lacks reliable sources, it is not enough to counter that *someone will publish about this website when it gets out of beta testing.*[3] This newcomer's argument fails to convincingly establish that there are reliable sources (because for Wikipedia, a reliable source should be published, independent, and subject to full editorial control), and may make things worse because it suggests that the sources are not independent. Rather, a convincing counterargument would explicitly address how the most relevant criteria are met.

3 Envisioned applications of argumentation mining

The manual annotations described above, of argumentation schemes and of factors, suggest several possibilities for automation. Scalable processes for analyzing messages are needed since Wikipedia has roughly 500 debates each week about deleting borderline articles. Argumentation mining could be the basis for several support tools, helping participants write more persuasive arguments, find weaknesses in others' arguments, and summarize the overall conclusions of the debate.

First consider how we might give participants feedback about their arguments. From our research, we know which argumentation schemes are viewed as acceptable and persuasive within the community. If real-time algorithms could identify the argumentation schemes used in the main argument, authors could be given personalized feedback even before their message is posted to the discussion. When the argumentation scheme used in a draft message is not generally accepted, the author could be warned that their message might not be persuasive, and given personalized suggestions. Thus debate participants might be nudged into writing more persuasive arguments.

Next consider how we could help participants find weaknesses in others' arguments. Automatically listing critical questions might benefit the discussion. Critical questions point out the possible weaknesses of an argument, based on the argumentation scheme pattern it uses. Listing these questions in concrete and contextualized form (drawing on the premises, inference rules, and conclusions to instantiate and contextualize them) would encourage participants to consider the possible flaws in reasoning and might prompt participants to request answers within the debate. In the authoring process, supplying the critical questions associated with argumentation schemes might also help the author (who could consider elaborating before submitting a message).

Finally, we could envision argumentation mining being used to summarize the debate. Macro-argumentation, such as the factors analysis described above, would be a natural choice for summarization, as it has already proven useful for filtering discussions. A more reasoning-intensive approach would be to calculate consistent outcomes (Wyner and van Engers, 2010), if debates can be easily formalized.

3.1 Challenges for argumentation mining

In previous work, argumentation schemes have been classified in constrained domains, especially in legal argumentation (Mochales and Moens, 2011) and by using (Feng, 2010; Feng and Hirst, 2011) the Araucaria corpus (Katzav et al., 2004).[4]

Each of our envisioned applications of argumentation has certain requirements. Automatically detecting the argumentation schemes used in a message could be used for supporting authoring and finding weaknesses of arguments, which focus on the interior of each message. In order to ask the

[3]This is a real argument from a newcomer from our corpus, slightly reworded for clarity.

[4]Further work is needed on argument scheme prevalence, which seems to vary by domain. Only 3 of Feng's 5 'most common argumentation schemes' appear in the top 14 most common schemes in our corpus, excluding *Argument from Example* and *Argument from Cause to Effect*.

appropriate critical questions, the premises, conclusions, and inference rules would first need to be detected. To get at the point of each message, the macro-level argumentation (for instance using factors and dimensions) would be useful for summarizing the debate, especially if we record rationales.

Another challenge is to create scaleable architectures for real-time or batch reprocessing of argumentation mining on the Web. In our scenarios above, support for authoring arguments would require real-time feedback (i.e. within minutes). Slower batch processing would be useful for the two other scenarios (support in challenging arguments with critical questions; support for summarizing debates) since Wikipedia's debates are generally open for 7 days.

3.2 Related scenarios

This is a single use case, but it represents a wide array of related ones. Open source and open knowledge projects are full of decision making discussions available widely in textual form. Rhetorical studies of them so far take place on a qualitative, discursive level. Examples include dissent and rhetorical devices in bug reporting (Ko and Chilana, 2011) and how Python listservs select enhancement proposals (Barcellini et al., 2005). Interestingly, the role of a participant in the Python community is related to the kinds of message they quote (Syntheses, Disagreements, Proposals, or Agreements), and Syntheses and Disagreements are the most quoted. The organizational relevance of these open decision making discussions in collaborative communities makes them a promising target for support, and argumentation mining technology is an appropriate tool to deploy towards that end.

4 Conclusions

This paper detailed how automated argumentation mining could be leveraged to support open online communities in making decisions through online debates about rationale. We first gave a basic overview of argumentation structures, describing arguments as consisting of Statements, Inference Rules, and (possibly) Attacks. Then we described our own work on manual identification of argumentation schemes in Wikipedia information quality debates. We envisioned three kinds support tools that could be developed from automated argumentation mining in the future, for authoring more persuasive arguments, finding weaknesses in others' arguments, and summarizing a debate's overall conclusions. Open online communities are a wide area of application where argumentation mining could help participants reason collectively.

References

Kevin D Ashley. 1991. *Modeling Legal Arguments: Reasoning with Cases and Hypotheticals.* MIT Press.

Flore Barcellini, Françoise Détienne, Jean-Marie Burkhardt, and Warren Sack. 2005. A study of online discussions in an open-source software community. In *Communities and Technologies 2005*, pages 301–320. Springer.

Trevor J M Bench-Capon and Edwina L Rissland. 2001. Back to the future: Dimensions revisited. In *Proceedings of JURIX 2001*, pages 41–52.

Jacob Cohen. 1960. A coefficient of agreement for nominal scales. *Educational and psychological measurement*, 20(1):37–46.

Morten Elvang-Gøransson, Paul J Krause, and John Fox. 1993. Acceptability of arguments as 'logical uncertainty'. In *Symbolic and Quantitative Approaches to Reasoning and Uncertainty*, pages 85–90. Springer.

Vanessa Wei Feng and Graeme Hirst. 2011. Classifying arguments by scheme. In *Proceedings of the 49th Annual Meeting of the Association for Computational Linguistics: Human Language Technologies–Volume 1*, pages 987–996.

Vanessa Wei Feng. 2010. Classifying arguments by scheme. Master's thesis, University of Toronto.

Joel Katzav, Chris Reed, and Glenn Rowe. 2004. Argument Research Corpus. In *Proceedings of the 2003 Conference on Practical Applications in Language and Computers*, pages 229–239. Peter Lang.

Andrew J Ko and Parmit K Chilana. 2011. Design, discussion, and dissent in open bug reports. In *Proceedings of the 2011 iConference*, pages 106–113.

Raquel Mochales and Marie-Francine Moens. 2011. Argumentation mining. *Artificial Intelligence and Law*, 19(1):1–22.

John L Pollock. 1994. Justification and defeat. *Artificial Intelligence*, 67(2):377–407.

Henry Prakken. 2010. An abstract framework for argumentation with structured arguments. *Argument and Computation*, 1(2):93–124.

Jodi Schneider, Alexandre Passant, and Stefan Decker. 2012. Deletion discussions in Wikipedia: Decision factors and outcomes. In *Proceedings of the International Symposium on Wikis and Open Collaboration*, pages 17:1–17:10.

Jodi Schneider, Krystian Samp, Alexandre Passant, and Stefan Decker. 2013. Arguments about deletion: How experience improves the acceptability of arguments in ad-hoc online task groups. In *Proceedings of the ACM conference on Computer Supported Cooperative Work*, pages 1069–1080.

Jodi Schneider. 2014. *Identifying, Annotating, and Filtering Arguments and Opinions in Open Collaboration Systems*. Ph.D. dissertation, Digital Enterprise Research Institute, National University of Ireland, Galway. Corpus and supplementary material also available online at `http://purl.org/jsphd`.

Gerard Vreeswijk. 1993. *Studies in Defeasible Argumentation*. Ph.D. dissertation, Free University Amsterdam.

Douglas Walton, Chris Reed, and Fabrizio Macagno. 2008. *Argumentation Schemes*. Cambridge.

Adam Wyner and Tom van Engers. 2010. Towards web-based mass argumentation in natural language. In *Proceedings of Knowledge Engineering and Knowledge Management 2010 Poster and Demo Track*.

Adam Z Wyner, Trevor J Bench-Capon, and Katie Atkinson. 2008. Three senses of "Argument". In *Computable Models of the Law: Languages, Dialogues, Games, Ontologies*, pages 146–161. Springer-Verlag.

A Benchmark Dataset for Automatic Detection of Claims and Evidence in the Context of Controversial Topics

Ehud Aharoni* IBM Haifa Research Lab, Haifa, Israel

Anatoly Polnarov* Hebrew University, Israel

Tamar Lavee† IBM Haifa Research Lab, Haifa, Israel

Daniel Hershcovich IBM Haifa Research Lab, Haifa, Israel

Ran Levy IBM Haifa Research Lab, Haifa, Israel

Ruty Rinott IBM Haifa Research Lab, Haifa, Israel

Dan Gutfreund IBM Haifa Research Lab, Haifa, Israel

Noam Slonim‡ IBM Haifa Research Lab, Haifa, Israel

Abstract

We describe a novel and unique argumentative structure dataset. This corpus consists of data extracted from hundreds of Wikipedia articles using a meticulously monitored manual annotation process. The result is 2,683 argument elements, collected in the context of 33 controversial topics, organized under a simple claim-evidence structure. The obtained data are publicly available for academic research.

1 Introduction

One major obstacle in developing automatic argumentation mining techniques is the scarcity of relevant high quality annotated data. Here, we describe a novel and unique benchmark data that relies on a simple argument model and elaborates on the associated annotation process. Most importantly, the argumentative elements were gathered in the context of pre-defined controversial topics, which distinguishes our work from other previous related corpora.[1] Two recent works that are currently under review [Rinott et al, Levy et al] have reported first results over different subsets of this data, which is now publically available for academic research upon request. We believe that this novel corpus should be of practical importance to many researches, and in particular to the emerging community of argumentation mining.

Unlike the classical Toulmin model (Freeley and Steinberg 2008), we considered a simple and robust argument structure comprising only two components – *claim* and associated supporting *evidence*. The argumentative structures were carefully annotated under a pre-defined *topic*, introduced as a debate motion. As the collected data covers a diverse set of 33 motions, we expect it could be used to develop generic tools for automatic detection and construction of argumentative structures in the context of new topics.

2 Data Model

We defined and implemented the following concepts:

Topic – a short, usually controversial statement that defines the subject of interest. **Context De-**

* These authors contributed equally to this manuscript.

† Present affiliation: Yahoo!

‡ Corresponding author, at noams@il.ibm.com

[1] E.g., AraucariaDB (Reed 2005, Moens et al 2007) and Vaccine/Injury Project (V/IP) Corpus (Ashley and Walker 2013).

Proceedings of the First Workshop on Argumentation Mining, pages 64–68,
Baltimore, Maryland USA, June 26, 2014.

pendent Claim (CDC) – a general concise statement that directly supports or contests the Topic. **Context Dependent Evidence (CDE)** – a text segment that directly supports a CDC in the context of a given Topic. Examples are given in Section 6.

Furthermore, since one can support a claim using different types of evidence (Rieke et al 2012, Seech 2008), we defined and considered three CDE types: **Study**: Results of a quantitative analysis of data given as numbers or as conclusions. **Expert**: Testimony by a person / group / committee / organization with some known expertise in or authority on the topic. **Anecdotal:** a description of specific event(s)/instance(s) or concrete example(s).

3 Labeling Challenges and Approach

The main challenge we faced in collecting the annotated data was the inherently elusive nature of concepts such as "claim" and "evidence." To address that we formulated two sets of criteria for CDC and CDE, respectively, and relied on a team of about 20 carefully trained in-house labelers whose work was closely monitored. To further enhance the quality of the collected data we adopted a two-stage labeling approach. First, a team of five labelers worked independently on the same text and prepared the initial set of candidate CDCs or candidate CDEs. Next, a team of five labelers—not necessarily the same five—independently crosschecked the joint list of the detected candidates, each of which was either confirmed or rejected. Candidates confirmed by at least three labelers were included in the corpus.

4 Labeling Guidelines

The labeling guidelines defined the concepts of Topic, CDC, CDE, and CDE types, along with relevant examples. According to these guidelines, given a Topic, a text fragment should be labeled as a CDC if and only if it complies with all of the following five CDC criteria: **Strength**: Strong content that directly supports or contests the provided Topic. **Generality**: General content that deals with a relatively broad idea. **Phrasing**: Is well phrased, or requires at most a single and minor "allowed" change.[2] **Keeping text spirit**: Keeps the spirit of the original text from which it was extracted. **Topic unity**: Deals with one, or at most two related topics. Four CDE criteria were defined in a similar way, given a Topic and a CDC, except for the generality criterion.

5 Labeling Details

The labeling process was carried out in the GATE environment (https://gate.ac.uk/). The 33 Topics were selected at random from the debate motions at http://idebate.org/ database. The labeling process was divided into five stages:

Search: Given a Topic, five labelers were asked to independently search English Wikipedia[3] for articles with promising content.

Claim Detection: At this stage, five labelers independently detected candidate CDCs supporting or contesting the Topic within each article suggested by the Search team.

Claim Confirmation: At this stage, five labelers independently cross-examined the candidate CDCs suggested at the Claim Detection stage, aiming to confirm a candidate and its sentiment as to the given Topic, or reject it by referring to one of the five CDC Criteria it fails to meet. The candidate CDCs confirmed by at least three labelers were forwarded to the next stage.

Evidence Detection: At this stage, five labelers independently detected candidate CDEs supporting a confirmed CDC in the context of the given Topic. The search for CDEs was done

[2] For example, anaphora resolution. The enclosed data set contains the corrected version as well, as proposed by the labelers.

[3] We considered the Wikipedia dump as of April 3, 2012.

only in the same article where the corresponding CDC was found.

Evidence Confirmation: This stage was carried out in a way similar to Claim Confirmation. The only difference was that the labelers were required to classify accepted CDE under one or more CDE types.

Labelers training and feedback: Before joining actual labeling tasks, novice labelers were assigned with several completed tasks and were expected to show a reasonable degree of agreement with a consensus solution prepared in advance by the project administrators. In addition, the results of each Claim Confirmation task were examined by one or two of the authors (AP and NS) to ensure the conformity to the guidelines. In case crude mistakes were spotted, the corresponding labeler was requested to revise and resubmit. Due to the large numbers of CDE candidates, it was impractical to rely on such a rigorous monitoring process in Evidence Confirmation. Instead, Evidence Consensus Solutions were created for selected articles by several experienced labelers, who first solved the tasks independently and then reached consensus in a joint meeting. Afterwards, the tasks were assigned to the rest of the labelers. Their results on these tasks were juxtaposed with the Consensus Solutions, and on the basis of this comparison individual feedback reports were drafted and sent to the team members. Each labeler received such a report on an approximately weekly basis.

6 Data Summary

For 33 debate motions, a total of 586 Wikipedia articles were labeled. The labeling process resulted in 1,392 CDCs distributed across 321 articles. In 12 debate motions, for which 350 distinct CDCs were confirmed across 104 articles, we further completed the CDE labeling, ending up with a total of 1,291 confirmed CDEs – 431 of type Study, 516 of type Expert, and 529 of type Anecdotal. Note that some CDEs were associated with more than one type (for example, 118 CDEs were classified both under the type Study and Expert).

Presented in Tables 1 and 2 are several examples of CDCs and CDEs gathered under the Topics we worked with, as well as some inacceptable candidates illustrating some of the subtleties of the performed work.

Topic	The sale of violent video games to minors should be banned
(Pro) CDC	*Violent video games can increase children's aggression*
(Pro) CDC	*Video game publishers unethically train children in the use of weapons* Note that a valid CDC is not necessarily factual.
(Con) CDC	*Violent games affect children positively*
Invalid CDC 1	*Video game addiction is excessive or compulsive use of computer and video games that interferes with daily life.* This statement defines a concept relevant to the Topic, not a relevant claim.
Invalid CDC 2	*Violent TV shows just mirror the violence that goes on in the real world.* This claim is not relevant enough to Topic.
Invalid CDC 3	*Violent video games should not be sold to children.* This candidate simply repeats the Topic and thus is not considered a valid CDC.
Invalid CDC 4	*"Doom" has been blamed for nationally covered school shooting.* This candidate fails the generality criterion, as it focuses on a specific single video game. Note that it could serve as CDE to a more general CDC.

Table 1: Examples of CDCs and invalid CDCs.

Topic 1	The sale of violent video games to minors should be banned
(Pro) CDC	*Violent video games increase youth violence*
CDE (*Study*)	*The most recent large scale meta-analysis—examining 130 studies with over 130,000 subjects worldwide—concluded that exposure to violent*

	video games causes both short term and long term aggression in players
CDE *(Anecdotal)*	*In April 2000, a 16-year-old teenager murdered his father, mother and sister proclaiming that he was on an "avenging mission" for the main character of the video game Final Fantasy VIII*
Invalid CDE	*While most experts reject any link between video games content and real-life violence, some media scholars argue that the connection exists.* Invalid, because it includes information that contests the CDC.
Topic 2	The use of performance enhancing drugs in sports should be permitted
(Con) CDC	*Drug abuse can be harmful to one's health and even deadly.*
CDE *(Expert)*	*According to some nurse practitioners, stopping substance abuse can reduce the risk of dying early and also reduce some health risks like heart disease, lung disease, and strokes*
Invalid CDE	*Suicide is very common in adolescent alcohol abusers, with 1 in 4 suicides in adolescents being related to alcohol abuse.* Although the candidate CDE does support the CDC, the notion of adolescent alcohol abusers is irrelevant to the Topic. Therefore, the candidate is invalid.

Table 2: Examples of CDE and invalid CDE

7 Agreement and Recall Results

To evaluate the labelers' agreement we used Cohen's kappa coefficient (Landis and Koch 1977). The average measure was calculated over all labelers' pairs, for each pair taking those articles on which the corresponding labelers worked together and omitting labeler pairs which labeled together less than 100 CDCs/CDEs. This strategy was chosen since no two labelers worked on the exact same tasks, so standard multi-rater agreement measures could not be applied. The obtained average kappa was 0.39 and 0.4 in the Claim confirmation and Evidence confirmation stages, respectively, which we consider satisfactory given the subtlety of the concepts involved and the fact that the tasks naturally required a certain extent of subjective decision making.

We further employed a simple method to obtain a rough estimate of the recall at the detection stages. For CDCs (and similarly for CDEs), let n be the number of CDCs detected and confirmed in a given article, and x be the unknown total number of CDCs in this article. Assuming the *i*-th labeler detects a ratio p_i of x, and taking a strong assumption of independence between the labelers, we get:

$$x \prod_i (1 - p_i) = x - n.$$

We estimated p_i from the observed data, and computed x for each article. We were then able to compute the estimated recall per motion, ending up with the estimated average recall of 90.6% and 90.0% for CDCs and CDEs, respectively.

8 Future Work and Conclusion

There are several natural ways to proceed further. First, a considerable increase in the quantity of gathered CDE data can be achieved by expanding the search scope beyond the article in which the CDC is found. Second, the argument model can be enhanced – for example, to include counter-CDE (i.e., evidence that contest the CDC). Third, one may look into ways to add more labeling layers on the top of the existing model (for example, distinguishing between factual CDCs, value CDCs, and so forth). Fourth, new topics and new sources besides Wikipedia can be considered.

The data is released and available upon request for academic research. We hope that it will prove useful for different data mining communities, and particularly for various purposes in the field of Argumentation Mining.

References

Austin J. Freeley and David L. Steinberg. 2008. *Argumentation and Debate*. Wadsworth, Belmont, California.

Chris Reed. 2005. "Preliminary Results from an Argument Corpus" in *Proceedings of the IX Symposium on Social Communication*, Santiago de Cuba, pp. 576-580.

J. Richard Landis and Gary G. Koch. 1977. "The measurement of observer agreement for categorical data." *Biometrics* 33:159-174.

Kevid D. Ashley and Vern R. Walker. 2013. "Toward Constructing Evidence-Based Legal Arguments Using Legal Decision Documents and Machine Learning" in *Proceedings of the Fourteenth International Conference on Artificial Intelligence and Law (ICAIL '13)*, Rome, Italy, pp. 176-180.

Marie-Francine Moens, Erik Boiy, Raquel Mochales Palau, and Chris Reed. 2007. "Automatic Detection of Arguments in Legal Texts" in *Proceedings of the International Conference on AI & Law (ICAIL-2007)*, Stanford, CA, pp. 225-230.

Richard D. Rieke, Malcolm O. Sillars and Tarla Rai Peterson. 2012. *Argumentation and Critical Decision Making (8e)*. Prentice Hall, USA.

Ran Levy, Yonatan Bilu, Daniel Hershcovich, Ehud Aharoni and Noam Slonim. "Context Dependent Claim Detection." Submitted

Ruty Rinott, Lena Dankin, Carlos Alzate, Ehud Aharoni and Noam Slonim. "Show Me Your Evidence – an Automatic Method for Context Dependent Evidence Detection." Submitted.

Zachary Seech. 2008. *Writing Philosophy Papers (5th edition)*. Wadsworth, Cengage Learning, Belmont, California.

Applying Argumentation Schemes for Essay Scoring

Yi Song Michael Heilman Beata Beigman Klebanov Paul Deane
Educational Testing Service
Princeton, NJ, USA
{ysong, mheilman, bbeigmanklebanov, pdeane}@ets.org

Abstract

Under the framework of the argumentation scheme theory (Walton, 1996), we developed annotation protocols for an argumentative writing task to support identification and classification of the arguments being made in essays. Each annotation protocol defined argumentation schemes (i.e., reasoning patterns) in a given writing prompt and listed questions to help evaluate an argument based on these schemes, to make the argument structure in a text explicit and classifiable. We report findings based on an annotation of 600 essays. Most annotation categories were applied reliably by human annotators, and some categories significantly contributed to essay score. An NLP system to identify sentences containing scheme-relevant critical questions was developed based on the human annotations.

1. Introduction

In this paper, we analyze the structure of arguments as a first step in analyzing their quality. Argument structure plays a critical role in identifying relevant arguments based on their content, so it seems reasonable to focus first on identifying characteristic patterns of argumentation and the ways in which such arguments are typically developed when they are explicitly stated. It is worthwhile to classify the arguments in a text and to identify their structure when they are extended to include whole text segments (Walton, 1996; Walton, Reed, and Macagno, 2008), but it is not clear how far human annotation can go in analyzing argument structure.

An analysis of the effectiveness and full complexity of argument structure is different than the identification of generic elements that might compose an argument, such as claims (e.g., a thesis sentence), main reasons (e.g., supporting topic sentences), evidence (e.g., elaborating segments), and other components, such as the introduction and conclusion (Burstein, Kukich, Wolff, Lu, Chodorow, Braden-Harder, & Harris, 1998; Burstein, Marcu, and Knight, 2003; Pendar & Cotos, 2008). In contrast, here we focus on analyzing specific types of arguments, what the literature terms *argumentation schemes* (Walton, 1996). Argumentation schemes include schematic content and take into account a pattern of possible argumentation moves in a larger persuasive dialog. Understanding these argumentation schemes is important for understanding the logic behind an argument. *Critical questions* associated with a particular argumentation scheme provide a normative standard that can be used to evaluate the relevance of an argument's justificatory structure (van Eemeren and Grootendorst, 1992; Walton, 1996; Walton et al., 2008).

We aimed to lay foundations for the automated analysis of argumentation schemes, such as the identification and classification of the arguments in an essay. Specifically, we developed annotation protocols for writing prompts in an argument analysis task from a graduate school admissions test. The task was designed to assess how well a student analyzes someone else's argument, which is provided by the prompt. The student must critically evaluate the logical soundness of the given argument. The annotation categories were designed to map student responses to the scheme-relevant critical questions. We examined whether this approach provides a useful framework for describing argumentation and whether human annotators can apply it reliably and consistently. Furthermore, we have begun work on automating the annotation process by developing a system to predict whether sentences contain scheme-relevant critical questions.

2. Theoretical Framework

As Nussbaum (2011) notes, there have been critical advances in the study of informal argument,

Proceedings of the First Workshop on Argumentation Mining, pages 69–78,
Baltimore, Maryland USA, June 26, 2014.

which takes place within a social context involving dialog among people with different beliefs, most notably the development of theories that provide relatively rich schemata for classifying informal arguments, such as Walton (1996).

An argumentation scheme is defined as "a more or less conventionalized way of representing the relation between what is stated in the argument and what is stated in the standpoint" (van Eemeren and Grootendorst, 1992, p. 96). It is a strategic pattern of argumentation linking premises to a conclusion and illustrating how the conclusion is derived from the premises. This "internal structure" of argumentation reflects justificatory standards that can be used to help evaluate the reasonableness of an argument (van Eemeren and Grootendorst, 2004). Argumentation schemes should be distinguished from the kinds of structures postulated in Mann and Thompson's (1988) Rhetorical Structure Theory (RST) because they focus on relations inherent in the meaning of the argument, regardless of whether they are explicitly realized in the discourse.

Consider, for instance, *argument from consequences*, which applies when the primary claim argues for or against a proposed policy (i.e., course of action) by citing positive or negative consequences that would follow if the policy were adopted (Walton, 1996). Elaborations of an argument from consequences are designed to defend against possible objections. For instance, an opponent could claim that the claimed consequences are not probable; or that they are not desirable; or that they are less important than other, undesirable consequences. Thus a sophisticated writer, in elaborating an *argument from consequences*, may provide information to reinforce the idea that the argued consequences are probable, desirable, and more important than any possible undesired effects. These moves correspond to what the literature calls *critical questions*, which function as a standard for evaluating the reasonableness of an argument based on its argumentation schemes (Walton, 1996).

Walton and his colleagues (2008) analyzed over 60 argumentation schemes, and identified critical questions associated with certain schemes as the logical moves in argumentative discourse. The range of possible moves is quite large, especially when people use multiple schemes. There have been several efforts to annotate corpora with argumentation scheme information to support future machine learning efforts (Mochales and Ieven, 2009; Palau and Moens, 2009; Rienks, Heylen, and Van der Weijden, 2005; Verbree, Rienks, and Heylen, 2006), to support argument representation (Atkinson, Bench-Capon, and McBurney, 2006; Rahwan, Banihashemi, Reed, Walton, and Abdallah, 2010), and to teach argumentative writing (Ferretti, Lewis, and Andrews-Weckerly, 2009; Nussbaum and Schraw, 2007; Nussbaum and Edwards, 2011; Song and Ferretti, 2013). In addition, Feng and Hirsh (2011) used the argumentation schemes to reconstruct the implicit parts (i.e., unstated assumptions) of the argument structure. In many previous studies, the data sets on argumentation schemes were relatively small and the inter-rater agreement was not measured.

We are particularly interested in exploring the relationship between the use of scheme-relevant critical questions and essay quality, as measured by holistic essay scores. The difference between an expert and a novice is that the expert knows which critical questions should be asked when the dynamic of the argument requires them, while the novice misses the essential moves to ask critical questions that help evaluate if the argument is valid or reasonable. Often, students presume information and fail to ask questions that would reveal potential fallacies. For example, they might use quotations from books, arguments from TV programs, or opinions posted online without evaluating whether the information is adequately supported by evidence.

Critically evaluating arguments is considered an important skill in college and graduate school. For example, a widely accepted graduate admissions test has a task to assess students' critical thinking and analytical writing skills. In this argument analysis task, students should demonstrate skills in critiquing other people's arguments, such as identifying unwarranted assumptions or discussing what specific evidence is need to support the argument. They must communicate their evaluation of the arguments clearly to the audience. To accomplish this task successfully, students need to evaluate the arguments against appropriate criteria. Therefore, their essays could be analyzed using an annotation approach based on the theory of argumentation schemes and critical questions.

Our research questions were as follows:

1. Can this scheme-based annotation approach be applied consistently by annotators to a corpus of argumentative essays?
2. Do annotation categories based on the theory of argumentation schemes contribute

significantly to the prediction of essay scores?

3. Can we use NLP techniques to train an automated classifier for distinguishing sentences that raise critical questions from sentences that contain no critical questions?

3 Development of Annotation Protocols

Although Walton's argumentation schemes provided a good framework for analyzing arguments, it was challenging to apply them in some cases of argument essays because various interpretations could be made on some argument structures. For instance, people were often confused with *argument from consequences*, *argument from correlation to cause*, and *argument from cause to effect* because all these three types of arguments indicate a causal relationship. While it is good that Walton tried to identify variations of a causal relationship, a side effect is that some schemes are not so distinguishable from each other, especially for someone who is not an expert in logic. This ambiguity makes it difficult to apply his theory directly to annotation. Thus, we modified Walton's schemes and created new schemes when necessary to achieve exclusive annotation categories and capture the features in the argument analysis task.

In this paper, we illustrate our annotation protocols on a policy argument because over half of the argument analysis prompts for the assessment we are working with deal with policy issues (i.e., issues involve the possibility of putting a practice into place). Here, we use the "Patriot Car" prompt as an example.

> The following appeared in a memorandum from the new president of the Patriot car manufacturing company.
>
> "In the past, the body styles of Patriot cars have been old-fashioned, and our cars have not sold as well as have our competitors' cars. But now, since many regions in this country report rapid increases in the numbers of newly licensed drivers, we should be able to increase our share of the market by selling cars to this growing population. Thus, we should discontinue our oldest models and concentrate instead on manufacturing sporty cars. We can also improve the success of our marketing campaigns by switching our advertising to the Youth Advertising agency, which has successfully promoted the country's leading soft drink."

Test takers are asked to analyze the reasoning in the argument, consider any assumptions, and discuss how well any evidence that is mentioned supports the conclusion.

The prompt states that the new president of the Patriot car manufacturing company pointed out a problem that the body styles of Patriot cars have been old-fashioned and their cars have not sold as well as their competitors' cars. The president proposed a plan to discontinue their oldest models and to concentrate on manufacturing sporty cars. He believed that this plan will lead to an increase in their market share (i.e., the goal). This is a policy issue because it involves whether the plan of discontinuing oldest car models and manufacturing sporty cars should be put into place. This prompt shows a typical pattern of many argument analysis prompts about policy issues: (1) a problem is stated; (2) a plan is proposed; and (3) a desirable goal will be achieved if the plan is implemented. Thus, we created a *policy* scheme that includes these three major components (i.e., problem, plan, and goal), and a causal relationship that bridges the plan to the goal in the policy scheme. Therefore, a *causal* scheme appears in a policy argument to represent the causal relationship from the proposed plan to the goal. This part is different from Walton's analysis. He uses the *argument from consequences* scheme for policy arguments, but it created confusions when applying it to annotation, especially when students unconsciously use the word "cause" to introduce a potential consequence that follows a policy. In addition, our *causal* scheme combines the argument from *correlation to cause* scheme and the argument from *cause to effect* scheme specified by Walton.

Accordingly, we revised or re-arranged some of the critical questions in Walton's theory. For example, challenges to arguments that use a *policy* scheme fall into the following six categories: (a) problem; (b) goal; (c) plan implementation; (d) plan definition; (e) side effect; and (f) alternative plan. When someone writes that the president should re-evaluate whether this is really a problem, it matches the question in the "problem" category; when someone questions if there is an alternative plan that could also help achieve the goal and is better than the plan proposed by the president, it should be categorized as a challenge in "alternative plan." We call these "specific questions" because they are attached to a par-

Scheme	Category	Critical Question
Policy	Problem	Is this really a problem? Is the problem well-defined?
	Goal	How desirable is this goal? Are there specific conflicting goals we do not wish to sacrifice?
	Plan Implementation	Is it practically possible to carry out this plan?
	Plan Definition	Is the plan well defined?
	Side Effects	Are there negative side effects that should be taken into account if we carry out our plan?
	Alternative plan	Are there better alternatives that could achieve the goal?
Causal	Causal Mechanism	Is there really a correlation? Is the correlation merely a coincidence (invalid causal relationship)? Are there alternative causal factors?
	Causal Efficacy	Is the causal mechanism strong enough to produce the desired effects?
	Applicability	Does this causal mechanism apply?
	Intervening Factors	Are there intervening factors that could undermine the causal mechanism?
Sample	Significance	Are the patterns we see in the sample clear-cut enough (and in the right direction) to support the desired inference?
	Representativeness	Is there any reason to think that this sample might not be representative of the group about which we wish to make an inference?
	Stability	Is there any reason to think this pattern will be stable across all the circumstances about which we wish to make an inference?
	Sample Size	Is there any reason to think that the sample may not be large enough and reliable enough to support the inference we wish to draw?
	Validity	Is the sample measured in a way that will give valid information on the population attributes about which we wish to make inferences?
	Alternatives	Are there external considerations that could invalidate the claims?

Table 1: Annotation protocols for three types of argumentation schemes

ticular prompt. In other words, specific questions are content dependent. Each category also includes one or more "general questions" that can be asked for any argument using the same argumentation scheme, and in this case, it is the *policy* scheme.

We have developed annotation protocols for various argumentation schemes. Table 1 includes part of the annotation protocols (i.e., scheme, category, and general critical questions) for three argumentation schemes: the *policy* argument scheme, the *causal argument* scheme, and the *argument from a sample* scheme. This study focuses on these three argumentation schemes and 16 associated categories.

4 Application of the Annotation Approach

This section focuses on applying the annotation approach and the following research question: Can this scheme-based annotation approach be applied consistently by raters to a corpus of argumentative essays?

4.1 Annotation Rules

The first step of the annotation is reading the entire essay. It is important to understand the writer's major arguments and the organization of the essay. Next, the annotator will identify and highlight any text segment (e.g., paragraph, sentence, or clause) that addresses a critical question. Usually, the minimal text segment is at the sentence-level, but it could be the case that the selection is at the phrase-level when a sentence includes multiple points that match more than one critical question. Thirdly, for a highlighted unit, the annotator will choose a topic, a category, and a second topic, if applicable. Only one category label can be assigned to each selected text unit.

"Generic" information will not be selected or assigned an annotation label. Generic information includes restatements of the text in the prompt, general statements that do not address any specific questions, rhetoric attacks, and irrelevant information. Note that this notion of generic information is related to "shell language," as described by Madnani et al (2012). However, our definition here focuses more closely on sentences that do not raise critical questions. Surface errors (e.g., grammar and spelling) can be ignored if they do not prevent people from understanding the meaning of the essay. Here is an example of annotated text.

> As stated by the president, there is a rapid increase in the number of newly licensed drivers which would be a marketable target. [However, there was no concrete evidence that these newly licensed drivers favored sporty cars over other model types.]$_{\textbf{Causal Applicability}}$ [On a similar note, there was no anecdotal evidence demonstrating that lack of sales was contributed to the old-fashion body styles of the Patriot cars.]$_{\textbf{Causal Mechanism}}$ [There could be numerous other factors contributing to their lack of sales: prices are not competitive, safety ratings are not as high, features are not as appealing. The best way to tackle this problem is to send out researches and surveys to get the opinions of consumers.]$_{\textbf{Causal Mechanism}}$

4.2 Annotation Tool

The annotation interface includes the following elements:

1. the original writing prompt;
2. topics that the prompt addresses;
3. categories associated with critical questions relevant to that type of argument;
4. general critical questions that can be used across prompts that possess the same argumentation scheme; and
5. specific critical questions for this particular prompt.

The annotators highlight text segments to be annotated and then clicked a button to choose a topic (e.g., body style versus advertising agency in the Patriot Car prompt) and a category to identify which critical questions were addressed.

4.3 Data and Annotation Procedures

In this section, we report our annotation on two selected argument analysis prompts in an assessment for graduate school admissions. The actual prompts are not included here because they may be used in future tests. Both prompts deal with policy issues and are involved in causal reasoning, but the second prompt also has a *sample* scheme (see Table 1). For each prompt, we randomly selected 300 essays to annotate. These essays were written between 2008 and 2010.

Four annotators with linguistics backgrounds who were not co-authors of the paper received training on the annotation approach. Training focused on the application to specific prompts because each prompt had a specific annotation protocol that covers the argumentation schemes and how they relate to the prompt's topics. The first author delivered the training sessions, and helped resolve differences of opinion during practice annotation rounds. After training and practice, the annotators annotated 20 pilot essays for a selected prompt to test their agreement. This pilot stage gave us another chance to find and clarify any confusion about the annotation categories. After that, the annotators worked on the sampled set of 300 essays, and these annotations were then used for analyses. For each prompt, 40 essays were randomly selected, and all 4 annotators annotated these 40 essays to check the inter-annotator agreement. For the experiments described later that involve the multiply-annotated set, we used the annotations from the annotator who seemed most consistent.

4.4 Inter-Annotator Agreement

To compute human-human agreement, we automatically split the essays into sentences. For each sentence, we computed the annotations that overlapped with at least part of the tence. Then, for each category, we computed human-human agreement across all sentences about whether that category should be marked or not. We also created a "Generic" label, as discussed in section 4.1, for sentences that were not marked by any of the other labels.

We computed two inter-annotator agreement statistics. Our primary statistic is Cohen's *kappa* between pairs of raters. Four annotators generated 6 pairs of *kappa* values, and in this report we only report the average *kappa* value for each annotation category. As an alternative statistic, we computed Krippendorff's *alpha*, a chance-corrected statistic for calculating the inter-annotator agreement between multiple coders (four annotators in our case), which is similar to multi *kappa* (Krippendorff, 1980).

Table 2 shows the *kappa* and *alpha* values for each annotation category, excluding those that were rare. To identify rare categories, we averaged the numbers of sentences annotated under a category among four annotators, which indicated how many sentences were annotated under this category in 40 essays. If the number was lower than 10, which means that no more than one sentence was annotated in every four essays, then the category was considered rare. Most rare categories had low inter-rater agreement, which is not surprising. It is not realistic to require annotators to always agree about rare categories.

From Table 2, we can see that the *kappa* value and the alpha value on the same category were close. The inter-annotator agreement on the "generic" category varied little across the two prompts (*kappa*: 0.572-0.604; *alpha*: 0.571-0.603), which indicates that the annotators had a fairly good agreement on this category. The annotators had good agreements on most of the commonly used categories (*kappa* ranged from 0.549 to 0.848, and *alpha* ranged from 0.537 to 0.843) except the "plan definition" under the *policy* scheme in prompt B (both *kappa* and alpha *values* were below 0.400). The major reason for this disagreement is that one annotator marked a significantly higher number of sentences (more than double) for this category than others did.

Prompt	Category	*Kappa*	*Alpha*
Prompt A			
	Generic	0.572	0.571
	Policy : Problem	0.644	0.640
	Policy : Side Effects	0.612	0.609
	Policy : Alternative Plan	0.665	0.666
	Causal : Causal Mechanism	0.680	0.676
	Causal : Applicability	0.557	0.555
Prompt B			
	Generic	0.604	0.603
	Policy : Problem	0.848	0.843
	Policy : Plan Definition	0.346	0.327
	Causal : Causal Mechanism	0.620	0.622
	Causal : Applicability	0.767	0.769
	Sample : Validity	0.549	0.537

Table 2: Inter-annotator agreement

5 Essay Score and Annotation Features

This section explores the second research question: Do annotation categories based on the theory of argumentation schemes contribute significantly to the prediction of essay scores? Answering this question would tell us whether we capture an important construct of the argument analysis task by recognizing these argumentation features. Specifically, we tested whether these features add predictive value to a model based the state-of-the-art e-rater essay scoring system (Burstein, Tetreault, and Madnani, 2013).

To explore the relationship between annotation categories and essay quality, we ran a multiple regression analysis for each prompt. Essay quality was the dependent variable and was measured by a final human score, on a scale from 0 to 6. The independent variables were nine high-level e-rater features and the annotation categories relevant to a prompt (Prompt A: 10 categories; Prompt B 16 categories). The e-rater features were designed to measure different aspects of writing (grammar, mechanics, style, usage, word choice, word length, sentence variety, development, and organization). We computed the percentage of sentences that were marked as belonging to each category (i.e., the number of sentences in a category divided by the total number of sentences) to factor out essay length.

Note that the generic category was negatively correlated with the essay score in both prompts, since it included responses judged irrelevant to the scheme-relevant critical questions. In other words, the generic responses are the parts of the text that do not present specific critical evaluations of the arguments in a given prompt. For the purposes of our evaluation, we used the inverse feature labeled "all critical questions": the proportion of the text that actually raises some critical question (i.e., is not generic), regardless of scheme. We believe this formulation more transparently expresses the underlying mechanism relating the feature to essay quality.

For each prompt, we split the 300 essays into two data sets: the training set and the testing set. The testing set had the 40 essays that were annotated by all four annotators, and the training set had the remaining 260. We trained three models with stepwise regression on the training set and evaluated them on the testing set:

1. A model that included only the e-rater features to examine how well the e-rater model works ("baseline")
2. A model with the baseline features and all the annotation category percentage variables except for the "generic" category variable ("baseline + categories")
3. A model with the baseline features and a feature corresponding to the inverse of the "generic" category ("baseline + all critical questions").

Table 3 presents the Pearson correlation coefficient r values for comparing model predictions to human scores for each of the models. In prompt A, three annotation categories (causal mechanism, applicability, and alternative plan) were selected by the stepwise regression because they significantly contributed to the essay score above the nine e-rater features. This model showed higher test set correlations than the baseline model (Δr = .014). The model with the general argument feature ("all critical questions") showed a similar increase (Δr = .014).

	Training Set r	Testing Set r	Testing Set Δr
Prompt A			
baseline	.838	.852	---
baseline + specific categories	.852	.866	.014
baseline + all critical questions	.858	.866	.014
Prompt B			
baseline	.818	.761	---
baseline + specific categories	.835	.817	.056
baseline + all critical questions	.845	.821	.060

Table 3: Performance of essay scoring models with and without argumentation features

Similar observations apply to prompt B. The causal mechanism category added prediction significantly above e-rater with an increase (Δr = .056). The model containing the general argument feature ("all critical questions") performed slightly better (Δr = .060).

These results suggest that annotation categories based on argumentation schemes contribute additional useful information about essay quality to a strong baseline essay scoring model. In the next section, we report on preliminary experiments testing whether these annotations can be automated, which would almost certainly be necessary for practical applications.

6 Argumentation Schemes NLP System

We developed an NLP system for automatically identifying the presence of scheme-relevant critical questions in essays, and we evaluated this system with annotated data from the two selected argument prompts. This addresses the third research question: Can we use NLP techniques to train an automated classifier for distinguishing sentences that raise critical questions from sentences that contain no critical questions?

6.1 Modeling

In this initial development of the NLP system, we focused on the task of predicting whether a sentence raises any critical questions or none (i.e., generic vs. nongeneric). As such, the task was binary classification at the level of the sentence. The system we developed uses the SKLL tool[1] to fit L2-penalized logistic regression models with the following features:

- Word n-grams: Binary indicators for the presence of contiguous subsequences of n words in the sentence. The value of n ranged from 1 to 3. These features had value 1 if a particular n-gram was present in a sentence and 0 otherwise.
- word n-grams of the previous and next sentences: These are analogous to the word n-gram features for the current sentence.
- sentence length bins: Binary indicators for whether the sentence is longer than $2t$ word tokens, where t ranges from 1 to 10.
- sentence position: The sentence number divided by the number of sentences in text.
- part of speech tags: Binary indicators for the presence of words with various parts of speech, as predicted by NLTK 2.0.4.
- prompt overlap: Three features based on lexical overlap between the sentence and the prompt for the essay: a) the Jaccard similarity between the sets of word n-grams in the sentence and prompt (n = 1, 2, 3), b) the Jaccard similarity between the sets of word unigrams (i.e., just n = 1) in the sentence and prompt, and c) the Jaccard similarity between the sets of "content" word unigrams in the sentence and prompt (for this, content words were defined as word tokens that contained only numbers and letters and did not appear in NLTK's English stopword list).

6.2 Experiments

For these experiments, we used the training and testing sets described in Section 5. We trained models on the training data for each prompt individually and on the combination of the training data for both prompts. To measure generalization across prompts, we tested these models on the testing data for each prompt and on the combina-

[1] https://github.com/EducationalTestingService/skll

tion of the testing data for the two prompts. We evaluated performance in terms of unweighted Cohen's *kappa*. The results are in Table 4.

Training	Testing	*Kappa*
combined	combined	.438
Prompt A		.350
Prompt B		.346
combined	Prompt A	.379
Prompt A		.410
Prompt B		.217
combined	Prompt B	.498
Prompt A		.285
Prompt B		.478

Table 4: Performance of the NLP Model

The model trained on data from both prompts performed relatively well compared to the other models. For the testing data for prompt B, the combined model outperformed the model trained on just data from prompt B. However, the prompt-specific model for prompt A slightly outperformed the combined model on the testing data for prompt A.

Although the performance of models trained with data from one prompt and tested with data from another prompt did not perform as well, there is evidence of some generalization across prompts. The model trained on data from prompt B and tested on data from prompt A had *kappa* = 0.217; the model trained on data from prompt A and tested on data from prompt B had *kappa* = 0.285. Of course, these human-machine agreement values were somewhat lower than human-human agreement values (0.572 and 0.604, respectively), leaving substantial room for improvement in future work.

We also examined the most strongly weighted features in the combined model. We observed that multiple hedge words (e.g., "perhaps", "may") had positive weights, which associated with the "generic" class. We also observed that words related to argumentation (e.g., "conclusions", "questions") had negative weights, which associated them with the nongeneric class, as one would expect. One issue of concern is that some words related to the specific topics discussed in the prompts received high weights as well, which may limit generalizability.

7 Conclusion

Our research focused on identification and classification of argumentation schemes in argumentative text. We developed annotation protocols that capture various argumentation schemes. The annotation categories corresponded to scheme-relevant critical questions, and for text segments that do not contain any critical questions, we assigned a "generic" category. In this paper, we reported the results based on an annotation of a large pool of student essays (both high-quality and low-quality essays). Results showed that most of the common annotation categories (e.g. causal mechanism, alternative plan) can be applied reliably by the four annotators.

However, the annotation work is labor-intensive. People need to receive sufficient training to apply the approach consistently. They must not only identify meaningful chunks of textual information but also assign the right annotation category label for the selected text. Despite these complexities, it is a worthwhile investigation. Developing a systematic classification of argument structures not only plays a critical role in this project, but also has a potential contribution to other assessments on argumentation skills aligned with the Common Core State Standards. This work would help improve the current automated scoring techniques for argumentative essays because this annotation approach takes into account the argument structure and its content.

We ran regression analyses and found that manual annotations grounded in the argumentation schemes theory predict essay quality. Our data showed that features based on manual argument scheme annotations significantly contributed to models of essay scores for both prompts. This is probably because our approach focused on the core of argumentation, rather than surface or word-level features (e.g., mechanics, grammar, usage, style, essay organization, and vocabulary) examined by the baseline model.

Furthermore, we have implemented an automated system for predicting the human annotations. This system focused only on predicting whether or not a sentence raises any critical questions (i.e., generic vs. nongeneric). In the future, we plan to test whether features based on automated annotations make contributions to essay scoring models that are similar to the contributions of manual annotations. We also plan to work on detecting specific critical questions and adding additional features, such as features from Feng and Hirst (2011).

Acknowledgements

We would like to thank Keelan Evanini, Jill Burstein, Aoife Cahill, and the anonymous reviewers of this paper for their helpful comments. We would also like to thank Michael Flor for helping set up the annotation interface, and Melissa Lopez, Matthew Mulholland, Patrick Houghton, and Laura Ridolfi for annotating the data.

References

Katie Atkinson, Trevor Bench-Capon, and Peter McBurney. 2006. Computational representation of practical argument. *Synthese, 152*: 157-206. Burstein, Jill, Karen Kukich, Susanne Wolff, Chi Lu, Martin Chodorow, Lisa Braden-Harder, and Mary Dee Harris. 1998. "Automated scoring using a hybrid feature identification technique." In *Proceedings of the 17th international conference on Computational linguistics-Volume 1*, pp. 206-210. Association for Computational Linguistics.

Jill Burstein, Daniel Marcu, and Kevin Knight. 2003. Finding the WRITE stuff: Automatic identification of discourse structure in student essays. *IEEE Transactions on Intelligent Systems, 18*(1): 32-39.

Jill Burstein, Joel Tetreault, and Nitin Madnani. 2013. The e-rater automated essay scoring system. In Sermis, M. D. and Burstein, J. (eds.), *Handbook of Automated Essay Evaluation: Current Applications and New Directions* (pp. 55-67). New York: Routledge.

Vanessa W. Feng and Graeme Hirst. 2011. Classifying arguments by scheme. Proceedings of the 49th Annual Meeting of the Association for Computational Linguistics, Portland, OR.

Ralph P. Ferretti, William E. Lewis, and Scott Andrews-Weckerly. 2009. Do goals affect the structure of students' argumentative writing strategies? *Journal of Educational Psychology, 101*: 577-589.

Klaus Krippendorff. 1980. *Content Analysis: An Introduction to its Methodology*. Beverly Hills, CA : Sage Publications.Mann, William C., and Sandra A. Thompson. 1988. "Rhetorical structure theory: Toward a functional theory of text organization." *Text* 8(3): 243-281.

Nitin Madnani, Michael Heilman, Joel Tetreault, and Martin Chodorow. 2012. Identifying High Level Organizational Elements in Argumentative Discourse. *Proceedings of the 2012 Conference of the North American Chapter of the Association for Computational Linguistics: Human Language Technologies*. (pp. 20-28). Association for Computational Linguistics.

Raquel Mochales and Asgje Ieven. 2009. Creating an argumentation corpus: do theories apply to real arguments?: a case study on the legal argumentation of the ECHR. In ICAIL '09: Proceedings of the 12th International Conference on Artificial Intelligence and Law.

Michael Nussbaum. 2011. Argumentation, dialogue theory, and probability modeling: alternative frameworks for argumentation research in education. *Educational Psychologist, 46*: 84-106.

Nussbaum, E. M. and Edwards, O.V. (2011). Critical questions and argument stratagems: A framework for enhancing and analyzing students' reasoning practices. *Journal of the Learning Sciences, 20*, 443-488.

Palau, R.M. and Moens, M. F. 2009. Automatic argument detection and its role in law and the semantic web. In Proceedings of the 2009 conference on law, ontologies and the semantic web. IOS Press, Amsterdam, The Netherlands.Pendar, Nick, and Elena Cotos. 2008. "Automatic identification of discourse moves in scientific article introductions." In *Proceedings of the Third Workshop on Innovative Use of NLP for Building Educational Applications*, pp. 62-70. Association for Computational Linguistics.

Rahwan, I., Banihashemi, B., Reed, C. Walton, D., and Abdallah, S. (2010). Representing and classifying arguments on the semantic web. *The Knowledge Engineering Review*.

Rienks, R., Heylen, D., and Van der Weijden, E. 2005. Argument diagramming of meeting conversations. In A. Vinciarelli, J. Odobez (Ed.), Proceedings of Multimodal Multiparty Meeting Processing, Workshop at the 7th International Conference on Multimodal Interfaces (pp. 85–92). Trento, Italy.

Yi Song and Ralph P. Ferretti. 2013. Teaching critical questions about argumentation through the revising process: Effects of strategy instruction on college students' argumentative essays. *Reading and Writing: An Interdisciplinary Journal, 26*(1): 67-90.

Stephen E. Toulmin. 1958. *The uses of argument*. Cambridge University Press, Cambridge, UK.

Frans H. van Eemeren and Rob Grootendorst. 1992. *Argumentation, communication, and fallacies: A pragma-dialectical perspective.* Mahwah, NJ: Erlbaum.

Frans H. van Eemeren and Rob Grootendorst. 2004. *A systematic theory of argumentation: A pragma-dialectical approach.* Cambridge, UK: Cambridge University Press.

Verbree, D., Rienks, H., and Heylen, D. (2006). First Steps Towards the Automatic Construction of Argument-Diagrams from Real Discussions. In Proceedings of the 2006 conference on Computational Models of Argument: Proceedings of COMMA 2006. IOS Press, Amsterdam, The Netherlands.

Douglas N. Walton. 1996. *Argumentation schemes for presumptive reasoning.* Mahwah, NJ: Lawrence Erlbaum.

Douglas N. Walton, Chris Reed, and Fabrizio Macagno. 2008. *Argumentation schemes.* New York, NY: Cambridge University Press.

Mining Arguments From 19th Century Philosophical Texts Using Topic Based Modelling

John Lawrence and **Chris Reed**
School of Computing,
University of Dundee, UK

Colin Allen
Dept of History & Philosophy of Science,
Indiana University, USA

Simon McAlister and **Andrew Ravenscroft**
Cass School of Education & Communities,
University of East London, UK

David Bourget
Centre for Digital Philosophy,
University of Western Ontario, Canada

Abstract

In this paper we look at the manual analysis of arguments and how this compares to the current state of automatic argument analysis. These considerations are used to develop a new approach combining a machine learning algorithm to extract propositions from text, with a topic model to determine argument structure. The results of this method are compared to a manual analysis.

1 Introduction

Automatic extraction of meaningful information from natural text remains a major challenge facing computer science and AI. As research on specific tasks in text mining has matured, it has been picked up commercially and enjoyed rapid success. Existing text mining techniques struggle, however, to identify more complex structures in discourse, particularly when they are marked by a complex interplay of surface features rather than simple lexeme choice.

The difficulties in automatically identifying complex structure perhaps suggest why there has been, to date, relatively little work done in the area of argument mining. This stands in contrast to the large number of tools and techniques developed for manual argument analysis.

In this paper we look at the work which has been done to automate argument analysis, as well as considering a range of manual methods. We then apply some of the lessons learnt from these manual approaches to a new argument extraction technique, described in section 3. This technique is applied to a small sample of text extracted from three chapters of "THE ANIMAL MIND: A Text-Book of Comparative Psychology" by Margaret Floy Washburn, and compared to a high level manual analysis of the same text. We show that despite the small volumes of data considered, this approach can be used to produce, at least, an approximation of the argument structure in a piece of text.

2 Existing Approaches to Extracting Argument from Text

2.1 Manual Argument Analysis

In most cases, manual argument analysis can be split into four distinct stages as shown in Figure 1.

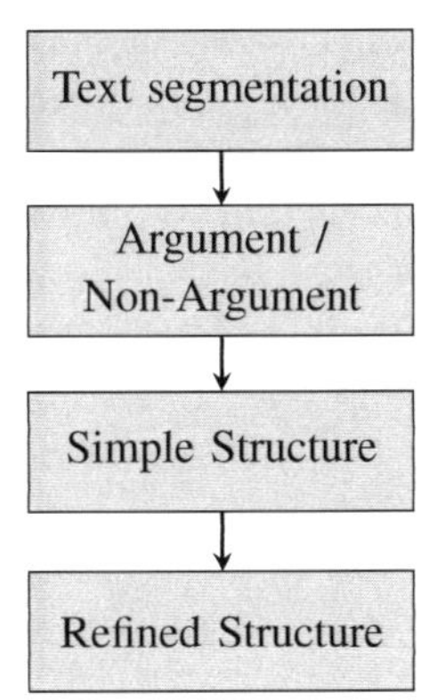

Figure 1: Steps in argument analysis

Text segmentation This involves selecting fragments of text from the original piece that will form the parts of the resulting argument structure. This can often be as simple as highlighting the section of text required, for example in OVA (Bex et al., 2013). Though in some cases, such as the AnalysisWall[1], this is a separate step carried out by a different user.

[1] http://arg.dundee.ac.uk/analysiswall

Proceedings of the First Workshop on Argumentation Mining, pages 79–87,
Baltimore, Maryland USA, June 26, 2014. ©2014 Association for Computational Linguistics

Argument / Non-Argument This step involves determining which of the segments previously identified are part of the argument being presented and which are not. For most manual analysis tools this step is performed as an integral part of segmentation: the analyst simply avoids segmenting any parts of the text that are not relevant to the argument. This step can also be performed after determining the argument structure by discarding any segments left unlinked to the rest.

Simple Structure Once the elements of the argument have been determined, the next step is to examine the links between them. This could be as simple as noting segments that are related, but usually includes determining support/attack relations.

Refined Structure Having determined the basic argument structure, some analysis tools allow this to be refined further by adding details such as the argumentation scheme.

2.2 Automatic Argument Analysis

One of the first approaches to argument mining, and perhaps still the most developed, is the work carried out by Moens et al. beginning with (Moens et al., 2007), which attempts to detect the argumentative parts of a text by first splitting the text into sentences and then using features of these sentences to classify each as either "Argument" or "Non-Argument". This approach was built upon in (Palau and Moens, 2009) where an additional machine learning technique was implemented to classify each Argument sentence as either premise or conclusion.

Although this approach produces reasonable results, with a best accuracy of 76.35% for Argument/Non-Argument classification and f-measures of 68.12% and 74.07% for classification as premise or conclusion, the nature of the technique restricts its usage in a broader context. For example, in general it is possible that a sentence which is not part of an argument in one situation may well be in another. Similarly, a sentence which is a conclusion in one case is often a premise in another.

Another issue with this approach is the original decision to split the text into sentences. While this may work for certain datasets, the problem here is that, in general, multiple propositions often occur within the same sentence and some parts of a sentence may be part of the argument while others are not.

The work of Moens et al. focused on the first three steps of analysis as mentioned in section 2.1, and this was further developed in (Feng and Hirst, 2011), which looks at fitting one of the top five most common argumentation schemes to an argument that has already undergone successful extraction of conclusions and premises, achieving accuracies of 63-91% for one-against-others classification and 80-94% for pairwise classification.

Despite the limited work carried out on argument mining, there has been significant progress in the related field of opinion mining (Pang and Lee, 2008). This is often performed at the document level, for example to determine whether a product review is positive or negative. Phrase-level sentiment analysis has been performed in a small number of cases, for example (Wilson et al., 2005) where expressions are classified as neutral or polar before determining the polarity of the polar expressions.

Whilst it is clear that sentiment analysis alone cannot give us anything close to the results of manual argument analysis, it is certainly possible that the ability to determine the sentiment of a given expression may help to fine-tune any discovered argument structure.

Another closely related area is Argumentative Zoning (Teufel et al., 1999), where scientific papers are annotated at the sentence level with labels indicating the rhetorical role of the sentence (criticism or support for previous work, comparison of methods, results or goals, etc.). Again, this information could assist in determining structure, and indeed shares some similarities to the topic modelling approach as described in section 3.2 .

3 Methodology

3.1 Text Segmentation

Many existing argument mining approaches, such as (Moens et al., 2007), take a simple approach to text segmentation, for example, simply splitting the input text into sentences, which, as discussed, can lead to problems when generally applied.

There have been some more refined attempts to segment text, combining the segmentation step with Argument/Non-Argument classification. For example, (Madnani et al., 2012) uses three methods: a rule-based system; a supervised probabilistic sequence model; and a principled hybrid version of the two, to separate argumentative discourse into language used to express claims and evidence, and language used to organise them ("shell"). Whilst this approach is instructive, it does not necessarily identify the atomic parts of the argument required for later structural analysis.

The approach that we present here does not consider whether a piece of text is part of an argument, but instead simply aims to split the text into propositions. Proposition segmentation is carried out using a machine learning algorithm to identify boundaries, classifying each word as either the beginning or end of a proposition. Two Naive Bayes classifiers, one to determine the first word of a proposition and one to determine the last, are generated using a set of manually annotated training data. The text given is first split into words and a list of features calculated for each word. The features used are given below:

word The word itself.

length Length of the word.

before The word before.

after The word after. Punctuation is treated as a separate word so, for example, the last word in a sentence may have an after feature of '.'.

pos Part of speech as identified by the Python Natural Language Toolkit POS tagger[2].

Once the classifiers have been trained, these same features can then be determined for each word in the test data and each word can be classified as either 'start' or 'end'. Once the classification has taken place, we run through the text and when a 'start' is reached we mark a proposition until the next 'end'.

3.2 Structure identification

Having extracted propositions from the text we next look at determining the simple structure of the argument being made and attempt to establish links between propositions. We avoid distinguishing between Argument and Non-Argument segments at this stage, instead assuming that any segments left unconnected are after the structure has been identified are Non-Argument.

In order to establish these links, we first consider that in many cases an argument can be represented as a tree. This assumption is supported by around 95% of the argument analyses contained in AIFdb (Lawrence et al., 2012) as well as the fact that many manual analysis tools including Araucaria (Reed and Rowe, 2004), iLogos[3], Rationale (Van Gelder, 2007) and Carneades (Gordon et al., 2007), limit the user to a tree format.

Furthermore, we assume that the argument tree is generated depth first, specifically that the conclusion is presented first and then a single line of supporting points is followed as far as possible before working back up through the points made. The assumption is grounded in work in computational linguistics that has striven to produce natural-seeming argument structures (Reed and Long, 1997). We aim to be able to construct this tree structure from the text by looking at the topic of each proposition. The idea of relating changes in topic to argument structure is supported by (Cardoso et al., 2013), however, our approach here is the reverse, using changes in topic to deduce the structure, rather than using the structure to find topic boundaries.

Based on these assumptions, we can determine structure by first computing the similarity of each proposition to the others using a Latent Dirichlet Allocation (LDA) model. LDA is a generative model which conforms to a Bayesian inference about the distributions of words in the documents being modelled. Each 'topic' in the model is a probability distribution across a set of words from the documents.

To perform the structure identification, a topic model is first generated for the text to be studied and then each proposition identified in the test data is compared to the model, giving a similarity score for each topic. The propositions are then processed in the order in which they appear in the test data. Firstly, the distance between the proposition and its predecessor is calculated as the Euclidean distance between the topic scores. If this is below a set threshold, the proposition is linked to its predecessor. If the threshold is exceeded, the distance is then calculated between the proposition and all the propositions that have come before, if the closest of these is then within a certain distance, an edge is added. If neither of these criteria

[2] http://www.nltk.org/

[3] http://www.phil.cmu.edu/projects/argument_mapping/

is met, the proposition is considered unrelated to anything that has gone before.

By adjusting the threshold required to join a proposition to its predecessor we can change how linear the structure is. A higher threshold will increase the chance that a proposition will instead be connected higher up the tree and therefore reduce linearity. The second threshold can be used to alter the connectedness of the resultant structure, with a higher threshold giving more unconnected sections.

It should be noted that the edges obtained do not have any direction, and there is no further detail generated at this stage about the nature of the relation between two linked propositions.

4 Manual Analysis

In order to train and test our automatic analysis approach, we first required some material to be manually analysed. The manual analysis was carried out by an analyst who was familiar with manual analysis techniques, but unaware of the automatic approach that we would be using. In this way we avoided any possibility of fitting the data to the technique. He also chose areas of texts that were established as 'rich' in particular topics in animal psychology through the application of the modelling techniques above, the assumption being that these selections would also contain relevant arguments.

The material chosen to be analysed was taken from "THE ANIMAL MIND: A TextBook of Comparative Psychology by Margaret Floy Washburn, 1908" made available to us through the Hathi Trust.

The analyst began with several selected passages from this book and in each case generated an analysis using OVA[4], an application which links blocks of text using argument nodes. OVA provides a drag-and-drop interface for analysing textual arguments. It is reminiscent of a simplified Araucaria, except that it is designed to work in an online environment, running as an HTML5 canvas application in a browser.

The analyst was instructed only to capture the argument being made in the text as well as they could. Arguments can be mapped at different levels depending upon the choices the analyst prioritises. This is particularly true of volumes such as those analysed here, where, in some cases, the same topic is pursued for a complete chapter and so there are opportunities to map the extended argument.

In this case the analyst chose to identify discrete semantic passages corresponding to a proposition, albeit one that may be compound. An example is shown in Figure 2. A section of contiguous text from the volume has been segmented and marked up using OVA, where each text box corresponds to such a passage. It is a problem of the era in which the chosen volume is written that there is a verbosity and indirectness of language, so a passage may stretch across several sentences. The content of each box was then edited to contain only argumentative content and a simple structure proposed by linking supporting boxes towards concluding or sub-concluding boxes. Some fifteen OVA maps were constructed to represent the arguments concerned with animal consciousness and with anthropomorphism.

In brief, this analysis approach used OVA as a formal modelling tool, or lens, to characterise and better understand the nature of argument within the texts that were considered, as well as producing a large set of argument maps. Therefore, it represented a data-driven and empirically authentic approach and set of data against which the automated techniques could be considered and compared.

5 Automatic Analysis Results

As discussed in section 4, the manual analysis is at a higher level of abstraction than is carried out in typical approaches to critical thinking and argument analysis (Walton, 2006; Walton et al., 2008), largely because such analysis is very rarely extended to arguments presented at monograph scale (see (Finocchiaro, 1980) for an exception). The manual analysis still, however, represents an ideal to which automatic processing might aspire. In order to train the machine learning algorithms, however, a large dataset of marked propositions is required. To this end, the manual analysis conducted at the higher level is complemented by a more fine-grained analysis of the same text which marks only propositions (and not inter-proposition structure). In this case a proposition was considered to correspond to the smallest span of text containing a single piece of information. It is this detailed analysis of the text which is used as training data for text segmentation.

[4] `http://ova.computing.dundee.ac.uk`

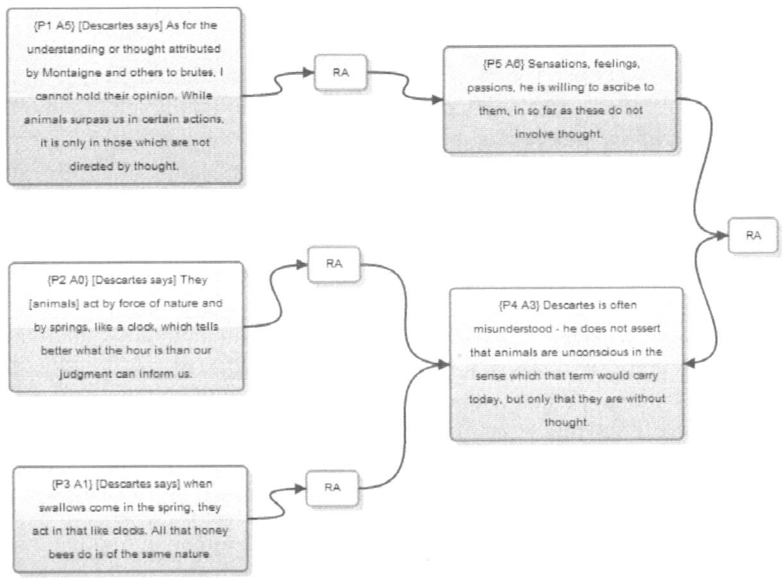

Figure 2: Sample argument map from OVA

5.1 Text segmentation

An obvious place to start, then, is to assess the performance of the proposition identification – that is, using discourse indicators and other surface features as described in section 3.1, to what extent do spans of text automatically extracted match up to spans annotated manually described in section 4? There are four different datasets upon which the algorithms were trained, with each dataset comprising extracted propositions from: (i) raw data directly from Hathi Trust taken only from Chapter 1 ; (ii) cleaned data (with these errors manually corrected) taken only from Chapter 1; (iii) cleaned data from Chapters 1 and 2; and (iv) cleaned data from Chapters 1, 2 and 4. All the test data is taken from Chapter 1, and in each case the test data was not included in the training dataset.

It is important to establish a base line using the raw text, but it is expected that performance will be poor since randomly interspersed formatting artifacts (such as the title of the chapter as a running header occurring in the middle of a sentence that runs across pages) have a major impact on the surface profile of text spans used by the machine learning algorithms.

The first result to note is the degree of correspondence between the fine-grained propositional analysis (which yielded, in total, around 1,000 propositions) and the corresponding higher level analysis. As is to be expected, the atomic argument components in the abstract analysis typically cover more than one proposition in the less abstract analysis. In total, however, 88.5% of the propositions marked by the more detailed analysis also appear in the more abstract. That is to say, almost nine-tenths of the material marked as argumentatively relevant in the detailed analysis was also marked as argumentatively relevant in the abstract analysis. This result not only lends confidence to the claim that the two levels are indeed examining the same linguistic phenomena, but also establishes a 'gold standard' for the machine learning – given that manual analysis achieves 88.5% correspondence, and it is this analysis which provides the training data, we would not expect the automatic algorithms to be able to perform at a higher level.

Perhaps unsurprisingly, only 11.6% of the propositions automatically extracted from the raw, uncleaned text exactly match spans identified as propositions in the manual analysis. By running the processing on cleaned data, this figure is improved somewhat to 20.0% using training data from Chapter 1 alone. Running the algorithms trained on additional data beyond Chapter 1 yields performance of 17.6% (for Chapters 1 and 2) and 13.9% (for 1, 2 and 4). This dropping off is quite surprising, and points to a lack of homogeneity in the book as a whole – that is, Chapters 1, 2 and 4 do not provide a strong predictive model for a small subset. This is an important observation, as it suggests the need for careful subsampling for training data. That is, establishing data sets upon which machine learning algorithms can be trained is a highly labour-intensive task. It is vital, therefore, to focus that effort where it will have the most effect. The tailing-off effect witnessed on this dataset suggests that it is more important to subsample 'horizontally' across a volume (or set of volumes), taking small extracts from each chapter, rather than subsampling 'vertically,' taking larger, more in-depth extracts from fewer places across the volume.

This first set of results is determined using strong matching criteria: that individual propositions must match exactly between automatic and manual analyses. In practice, however, artefacts of the text, including formatting and punctuation, may mean that although a proposition has indeed been identified automatically in the correct way, it is marked as a failure because it is including or excluding a punctuation mark, connective word or other non-propositional material. To allow for this, results were also calculated on the basis of a tolerance of ± 3 words (i.e. space-delimited character strings). On this basis, performance with unformatted text was 17.4% – again, rather poor as is to be expected. With cleaned text, the match rate between manually and artificially marked proposition boundaries was 32.5% for Chapter 1 text alone. Again, performance drops over a larger training dataset (reinforcing the observation above regarding the need for horizontal subsampling), to 26.5% for Chapters 1 and 2, and 25.0% for Chapters 1, 2 and 4.

A further liberal step is to assess automatic proposition identification in terms of argument relevance – i.e. to review the proportion of automatically delimited propositions that are included at all in manual analysis. This then stands in direct comparison to the 88.5% figure mentioned above, representing the proportion of manually identified propositions at a fine-grained level of analysis that are present in amongst the propositions at the coarse-grained level. With unformatted text, the figure is still low at 27.3%, but with cleaned up text, results are much better: for just the text of Chapter 1, the proportion of automatically identified propositions which are included in the manual, coarse-grained analysis is 63.6%, though this drops to 44.4% and 50.0% for training datasets corresponding to Chapters 1 and 2, and to Chapters 1, 2 and 4, respectively. These figures compare favourably with the 88.5% result for human analysis: that is, automatic analysis is relatively good at identifying text spans with argumentative roles.

These results are summarised in Table 1, below. For each of the four datasets, the table lists the proportion of automatically analysed propositions that are identical to those in the (fine-grained level) manual analysis, the proportion that are within three words of the (fine-grained level) manual analysis, and the proportion that are general substrings of the (coarse-grained level) manual analysis (i.e. a measure of argument relevance).

	Identical	**$\pm$3Words**	**Substring**
Unformatted	11.6	17.4	27.3
Ch. 1	20.0	32.5	63.6
Ch. 1&2	17.6	26.5	44.4
Ch. 1,2&4	13.9	25.0	50.0

Table 1: Results of automatic proposition processing

5.2 Structure identification

Clearly, identifying the atoms from which argument 'molecules' are constructed is only part of the problem: it is also important to recognise the structural relations. Equally clearly, the results described in section 5.1 have plenty of room for improvement in future work. They are, however, strong enough to support further investigation of automatic recognition of structural features (i.e., specifically, features relating to argument structure).

In order to tease out both false positives and false negatives, our analysis here separates precision and recall. Furthermore, all results are given with respect to the coarse-grained analysis of section 4, as no manual structure identification was performed on the fine-grained analysis.

As described in section 3.2, the automatic structure identification currently returns connectedness, not direction (that is, it indicates two argument atoms that are related together in an argument structure, but do not indicate which is premise and which conclusion). The system uses propositional boundaries as input, so can run equally on manually segmented propositions (those used as training data in section 5.1) or automatically segmented propositions (the results for which were described in Table 1). In the results which follow, we compare performance between manually annotated and automatically extracted propositions. Figures 3 and 4 show sample extracts from the automatic structure recognition algorithms running on manually segmented and automatically segmented propositions respectively.

For all those pairs of (manually or automatically) analysed propositions which the automatic structure recognition algorithms class as being connected, we examine in the manual structural analysis connectedness between propositions in which the text of the analysed propositions appears. Thus, for example, if our analysed propositions are the strings xxx and yyy, and the automatic structure recognition system classes them as connected, we first identify the two propositions (P1 and P2) in the manual analysis which include amongst the text with which they are associated the strings xxx and yyy. Then we check to see if P1 and P2 are (immediately) structurally related. For automatically segmented propositions, precision is 33.3% and recall 50.0%, whilst for manually segmented propositions, precision is 33.3% and recall 18.2%. For automatically extracted propositions, the overlap with the coarse-grained analysis was small – just four propositions – so the results should be treated with some caution. Precision and recall for the manually extracted propositions however is based on a larger dataset (n=26), so the results are disappointing. One reason is that with the manual analysis at a significantly more coarse-grained level, propositions that were identified as being structurally connected were quite often in the same atomic unit in the manual analysis, thus being rejected as a false positive by the analysis engine. As a result, we also consider a more liberal definition of a correctly identified link between propositions, in which success is recorded if either:

(a) for any two manually or automatically analysed propositions (p1, p2) that the automatic structure recognition indicates as connected, there is a structural connection between manually analysed propositions (P1, P2) where p1 is included in P1 and p2 included in P2

or

(b) for any two manually or automatically analysed propositions (p1, p2) that the automatic structure recognition indicates as connected, there is a single manually analysed propositions (P1) where p1 and p2 are both included in P1

Under this rubric, automatic structure recognition with automatically segmented propositions has precision of 66.6% and recall of 100% (but again, only on a dataset of n=4), and more significantly, automatic structure recognition with manually segmented propositions has precision 72.2% and recall 76.5% These results are summarised in Table 2.

	Automatically segmented propositions	**Manually segmented propositions**
In separate propositions	n=4, P=33.3%, R=50.0%	n=26, P=33.3%, R=18.2%
In separate or the same proposition	n=4, P=66.6%, R=100.0%	n=26, P=72.2%, R=76.5%

Table 2: Results of automatic structure generation

The results are encouraging, but larger scale analysis is required to further test the reliability of the extant algorithms.

6 Conclusion

With fewer than one hundred atomic argument components analysed at the coarse-grained level, and barely 1,000 propositions at the fine-grained level, the availability of training data is a major hurdle. Developing these training sets is demanding and extremely labour intensive. One possibility is to increasingly make available and reuse datasets between projects. Infrastructure efforts such as `aifdb.org` make this more realistic, with around 15,000 analysed propositions in around 1,200 arguments, though as scale increases, quality management (e.g. over crowdsourced contributions) becomes an increasing challenge.

With sustained scholarly input, however, in conjunction with crossproject import and export, we would expect these datasets to increase 10 to 100 fold over the next year or two, which will support rapid expansion in training and test data sets for the next generation of argument mining algorithms.

Despite the lack of training data currently available, we have shown that automatic segmentation of propositions in a text on the basis of relatively simple features at the surface and syntactic levels

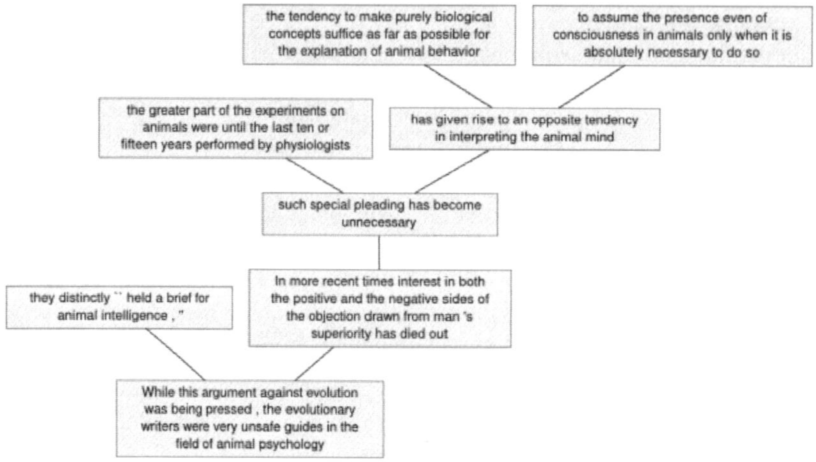

Figure 3: Example of automated structure recognition using manually identified propositions

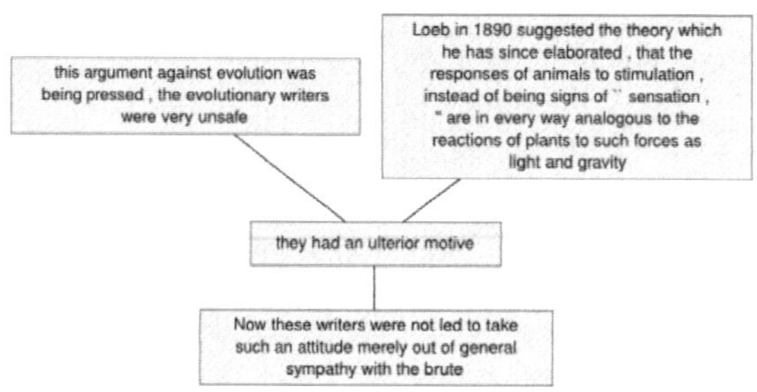

Figure 4: Example of automated structure recognition using automatically identified propositions

is feasible, though generalisation between chapters, volumes and, ultimately, genres, is extremely demanding.

Automatic identification of at least some structural features of argument is surprisingly robust, even at this early stage, though more sophisticated structure such as determining the inferential directionality and inferential type is likely to be much more challenging.

We have also shown that automatic segmentation and automatic structure recognition can be connected to determine at least an approximation of the argument structure in a piece of text, though much more data is required to test its applicability at scale.

6.1 Future Work

Significantly expanded datasets are crucial to further development of these techniques. This will require collaboration amongst analysts as well as the further development of tools for collaborating on and sharing analyses.

Propositional segmentation results could be improved by making more thorough use of syntactic information such as clausal completeness. Combining a range of techniques to determine propositions would counteract weaknesses that each may face individually.

With a significant foundation for argument structure analysis, it is hoped that future work can focus on extending and refining sets of algorithms and heuristics based on both statistical and deep learning mechanisms for exploiting not just topical information, but also the logical, semantic, inferential and dialogical structures latent in argumentative text.

7 Acknowledgements

The authors would like to thank the Digging Into Data challenge funded by JISC in the UK and NEH in the US under project CIINN01, "Digging By Debating" which in part supported the research reported here.

References

F. Bex, J. Lawrence, M. Snaith, and C.A. Reed. 2013. Implementing the argument web. *Communications of the ACM*, 56(10):56–73.

P.C. Cardoso, M. Taboada, and T.A. Pardo. 2013. On the contribution of discourse structure to topic segmentation. In *Proceedings of the Special Interest Group on Discourse and Dialogue (SIGDIAL)*, pages 92–96. Association for Computational Linguistics.

V.W. Feng and G. Hirst. 2011. Classifying arguments by scheme. In *Proceedings of the 49th Annual Meeting of the Association for Computational Linguistics: Human Language Technologies-Volume 1*, pages 987–996. Association for Computational Linguistics.

Maurice A. Finocchiaro. 1980. Galileo and the art of reasoning. rhetorical foundations of logic and scientific method. *Boston Studies in the Philosophy of Science New York, NY*, 61.

Thomas F Gordon, Henry Prakken, and Douglas Walton. 2007. The carneades model of argument and burden of proof. *Artificial Intelligence*, 171(10):875–896.

John Lawrence, Floris Bex, Chris Reed, and Mark Snaith. 2012. Aifdb: Infrastructure for the argument web. In *COMMA*, pages 515–516.

N. Madnani, M. Heilman, J. Tetreault, and M. Chodorow. 2012. Identifying high-level organizational elements in argumentative discourse. In *Proceedings of the 2012 Conference of the North American Chapter of the Association for Computational Linguistics: Human Language Technologies*, pages 20–28. Association for Computational Linguistics.

M.F. Moens, E. Boiy, R.M. Palau, and C. Reed. 2007. Automatic detection of arguments in legal texts. In *Proceedings of the 11th international conference on Artificial intelligence and law*, pages 225–230. ACM.

R.M. Palau and M.F. Moens. 2009. Argumentation mining: the detection, classification and structure of arguments in text. In *Proceedings of the 12th international conference on artificial intelligence and law*, pages 98–107. ACM.

Bo Pang and Lillian Lee. 2008. *Opinion mining and sentiment analysis*. Now Pub.

Chris Reed and Derek Long. 1997. Content ordering in the generation of persuasive discourse. In *IJCAI (2)*, pages 1022–1029. Morgan Kaufmann.

Chris Reed and Glenn Rowe. 2004. Araucaria: Software for argument analysis, diagramming and representation. *International Journal on Artificial Intelligence Tools*, 13(04):961–979.

S. Teufel, J. Carletta, and M. Moens. 1999. An annotation scheme for discourse-level argumentation in research articles. In *Proceedings of the ninth conference on European chapter of the Association for Computational Linguistics*, pages 110–117. Association for Computational Linguistics.

Tim Van Gelder. 2007. The rationale for rationale. *Law, probability and risk*, 6(1-4):23–42.

D Walton, C Reed, and F Macagno. 2008. *Argumentation Schemes*. Cambridge University Press.

D Walton. 2006. *Fundamentals of critical argumentation*. Cambridge University Press.

Theresa Wilson, Janyce Wiebe, and Paul Hoffmann. 2005. Recognizing contextual polarity in phrase-level sentiment analysis. In *Proceedings of the conference on human language technology and empirical methods in natural language processing*, pages 347–354. Association for Computational Linguistics.

Towards segment-based recognition of argumentation structure in short texts

Andreas Peldszus
Applied Computational Linguistics
University of Potsdam
peldszus@uni-potsdam.de

Abstract

Despite recent advances in discourse parsing and causality detection, the automatic recognition of argumentation structure of authentic texts is still a very challenging task. To approach this problem, we collected a small corpus of German microtexts in a text generation experiment, resulting in texts that are authentic but of controlled linguistic and rhetoric complexity. We show that trained annotators can determine the argumentation structure on these microtexts reliably. We experiment with different machine learning approaches for automatic argumentation structure recognition on various levels of granularity of the scheme. Given the complex nature of such a discourse understanding tasks, the first results presented here are promising, but invite for further investigation.

1 Introduction

Automatic argumentation recognition has many possible applications, including improving document summarization (Teufel and Moens, 2002), retrieval capabilities of legal databases (Palau and Moens, 2011), opinion mining for commercial purposes, or also as a tool for assessing public opinion on political questions.

However, identifying and classifying arguments in naturally-occurring text is a very challenging task for various reasons: argumentative strategies and styles vary across texts genres; classifying arguments might require domain knowledge; furthermore, argumentation is often not particularly explicit – the argument proper is being infiltrated with the full range of problems of linguistic expression that humans have at their disposal.

Although the amount of available texts featuring argumentative behaviour is growing rapidly in the web, we suggest there is yet one resource missing that could facilitate the development of automatic argumentation recognition systems: Short texts with explicit argumentation, little argumentatively irrelevant material, less rhetorical gimmicks (or even deception), in clean written language.

For this reason, we conducted a text generation experiment, designed to control the linguistic and rhetoric complexity of written 'microtexts'. These texts have then been annotated with argumentation structures. We present first results of automatic classification of these arguments on various levels of granularity of the scheme.

The paper is structured as follows: In the next section we describe related work. Section 3 presents the annotation scheme and an agreement study to prove the reliability. Section 4 describes the text generation experiment and the resulting corpus. Section 5 and 6 present the results of our first attempts in automatically recognizing the argumentative structure of those texts. Finally, Section 7 concludes with a summary and an outlook on future work.

2 Related Work

There exist a few ressources for the study of argumentation, most importantly perhaps the AIF database, the successor of the Araucaria corpus (Reed et al., 2008), that has been used in different studies. It contains several annotated English datasets, most interestingly for us one covering online newspaper articles. Unfortunately, the full source text is not part of the downloadable database, which is why the linguistic material surrounding the extracted segments is not easy to retrieve for analysis. Instead of manually annotating, Cabrio and Villata (2012) created an argumentation resource by extracting argumentations from collaborative debate portals, such as debatepedia.org, where arguments are already classified into pro and con classes by the

Proceedings of the First Workshop on Argumentation Mining, pages 88–97,
Baltimore, Maryland USA, June 26, 2014.

users. Unfortunately, those arguments are themselves small texts and their internal argumentative structure is not marked up. Finally, to the best of our knowledge, the only existing corpus of German newspaper articles, essays or editorials annotated with argumentation structure is that used by Stede and Sauermann (2008), featuring ten commentaries from the Potsdam Commentary Corpus (Stede, 2004). Although short, these texts are rhetorically already quite complex and often have segments not relevant to the argument.[1]

In terms of automatic recognition, scientific documents of different fields have been studied intensively in the Argumentative Zoning approach or in similar text zoning approaches (Teufel and Moens, 2002; Teufel et al., 2009; Teufel, 2010; Liakata et al., 2012; Guo et al., 2013). Here, sentences are classified into different functional or conceptual roles, grouped together with adjacent sentences of the same class to document zones, which induces a flat partitioning of the text. A variety of machine learning schemes have been applied here.

Another line of research approaches argumentation from the perspective of Rhetorical Structure Theory (RST) (Mann and Thompson, 1988) and works with argumentation-enriched RST trees (Azar, 1999; Green, 2010). However, we do not consider RST to be the best level for representing argumentation, due to its linearization constraints (Peldszus and Stede, 2013a, sec. 3). Nevertheless, noteworthy advances have been made recently in rhetorical parsing (Hernault et al., 2010; Feng and Hirst, 2012). Whether hybrid RST argumentation structures will profit similarly remains to be shown. A more linguistically oriented approach is given with the TextCoop platform (Saint-Dizier, 2012) for analyzing text on the discourse level with emphasis on argumentation.

One step further, Feng and Hirst (2011) concentrate on types of arguments and use a statistical approach to classify already identified premises and conclusions into five common argumentation schemes (Walton et al., 2008).

3 Annotation Scheme

Our representation of the argumentation structure of a text is based on Freeman's theory of argumentation structure (Freeman, 1991; Freeman, 2011).[2] Its central idea is to model argumentation as a hypothetical dialectical exchange between the proponent, who presents and defends his claims, and the opponent, who critically questions them in a regimented fashion. Every move in such a dialectical exchange corresponds to a structural element in the argument graph. The nodes of this graph represent the propositions expressed in text segments (round nodes are proponent's nodes, square ones are opponent's nodes), the arcs between those nodes represent different supporting (arrow-head links) and attacking moves (circle-head links). The theory distinguishes only a few general supporting and attacking moves. Those could be specified further with a more fine grained set, as provided for example by the theory of argumentation schemes (Walton et al., 2008). Still, we focus on the coarse grained set, since this reduces the complexity of the already sufficiently challenging task of automatic argument identification and classifcation. Our adaption of Freeman's theory and the resulting annotation scheme is described in detail and with examples in (Peldszus and Stede, 2013a).

3.1 Reliability of annotation

The reliability of the annotation scheme has been evaluated in two experiments. We will first recapitulate the results of a previous study with naive annotators and then present the new results with expert annotators.

Naive annotators: In (Peldszus and Stede, 2013b), we presented an agreement study with 26 naive and untrained annotators: undergraduate students in a "class-room annotation" szenario, where task introduction, guideline reading and the actual annotation is all done in one obligatory 90 min. session and the subjects are likely to have different experience with annotation in general, background knowledge and motivation. We constructed a set of 23 microtexts (each 5 segments long) covering different linearisations of several combinations of basic argumentation constructs. An example text and the corresponding argumentation structure graph is shown in Figure 1. On these texts, the annotators achieved moderate agreement[3] for certain aspects of the ar-

[1] We intend to use this resource, when we move on to experiment with more complex texts.

[2] The theory aims to integrate the ideas of Toulmin (1958) into the argument diagraming techniques of the informal logic tradition (Beardsley, 1950; Thomas, 1974) in a systematic and compositional way.

[3] Agreement is measured in Fleiss κ (Fleiss, 1971).

gument graph (e.g. κ=.52 in distinguishing proponent and opponent segments, or κ=.58 in destinguishing supporting and attacking segments), yet only a marginal agreement of κ=.38 on the full labelset describing all aspects of the argument graph. However, we could systematically identify subgroups performing much better than average using clustering techniques: e.g. a subgroup of 6 annotators reached a relatively high IAA agreement of κ=.69 for the full labelset and also high agreement with gold data.

Expert annotators: Here, we present the results of an agreement study with three expert annotators: two of them are the guideline authors, one is a postdoc in computational linguistics. All three are familiar with discourse annotation tasks in general and specifically with this annotation scheme. They annotated the same set of 23 microtexts and achieved a high agreement of κ=.83 on the full labelset describing all aspects of the argument graph. The distinction between supporting and attacking was drawn with very high agreement of κ=.95, the one between proponent and opponent segments even with perfect agreement.

Since argumentation structures can be reliably annotated using this scheme, we decided to create a small corpus of annotated microtexts.

4 Dataset

The corpus used in this study consists of two parts: on the one hand, the 23 microtexts used in the annotation experiments just described; on the other hand, 92 microtexts that have been collected in a controlled text generation experiment. We will describe this experiment in the following subsection.

4.1 Microtext generation experiment

We asked 23 probands to discuss a controversial issue in a short text of 5 segments. A list of 17 of these issues was given, concerning recent political, moral, or everyday's life questions. Each proband was allowed to discuss at maximum five of the given questions. Probands were instructed to first think about the pros & cons of the controversial question, about possible refutation and counter-refutations of one side to the other. On this basis, probands should decide for one side and write a short persuasive text (corresponding to the standards of the written language), arguing in favour of their chosen position.

The written texts were required to have a length of five segments. We decided not to bother our probands with an exact definition of a segment, as this would require the writers to reliably identify different complex syntactic constructions. Instead, we simply characterized it as a clause or a sentence, expressing an argumentative point on its own. We also required all segments to be argumentatively relevant, in the sense that they either formulate the main claim of the text, support the main claim or another segment, or attack the main claim or another segment. This requirement was put forward in order to prevent digression and argumentatively irrelevant but common segment types, such as theme or mood setters, as well as background information. Furthermore, we demanded that at least one possible objection to the main claim be considered in the text, leaving open the choice of whether to counter that objection or not. Finally, the text should be written in such a way that it would be understandable without having the question as a headline.

In total, 100 microtexts have been collected. The five most frequently chosen issues are:

- Should the fine for leaving dog excrements on sideways be increased?
- Should shopping malls generally be allowed to open on Sundays?
- Should Germany introduce the death penalty?
- Should public health insurance cover treatments in complementary and alternative medicine?
- Should only those viewers pay a TV licence fee who actually want to watch programs offered by public broadcasters?

4.2 Cleanup and annotation

Since we aim for a corpus of clean, yet authentic argumentation, all texts have been checked for spelling and grammar errors. As a next step, the texts were segmented into elementary units of argumentation. Due to the (re-)segmentation, not all texts conform to the length restriction of five segments, they can be one segment longer or shorter. Unfortunately, some probands wrote more than five main clauses, yielding texts with up to ten segments. We decided to shorten these texts down to six segments by removing segments that appear redundant or negligible. This removal also required modifications in the remaining segments to maintain text coherence, which we made as

[*Energy-saving light bulbs contain a considerable amount of toxic substances.*]1 [*A customary lamp can for instance contain up to five milligrams of quicksilver.*]2 [*For this reason, they should be taken off the market,*]3 [*unless they are virtually unbreakable.*]4 [*This, however, is simply not case.*]5

(a)

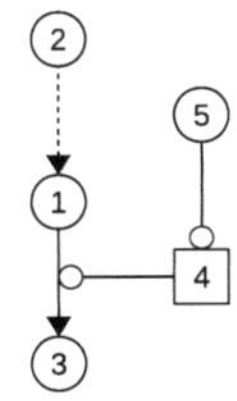

(b)

node id	rel. id	full label	target
1	1	PSNS	(n+2)
2	2	PSES	(n-1)
3	3	PT	(0)
4	4	OAUS	(r-3)
5	5	PARS	(n-1)

(c)

Figure 1: An example microtext: the (translated) segmented text in (a), the argumentation structure graph in (b), the segment-based labeling representation in (c).

minimal as possible. Another source of problems were segments that do not meet our requirement of argumentative relevance. Some writers did not concentrate on discussing the thesis, but moved on to a different issue. Others started the text with an introductory presentation of background information, without using it in their argument. We removed those segments, again with minimal changes in the remaining segments. Some texts containing several of such segments remained too short after the removal and have been discarded from the dataset.

After cleanup, 92 of the 100 written texts remained for annotation of argumentation structure. We found that a few texts did not meet the requirement of considering at least one objection to the own position. In a few other texts, the objection is not present as a full segment, but rather implicitly mentioned (e.g. in a nominal phrase or participle) and immediatly rejected in the very same segment. Those segments are to be annotated as a supporting segment according to the guidelines, since the attacking moves cannot be expressed as a relation between segments in this case.

We will present some statistics of the resulting dataset at the end of the following subsection.

5 Modelling

In this section we first present, how the argumentation structure graphs can be interpreted as a segment-wise labelling that is suitable for automatic classification. We then describe the set of extracted features and the classifiers set up for recognition.

5.1 Preparations

In the annotation process, every segment is assigned one and only one function, i.e. every node in the argumentative graph has maximally one outgoing arc. The graph can thus be reinterpreted as a list of segment labels.

Every segment is labeled on different levels: The 'role'-level specifies the dialectical role (proponent or opponent). The 'typegen'-level specifies the general type, i.e. whether the segment presents the central claim (thesis) of the text, supports or attacks another segment. The 'type'-level additionally specifies the kind of support (normal or example) and the kind of attack (rebutter or undercutter). Whether a segment's function holds only in combination with that of another segment (combined) or not (simple) is represented on the 'combined'-level. The target is finally specified by a position relative identifier: The offset *-x*. . . *0*. . . *+x* identifies the targeted segment, relative from the position of the current segment. The prefix 'n' states that the proposition of the node itself is the target, while the prefix 'r' states that the relation coming from the node is the target.[4]

The labels of each separate level can be merged to form a complex tagset. We interpret the result as a hierarchical tagset as it is presented in Figure 2. The label 'PSNS(n+2)' for example stands for a proponent's segment, giving normal, non-combined support to the next but one segment, while 'OAUS(r-1)' represents an opponent's segment, undercutting the relation established by the immediately previous segment, not combined. Figure 1c illustrates the segment-wise labelling for the example microtext.

The dataset with its 115 microtexts has 8183 word tokens, 2603 word types and 579 segments in total. The distribution of the basic labels and the complex 'role+type' level is presented in Table 1. The label distribution on the 'role+type' level shows that most of the opponent's attacks are rebutting attacks, directed against the central claim

[4]Segments with combined function (as e.g. linked supporting arguments) are represented by equal relation ids, which is why segments can have differing node and relation ids. However, for the sake of simplicity, we will only consider example of non-combined nature in this paper.

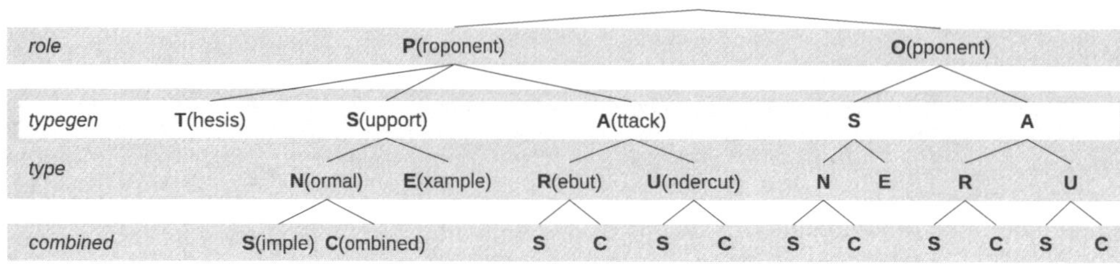

Figure 2: The hierarchy of segment labels.

or its premises directly (OAR>OAU). In contrast, the proponent's counters of these attack are typically untercutting attacks, directed against the attack relation (PAU>PAR). This is due to the author's typical strategy of first conceding some aspect in conflict with the main claim and then rendering it irrelevant or not applicable without directly challenging it. Note however, that about 40% of the opponents objections have not been countered by the proponent (OA*>PA*).

5.2 Features

All (unsegmented) texts have been automatically split into sentences and been tokenized by the OpenNLP-tools. The mate-pipeline then processed the tokenized input, yielding lemmatization, POS-tags, word-morphology and dependency parses (Bohnet, 2010). The annotated gold-standard segmentation in the dataset was then automatically mapped to the automatic sentence-splitting/tokenization, in order to be able to extract exactly those linguistic features present in the gold-segments. Using this linguistic output and several other resources, we extracted the following features:

Lemma Unigrams: We add a set of binary features for every lemma found in the present segment, in the preceding and the subsequent segment in order to represent the segment's context in a small window.

Lemma Bigrams: We extracted lemma bigramms of the present segment.

POS Tags: We add a set of binary features for every POS tag found in the present, preceding and subsequent segment.

Main verb morphology: We added binary features for tempus and mood of the segment's main verb, as subjunctive mood might indicate anticipated objections and tempus might help to identify the main claim.

Dependency triples: The dependency parses were used to extract features representing dependency triples (relation, head, dependent) for each token of the present segment. Two features sets were built, one with lemma representations, the other with POS tag representations of head and dependent.

Sentiment: We calculate the sentiment value of the current segment by summing the values of all lemmata marked as positive or negative in SentiWS (Remus et al., 2010).[5]

Discourse markers: For every lemma in the segment that is listed as potentially signalling a discourse relation (cause, concession, contrast, asymmetriccontrast) in a lexicon of German discourse markers (Stede, 2002) we add a binary feature representing the occurance of the marker, and one representing the occurance of the relation. Again, discourse marker / relations in the preceding and subsequent segment are registered in separate features.

First three lemmata: In order to capture sentence-initial expressions that might indicate argumentative moves, but are not strictly defined as discourse markers, we add binary features representing the occurance of the first three lemmata.

Negation marker presence: We use a list of 76 German negation markers derived in (Warzecha, 2013) containing both closed class negation operators (negation particles, quantifiers and adverbials etc.) and open class negation operators (nouns like "denial" or verbs like "refuse") to detect negation in the segment.

Segment position: The (relative) position of the segment in the text might be helpful to identify typical linearisation strategies of argumentation.

In total a number of ca. 19.000 features has been extracted. The largest chunks are bigrams and lemma-based dependencies with ca. 6.000 features each. Each set of lemma unigrams (for

[5]We are aware that this summation is a rather trivial and potentially error-prone way of deriving an overall sentiment value from the individual values of the tokens, but postpone the use of more sophisticated methods to future work.

level	role	typegen	type	comb	target	role+type
labels	P (454)	T (115)	T (115)	/ (115)	n-4 (26)	PT (115)
	O (125)	S (286)	SN (277)	S (426)	n-3 (52)	PSN (265)
		A (178)	SE (9)	C (38)	n-2 (58)	PSE (9)
			AR (112)		n-1 (137)	PAR (12)
			AU (66)		0 (115)	PAU (53)
					n+1 (53)	OSN (12)
					n+2 (35)	OSE (0)
					r-1 (54)	OAR (100)
					r-2 (7)	OAU (13)
					...	
# of lbls	2	3	5	3	16	9

Table 1: Label distribution on the basic levels and for illustration on the complex 'role+type' level. Labels on remaining complex level combine accordingly: 'role+type+comb' with in total 12 different labels and 'role+type+comb+target' with 48 different labels found in the dataset.

the present, preceding, and subsequent segment) has around 2.000 features.

5.3 Classifiers

For automatic recognition we compare classifiers that have frequently been used in related work: Naïve Bayes (NB) approaches as in (Teufel and Moens, 2002), Support Vector Machines (SVM) and Conditional Random Fields (CRF) as in (Liakata et al., 2012) and maximum entropy (MaxEnt) approaches as in (Guo et al., 2013) or (Teufel and Kan, 2011). We used the Weka data mining software, v.3.7.10, (Hall et al., 2009) for all approaches, except MaxEnt and CRF.

Majority: This classifier assignes the most frequent class to each item. We use it as a lower bound of performance. The used implementation is Weka's ZeroR.

One Rule: A simple but effective baseline is the one rule classification approach. It selects and uses the one feature whose values can describe the class majority with the smallest error rate. The used implementation is Weka's OneR with standard parameters.

Naïve Bayes: We chose to apply a feature selected Naïve Bayes classifier to better cope with the large and partially redundant feature set.[6] Before training, all features are ranked accoring to their information gain observed on the training set. Features with information gain $\ngtr 0$ are excluded.

SVM: For SVMs, we used Weka's wrapper to LibLinear (Fan et al., 2008) with the Crammer and Singer SVM type and standard wrapper parameters.

MaxEnt: The maximum entropy classifiers are trained and tested with the MaxEnt toolkit (Zhang, 2004). We used at maximum 50 iterations of L-BFGS parameter estimation without a Gaussian prior.

CRF: For the implementation of CRFs we chose Mallet (McCallum, 2002). We used the SimpleTagger interface with standard parameters.

Nonbinary features have been binarized for the MaxEnt and CRF classifiers.

6 Results

All results presented in this section have been produced in 10 repetitions (with different random seeds) of 10-fold cross validation, i.e. for each score we have 100 fold-specific values of which we can calculate the average and the standard deviation. We report A(ccuracy), micro-averaged F(1-score) as a class-frequency weighted measure and Cohen's κ (Cohen, 1960) as a measure focussing on less frequent classes. All scores are given in percentages.

6.1 Comparing classifiers

A comparison of the different classifiers is shown in Table 2. Due to the skewed label distribution, the majority classifier places the lower bounds already at a quite high level for the 'role' and 'comb'-level. Also note that the agreement between predicted and gold for the majority classifier is equivalent to chance agreement and thus κ is 0 on every level, even though there are F-scores near the .70.

Bold values in Table 2 indicate highest average. However note, that differences of one or two percent points between the non-baseline classifiers are not significant, due to the variance over the

[6] With feature selection, we experienced better scores with the Naïve Bayes classifier, the only exception being the most complex level 'role+type+comb+target', where only very few features reached the information gain threshold.

level	Majority			OneR			CRF		
	A	F	κ	A	F	κ	A	F	κ
role	78±1	69±1	0±0	83±3	79±4	33±13	86±5	84±6	49±16
typegen	49±1	33±1	0±0	58±3	47±3	23±7	68±7	67±8	46±12
type	48±1	31±1	0±0	56±3	45±3	22±6	62±7	58±8	38±10
comb	74±1	62±1	0±0	81±4	77±4	44±12	**84**±5	**81**±7	55±13
target	24±1	9±1	0±0	37±5	29±4	24±6	47±11	**45**±11	**38**±12
role+typegen	47±1	30±1	0±0	56±3	45±3	22±6	67±7	65±8	49±11
role+type	46±1	29±1	0±0	54±3	43±3	21±6	61±7	56±8	38±11
role+type+comb	41±1	24±1	0±0	50±4	38±3	19±6	56±7	51±8	36±9
role+type+comb+target	20±1	7±1	0±0	28±4	19±3	18±5	36±10	30±9	28±10
level	Naïve Bayes			MaxEnt			LibLinear		
	A	F	κ	A	F	κ	A	F	κ
role	84±5	84±5	**52**±14	**86**±4	**85**±5	**52**±15	**86**±4	84±4	50±14
typegen	**74**±5	**74**±5	**57**±8	70±6	70±6	51±10	71±5	71±5	53±9
type	**68**±5	**67**±5	**52**±8	63±6	62±6	43±9	65±6	62±6	44±9
comb	74±6	75±5	42±11	**84**±5	**81**±7	**56**±12	**84**±3	**81**±4	54±10
target	38±6	38±6	29±6	47±8	44±8	37±9	**48**±5	44±5	**38**±6
role+typegen	**69**±6	**69**±6	**55**±9	68±7	67±7	51±10	**69**±5	67±6	52±9
role+type	61±5	**61**±5	**45**±7	63±6	**61**±6	**45**±9	**64**±5	60±5	**45**±8
role+type+comb	53±6	51±6	36±8	58±6	54±7	41±8	61±5	56±5	44±8
role+type+comb+target	22±4	19±4	16±4	36±6	**33**±6	29±6	**39**±5	32±4	**31**±5

Table 2: Classifier performance comparison: Percent average and standard deviation in 10 repetitions of 10-fold cross-validation of A(ccuracy), micro averages of F1-scores, and Cohen's κ.

folds on this rather small dataset.

The Naïve Bayes classifier profits from the feature selection on levels with a small number of labels and gives best results for the 'type(gen)' and 'role+typegen' levels. On the most complex level with 48 possible labels, however, performance drops even below the OneR baseline, because features do not reach the information gain threshold. The MaxEnt classifier performs well on the 'role' and 'comb', as well as on the 'role+type' levels. It reaches the highest F-score on the most complex level, although the highest accuracy and agreement on this levels is achieved by the SVM, indicating that the SVM accounted better for the less frequent labels. The SVM generally performs well in terms of accuracy and specifically on the most interesting levels for future applications, namely in target identification and the complex 'role+type' and 'role+type+comb+target' levels. For the CRF classifier, we had hoped that approaching the dataset as a sequence labelling problem would be of advantage. However, applied out of the box as done here, it did not perform as well as the segment-based MaxEnt or SVM classifier.

6.2 Feature ablation on 'role+type' level

We performed feature ablation tests with multiple classifiers on multiple levels. For the sake of brevity, we only present the results of the SVM and MaxEnt classifiers here on the 'role+type' level. The results are shown in Table 3. Bold values indicate greatest impact, i.e. strongest loss in the upper leave-one-feature-out half of the table and highest gain in the lower only-one-feature half of the table.

The greatest loss is produced by leaving out the discourse marker features. We assume that this impact can be attributed to the useful abstraction of introducing the signalled discourse relation as a features, since the markers are also present in other features (as lemma unigrams, perhaps first three lemma or even lemma dependencies) that produce minor losses.

For the single feature runs, lemma unigrams produce the best results, followed by discourse markers and other lemma features as bigrams, first three lemma and lemma dependencies. Note that negation markers, segment position and sentiment perform below or equal to the majority baseline. Whether at least the sentiment feature can prove more useful when we apply a more sophisticated calculation of a segment's sentiment value is something we want to investigate in future work. POS-tag based features are around the OneR baseline in terms of F-score and κ, but less accurate.

Interestingly, when using the LibLinear SVM, lemma bigrams have a larger impact on the overall performance than lemma based dependency triples in both tests, even for a language with a relatively free word order as German. This indicates that the costly parsing of the sentences might not be required after all. However, this difference is not

Features	LibLinear			MaxEnt		
	A	F	κ	A	F	κ
all	64±5	60±5	45±8	63±6	61±6	45±9
all w/o dependencies lemma	64±5	60±5	46±8	62±6	60±6	44±9
all w/o dependencies pos	65±5	61±5	46±8	63±6	61±7	45±9
all w/o discourse markers	**62**±5	**59**±5	**43**±8	**61**±7	**58**±7	**42**±9
all w/o first three lemma	64±5	60±5	44±8	63±6	60±7	44±9
all w/o lemma unigrams	63±5	60±5	45±8	62±6	60±7	44±9
all w/o lemma bigrams	63±5	60±5	44±8	62±6	60±6	44±9
all w/o main verb morph	64±5	60±5	45±8	62±6	60±6	43±9
all w/o negation marker	64±5	60±6	45±8	63±6	61±7	45±9
all w/o pos	64±5	61±5	45±8	63±6	60±7	44±8
all w/o segment position	64±5	60±5	45±8	63±6	61±6	45±9
all w/o sentiment	64±5	60±5	45±8	62±6	60±6	44±9
only dependencies lemma	56±4	47±4	27±6	56±6	49±7	30±8
only dependencies pos	42±6	41±6	18±8	41±7	40±7	16±9
only discourse markers	56±6	53±6	34±9	53±6	52±7	30±10
only first three lemma	54±6	52±6	33±9	50±6	48±6	26±8
only lemma unigrams	**59**±5	**55**±5	**37**±8	**59**±6	**56**±7	**38**±8
only lemma bigrams	**59**±4	53±5	34±8	55±7	51±7	30±9
only main verb morph	49±6	39±4	16±7	52±5	41±6	20±6
only negation marker	25±14	19±8	0±4	46±5	29±5	0±0
only pos	45±6	45±6	24±9	46±8	45±7	23±10
only segment position	31±12	25±10	4±7	46±5	29±6	0±0
only sentiment	22±14	15±11	-1±3	46±5	29±6	0±0

Table 3: Feature ablation tests on the 'role+type' level: Percent average and standard deviation in 10 repetitions of 10-fold cross-validation of A(ccuracy), micro averages of F1-scores, and Cohen's κ.

as clear for the MaxEnt classifier.

6.3 Class specific results

Finally, we present class-specific results of the MaxEnt classifier for the 'role+type' level in Table 4. Frequent categories give good results, but for low-frequency classes there are just not enough instances in the dataset. We hope improve this by extending the corpus by corresponding examples.

label	Precision	Recall	F1-score
PT	75±12	74±13	74±11
PSN	65±8	79±7	71±6
PSE	1±6	1±6	1±6
PAR	12±29	12±27	11±24
PAU	57±26	49±24	50±22
OSN	1±12	1±12	1±12
OAR	54±18	42±16	46±13
OAU	8±27	7±23	7±23

Table 4: MaxEnt class-wise results on the 'role+type' level: Percent average and standard deviation in 10 repetitions of 10-fold cross-validation of Precision, Recall and F1-score.

7 Summary and outlook

We have presented a small corpus of German microtexts that features authentic argumentations, yet has been collected in a controlled fashion to reduce the amount of distracting or complicated rhetorical phenomena, focussing instead on the argumentative moves. The corpus has been annotated with a scheme that –as we have shown– can be reliably used by trained and experienced annotators. To get a first impression of the performance of frequently used modelling approaches on our dataset, we experimented with different classifiers with rather out-of-the-box parameter settings on various levels of granularity of the scheme. Given the complex nature of such a discourse understanding tasks, the first results presented here are promising, but invite for further investigation.

We aim to generate a significantly larger corpus of argumentative microtexts by a crowd-sourced experiment. For the improvement of models, we consider various strategies: Integrating top down constraints on the argumentation structure, as done in (Guo et al., 2013) for the zoning of scientific documents, is one option. Hierarchical models that apply classifiers along the levels of our label hierarchy are another option. Furthermore, we want to explore sequence labelling models in more detail. Ultimately, the goal will be to apply these methods to authentic news-paper commentaries.

Acknowledgments

Thanks to Manfred Stede and to the anonymous reviewers for their helpful comments. The author was supported by a grant from Cusanuswerk.

References

Moshe Azar. 1999. Argumentative text as rhetorical structure: An application of rhetorical structure theory. *Argumentation*, 13:97–114.

Monroe C. Beardsley. 1950. *Practical Logic*. Prentice-Hall, New York.

Bernd Bohnet. 2010. Very high accuracy and fast dependency parsing is not a contradiction. In *Proceedings of the 23rd International Conference on Computational Linguistics*, COLING '10, pages 89–97, Stroudsburg, PA, USA. Association for Computational Linguistics.

Elena Cabrio and Serena Villata. 2012. Natural language arguments: A combined approach. In Luc De Raedt, Christian Bessiere, Didier Dubois, Patrick Doherty, Paolo Frasconi, Fredrik Heintz, and Peter J. F. Lucas, editors, *ECAI*, volume 242 of *Frontiers in Artificial Intelligence and Applications*, pages 205–210. IOS Press.

Jacob Cohen. 1960. A Coefficient of Agreement for Nominal Scales. *Educational and Psychological Measurement*, 20(1):37–46.

Rong-En Fan, Kai-Wei Chang, Cho-Jui Hsieh, Xiang-Rui Wang, and Chih-Jen Lin. 2008. Liblinear: A library for large linear classification. *J. Mach. Learn. Res.*, 9:1871–1874, June.

Vanessa Wei Feng and Graeme Hirst. 2011. Classifying arguments by scheme. In *Proceedings of the 49th Annual Meeting of the Association for Computational Linguistics: Human Language Technologies - Volume 1*, HLT '11, pages 987–996, Stroudsburg, PA, USA. Association for Computational Linguistics.

Vanessa Wei Feng and Graeme Hirst. 2012. Text-level discourse parsing with rich linguistic features. In *Proceedings of the 50th Annual Meeting of the Association for Computational Linguistics: Long Papers - Volume 1*, ACL '12, pages 60–68, Stroudsburg, PA, USA. Association for Computational Linguistics.

Joseph L. Fleiss. 1971. Measuring nominal scale agreement among many raters. *Psychological Bulletin*, 76(5):378–382.

James B. Freeman. 1991. *Dialectics and the Macrostructure of Argument*. Foris, Berlin.

James B. Freeman. 2011. *Argument Structure: Representation and Theory*. Argumentation Library (18). Springer.

Nancy L. Green. 2010. Representation of argumentation in text with rhetorical structure theory. *Argumentation*, 24:181–196.

Yufan Guo, Roi Reichart, and Anna Korhonen. 2013. Improved information structure analysis of scientific documents through discourse and lexical constraints. In *Proceedings of the 2013 Conference of the North American Chapter of the Association for Computational Linguistics: Human Language Technologies*, pages 928–937, Atlanta, Georgia, June. Association for Computational Linguistics.

Mark Hall, Eibe Frank, Geoffrey Holmes, Bernhard Pfahringer, Peter Reutemann, and Ian H. Witten. 2009. The weka data mining software: An update. *SIGKDD Explor. Newsl.*, 11(1):10–18, November.

Hugo Hernault, Hemut Prendinger, David duVerle, and Mitsuru Ishizuka. 2010. HILDA: A discourse parser using support vector machine classification. *Dialogue and Discourse*, 1(3):1–33.

Maria Liakata, Shyamasree Saha, Simon Dobnik, Colin R. Batchelor, and Dietrich Rebholz-Schuhmann. 2012. Automatic recognition of conceptualization zones in scientific articles and two life science applications. *Bioinformatics*, 28(7):991–1000.

William Mann and Sandra Thompson. 1988. Rhetorical structure theory: Towards a functional theory of text organization. *TEXT*, 8:243–281.

Andrew Kachites McCallum. 2002. Mallet: A machine learning for language toolkit. http://mallet.cs.umass.edu.

Raquel Mochales Palau and Marie-Francine Moens. 2011. Argumentation mining. *Artificial Intelligence and Law*, 19(1):15–22.

Andreas Peldszus and Manfred Stede. 2013a. From argument diagrams to automatic argument mining: A survey. *International Journal of Cognitive Informatics and Natural Intelligence (IJCINI)*, 7(1):1–31.

Andreas Peldszus and Manfred Stede. 2013b. Ranking the annotators: An agreement study on argumentation structure. In *Proceedings of the 7th Linguistic Annotation Workshop and Interoperability with Discourse*, pages 196–204, Sofia, Bulgaria, August. Association for Computational Linguistics.

Chris Reed, Raquel Mochales Palau, Glenn Rowe, and Marie-Francine Moens. 2008. Language resources for studying argument. In Nicoletta Calzolari (Conference Chair), Khalid Choukri, Bente Maegaard, Joseph Mariani, Jan Odijk, Stelios Piperidis, and Daniel Tapias, editors, *Proceedings of the Sixth International Conference on Language Resources and Evaluation (LREC'08)*, Marrakech, Morocco, may. European Language Resources Association (ELRA).

Robert Remus, Uwe Quasthoff, and Gerhard Heyer. 2010. SentiWS - A Publicly Available German-language Resource for Sentiment Analysis. In Nicoletta Calzolari (Conference Chair), Khalid Choukri, Bente Maegaard, Joseph Mariani, Jan Odijk, Stelios Piperidis, Mike Rosner, and Daniel Tapias, editors, *Proceedings of the 7th International Conference on Language Resources and Evaluation (LREC'10)*, pages 1168–1171, Valletta, Malta, May. European Language Resources Association (ELRA).

Patrick Saint-Dizier. 2012. Processing natural language arguments with the TextCoop platform. *Journal of Argumentation and Computation*, 3(1):49–82.

Manfred Stede and Antje Sauermann. 2008. Linearization of arguments in commentary text. In *Proceedings of the Workshop on Multidisciplinary Approaches to Discourse*. Oslo.

Manfred Stede. 2002. DiMLex: A Lexical Approach to Discourse Markers. In Vittorio Di Tomaso Alessandro Lenci, editor, *Exploring the Lexicon - Theory and Computation*. Edizioni dell'Orso, Alessandria, Italy.

Manfred Stede. 2004. The Potsdam Commentary Corpus. In *Proceedings of the ACL Workshop on Discourse Annotation*, pages 96–102, Barcelona.

Simone Teufel and Min-Yen Kan. 2011. Robust argumentative zoning for sensemaking in scholarly documents. In Raffaella Bernadi, Sally Chambers, Björn Gottfried, Frédérique Segond, and Ilya Zaihrayeu, editors, *Advanced Language Technologies for Digital Libraries*, volume 6699 of *Lecture Notes in Computer Science*, pages 154–170. Springer Berlin Heidelberg.

Simone Teufel and Marc Moens. 2002. Summarizing scientific articles: Experiments with relevance and rhetorical status. *Comput. Linguist.*, 28(4):409–445, December.

Simone Teufel, Advaith Siddharthan, and Colin Batchelor. 2009. Towards discipline-independent argumentative zoning: evidence from chemistry and computational linguistics. In *Proceedings of the 2009 Conference on Empirical Methods in Natural Language Processing: Volume 3*, EMNLP '09, pages 1493–1502, Stroudsburg, PA, USA. Association for Computational Linguistics.

Simone Teufel. 2010. *The Structure of Scientific Articles: Applications to Citation Indexing and Summarization*. CSLI Studies in Computational Linguistics. CSLI Publications.

Stephen N. Thomas. 1974. *Practical Reasoning in Natural Language*. Prentice-Hall, New York.

Stephen Toulmin. 1958. *The Uses of Argument*. Cambridge University Press, Cambridge.

Douglas Walton, Chris Reed, and Fabrizio Macagno. 2008. *Argumentation Schemes*. Cambridge University Press.

Saskia Warzecha. 2013. Klassifizierung und Skopusbestimmung deutscher Negationsoperatoren. Bachelor thesis, Potsdam University.

Le Zhang, 2004. *Maximum Entropy Modeling Toolkit for Python and C++*, December.

Titles That Announce Argumentative Claims in Biomedical Research Articles

Heather Graves
Roger Graves
Department of English and Film Studies
The University of Alberta
Edmonton, Alberta, Canada
graves1,hgraves@ualberta.ca

Robert E. Mercer
Mahzereen Akter
Department of Computer Science
The University of Western Ontario
London, Ontario, Canada
mercer@csd.uwo.ca

Abstract

In the experimental sciences authors use the scientific article to express their findings by making an argumentative claim. While past studies have located the claim in the Abstract, the Introduction, and in the Discussion section, in this paper we focus on the article title as a potential source of the claim. Our investigation has suggested that titles which contain a tensed verb almost certainly announce the argument claim while titles which do not contain a tensed verb have varied announcements. Another observation that we have confirmed in our dataset is that the frequency of verbs in titles of experimental research articles has increased over time.

1 Introduction

In this paper we are interested in determining what is being claimed in articles in experimental (not clinical) biomedical literature, in particular. Claims have been studied in the argumentation literature from many different standpoints (White, 2009). Rhetorical structure theory was developed from systemic functional linguistics to map connections among texts (Mann and Thompson, 1987); Argumentative zoning was developed from Swales' CARS model of moves made in research articles (Teufel, 1999; Teufel and Moens, 1999; Teufel and Moens, 2002). Toulmin-based analysis has also been used to map the argumentative structure of articles (Toulmin, 1958 2003; Jenicek, 2006; Reed and Rowe, 2006; Graves et al., 2013; Graves, 2013). With these models of argument in mind, we view the claim of a scientific argument as the conclusion that the authors infer from known information and new information (results from an experiment or other forms of observations). Past studies locate the claim in the Abstract (Kanoksilapatham, 2013), at the end of the Introduction (Swales, 1990; Swales and Najjar, 1987; Kanoksilapatham, 2005; Kanoksilapatham, 2012), and in the Discussion section (Kanoksilapatham, 2005). Our observations of changes in the genre of the research article have led us to perform a preliminary investigation of titles with the outcome being a provisional typology.

2 Method

The Genia Tagger uses the Penn Treebank Tagset. In the following we mention the verb tags from this tagset: VB – base form, VBD – past tense, VBG – gerund, VBN – past participle, VBP – present tense non-3rd person singular, VBZ – present tense 3rd person singular. We applied these tags to the dataset of biomedical article titles and abstracts used in this preliminary study has been taken from MEDLINE, the well-known biomedical bibliographic repository that contains over 19 million citations and abstracts for about 81% of these citations from approximately 5600 journals (NLM, 2013 accessed 3 February 2014). We have curated a small database using *biotextEngine* and some locally developed tools.

3 Analysis

For each title we collect the following:

- cumulative frequency of all verb categories
- whether the title contains a VBP, VBZ, or passive verb
- whether the title contains a nominalization

4 Findings

Our analysis so far has identified three typologies. The articles can be categorized according to genre, purpose and structure. For titles with verbs the claim of the title is repeated several times: in the

Proceedings of the First Workshop on Argumentation Mining, pages 98–99,
Baltimore, Maryland USA, June 26, 2014.

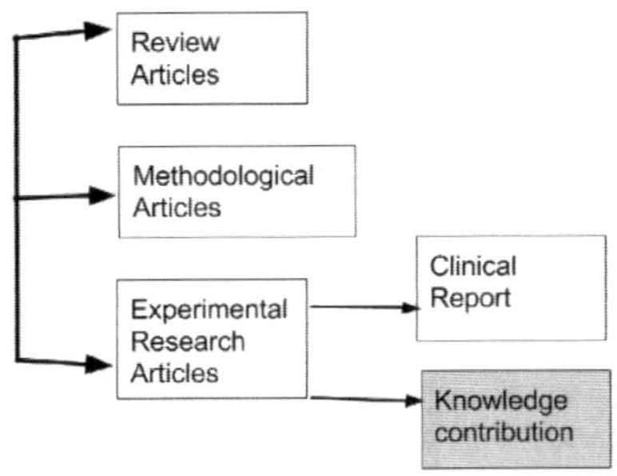

Figure 1: Genre typology

Abstract, Introduction, and Discussion sections. For articles without verbs, the claim does not appear in the title or introduction (it does appear in the abstract and discussion sections). A third finding: the frequency of verbs in titles of experimental research articles has increased over time.

5 Discussion

We believe that our methods for identifying titles could lead to better literature search techniques. If researchers are able to identify the claim of an article from a search of titles alone, they will be able to evaluate the relevance of each article more efficiently. We suspect that the increase in titles with verbs and claims in them is an emerging trend, possibly the result of explicit editorial policy. One side effect of including claims in titles may be higher quality writing by the authors. Another result from using verbs in titles could be the automation of claim extraction. Finally, having research scientists use clear language to state their claim can have the added benefit of making knowledge translation more effective by lessening the difficulty of reading scientific texts. This, in turn, might afford greater access to the research outcomes by clinical practitioners (one of the main readerships of biomedical research).

References

Heather Graves, Shahin Moghaddasi, and Azirah Hashim. 2013. Mathematics is the method: Exploring the macro-organizational structure of research articles in mathematics. *Discourse Studies*, 15:421–438.

Heather Graves. 2013. The trouble with Toulmin for teaching argument in science. In *11th Annual Technology for Second Language Learning Conference: Technology and Teaching Writing for Academic Disciplines*. ms.

Milos Jenicek. 2006. How to read, understand, and write discussion sections in medical articles: An exercise in critical thinking. *Med. Sci. Monitor*, 12.

Budsaba Kanoksilapatham. 2005. Rhetorical structure of biochemistry research articles. *English for Specific Purposes*, 24:269–292.

Budsaba Kanoksilapatham. 2012. Structure of research article introductions in three engineering subdisciplines. *IEEE Transactions on Professional Communication*, 55:294–309.

Budsaba Kanoksilapatham. 2013. Generic characterisation of civil engineering research article abstracts. *3L: The Southeast Asian Journal of English Language Studies*, 19:1–10.

William C. Mann and Sandra A. Thompson. 1987. Rhetorical structure theory: Description and construction of text structures. In G. Kempen, editor, *Natural language generation: New results in artificial intelligence, psychology and linguistics*, pages 85–95. Dordrecht: Martinus Nijhoff.

U.S. National Library of Medicine NLM. 2013 (accessed 3 February 2014). "ncbi: Pubmed overview. `http://www.ncbi.nlm.nih.gov/entrez/query/static/overview.html`.

Chris Reed and Glenn Rowe. 2006. Translating Toulmin diagrams: Theory neutrality in argument representation. In David Hitchcock and Bart Verheij, editors, *Arguing on the Toulmin model: New essays in argument analysis and evaluation*, pages 341–358. Dordrecht: Springer.

John Swales and Hazem Najjar. 1987. The writing of research article introductions. *Written Communication*, 4:175–192.

John Swales. 1990. *Genre Analysis: English in Academic and Research Settings*. Cambridge Applied Linguistics. Cambridge University Press.

Simone Teufel and Mark Moens. 1999. Argumentative classification of extracted sentences as a first step towards flexible abstracting. In Inderjeet Mani and Mark Maybury, editors, *Advances in automatic text summarization*, pages 155–171. MIT Press.

Simone Teufel and Marc Moens. 2002. Summarizing scientific articles: Experiments with relevance and rhetorical status. *Computational Linguistics*, 28(4):409–445.

Simone Teufel. 1999. *Argumentative Zoning : Information Extraction from Scientific Text*. Ph.D. thesis, School of Cognitive Science, University of Edinburgh.

Stephen Toulmin. 1958-2003. *The uses of argument*. Cambridge University Press.

Barbara White. 2009. *Annotating a corpus of biomedical research texts: Two models of rhetorical analysis*. Ph.D. thesis, The University of Western Ontario, Canada.

Extracting Higher Order Relations From Biomedical Text

Syeed Ibn Faiz
Department of Computer Science
The University of Western Ontario
syeedibnfaiz@gmail.com

Robert E. Mercer
Department of Computer Science
The University of Western Ontario
mercer@csd.uwo.ca

Abstract

Argumentation in a scientific article is composed of unexpressed and explicit statements of old and new knowledge combined into a logically coherent textual argument. Discourse relations, linguistic coherence relations that connect discourse segments, help to communicate an argument's logical steps. A biomedical relation exhibits a relationship between biomedical entities. In this paper, we are primarily concerned with the extraction of connections between biomedical relations, a connection that we call a higher order relation. We combine two methods, namely biomedical relation extraction and discourse relation parsing, to extract such higher order relations from biomedical research articles. Finding and extracting these relations can assist in automatically understanding the scientific arguments expressed by the author in the text.

1 Introduction

We use the term ***higher order relation*** to denote a relation that relates two biomedical relations. Consider, for example, the following sentence:

(1) Aspirin appeared to prevent VCAM-1 transcription, since it dose-dependently inhibited induction of VCAM-1 mRNA by TNF.

We can find two biomedical relations involving Aspirin: Aspirin–*prevents*–VCAM-1 transcription and Aspirin–*inhibits*–induction of VCAM-1 mRNA. These two relations are connected by the word *since*. The higher order relation conveys a causal sense, which indicates that the latter relation causes the earlier one. In genetic transcription mRNA is generated (a process known by the reader, so not expressed in the argument). This piece of the author's argument is that by observing inhibition of mRNA induction (the genetic process that activates transcription) by different doses of aspirin, the inference that aspirin prevents the transcription can be made. This inference is textually signalled by the discourse connective *since*.

Formally, we define a higher order relation as a binary relation that relates one biomedical relation with another biomedical relation. In this paper we propose a method for these extracting higher order relations using discourse relation parsing and biomedical relation extraction.

2 Extracting Higher Order Relations

There are two stages in our method for extracting higher order relations from text. In the first stage we use a discourse relation parser to extract the explicit discourse relations from text. In the second stage we analyze each extracted explicit discourse relation to determine whether it can produce a higher order relation. We use a biomedical relation extraction system in this process. For each argument of an explicit discourse relation we find all occurrences of biomedical relations in it. Higher order relations are then constructed by pairing the biomedical relations or observations found in the discourse arguments. The sense of the explicit discourse relation is used to interpret all the higher order relations derived from it.

Parsing an explicit discourse relation involves three steps: identifying the explicit discourse connective, the arguments and the sense. In (Faiz and Mercer, 2013) we showed how to use syntactic and surface level context to achieve a state-of-the-art result for identifying discourse connectives from text. Our work on a complete explicit discourse relation parser is presented in (Faiz, 2012). For identifying the arguments of discourse connectives we use the head-based representation proposed by Wellner and Pustejovsky (Wellner and Pustejovsky, 2007). We found that this head-based

Proceedings of the First Workshop on Argumentation Mining, pages 100–101,
Baltimore, Maryland USA, June 26, 2014.

representation is very suitable for the task of extracting higher order relations. The head of an argument plays an important role in selecting a biomedical relation as an argument to a higher order relation.

This observation regarding the heads of the discourse arguments has another useful implication. Since the biomedical relations that we have to consider need to involve the argument head, we only have to extract the portion of the argument that is influenced or dominated by the head. One simple way to do this is to consider the dependents of the head in the dependency representation. Wellner (2009) reported that finding the dependents of the syntactic head of an argument often gives a good approximation of the argument extent .

3 Evaluation

Our algorithm for extracting higher order relations depends on discourse parsing and biomedical relation extraction. We have discussed our implementation of these components and evaluated their performance in previous work (Faiz, 2012; Faiz and Mercer, 2013). We have evaluated the algorithm we present in this paper in terms of how accurately it can use those components in order to find higher order relations. More specifically, we will measure how accurately it can determine the part of the full argument extent that contains the biomedical entities in it.

For this evaluation we used the AIMed corpus (Bunescu et al., 2005). This corpus contains an annotation for protein-protein interactions. From this corpus we collected 69 discourse relations.

For both ARG1 and ARG2 we performed two tests. We measured from the argument heads how many protein mentions occurring within the argument extent (the *True Positives*) are found and how many protein mentions that lie beyond the argument extent (the *False Positives*) are found. For ARG1, we found that our algorithm missed only one protein mention and incorrectly found three proteins from outside the argument extent, a precision of 98% and a recall of 99.32%. For ARG2, we obtained a 100% precision and a 99% recall.

We conducted another experiment, which is similar to the previous one except that now instead of counting only the protein mentions, we counted all the words that can be reached from an argument head. In other words, this experiment evaluates our algorithm in terms of how accurately it can identify the full argument extent (i.e., the words in it). For ARG1 and ARG2 we got an F-score of 91.98% and 92.98% respectively.

4 Discussion

Extraction of many higher order relations is dependent on coreference resolution. For example, in (1), Aspirin is anaphorically referred to in ARG2. In our current implementation we lack coreference resolution. Therefore, augmenting a coreference resolution module in our pipeline would be an immediate improvement.

In our implementation, we used a simple but imperfect method to determine whether a biomedical relation involves the head of a discourse argument. We checked whether the head appears between the biomedical entities or within a short distance from either one in the sentence. However, this simple rule may produce spurious higher order relations. One way to improve this method would be to consider the rules we presented for rule-based biomedical relation extraction. Most of the rules give a dependency path corresponding to the relation they can extract. That path can then be analyzed to determine whether the relation depends on the head.

Acknowledgments

This work was partially funded by a Natural Sciences and Engineering Research Council of Canada (NSERC) Discovery Grant to R. Mercer.

References

Razvan Bunescu, Ruifang Ge, Rohit J. Kate, Edward M. Marcotte, Raymond J. Mooney, Arun K. Ramani, and Yuk W. Wong. 2005. Comparative experiments on learning information extractors for proteins and their interactions. *Artificial Intelligence in Medicine*, 33(2):139–155, February.

Syeed Ibn Faiz and Robert E. Mercer. 2013. Identifying explicit discourse connectives in text. In *Canadian Conference on AI*, pages 64–76.

Syeed Ibn Faiz. 2012. Discovering higher order relations from biomedical text. Master's thesis, University of Western Ontario, London, ON, Canada.

Ben Wellner and James Pustejovsky. 2007. Automatically identifying the arguments of discourse connectives. In *EMNLP-CoNLL*, pages 92–101. ACL.

Ben Wellner. 2009. *Sequence models and ranking methods for discourse parsing*. Ph.D. thesis, Brandeis University, Waltham, MA, USA. AAI3339383.

Survey in sentiment, polarity and function analysis of citation

Myriam Hernández A
Escuela Politécnica Nacional
Facultad de Ingeniería de Sistemas
Quito, Ecuador
myriam.hernandez@epn.edu.ec

José M. Gómez
Universidad de Alicante
Dpto de Lenguajes y Sistemas Informáticos
Alicante, España
jmgomez@ua.es

Abstract

In this paper we proposed a survey in sentiment, polarity and function analysis of citations. This is an interesting area that has had an increased development in recent years but still has plenty of room for growth and further research. The amount of scientific information in the web makes it necessary innovate the analysis of the influence of the work of peers and leaders in the scientific community. We present an overview of general concepts, review contributions to the solution of related problems such as context identification, function and polarity classification, identify some trends and suggest possible future research directions.

1 Extended abstract

The number of publications in science grows exponentially each passing year. To understand the evolution of several topics, researchers and scientist require locating and accessing available contributions from among large amounts of available electronic material that can only be navigated through citations. Citation analysis is a way of evaluating the impact of an author, a published work or a scientific media.

Sugiyama (2010) established that there are two types of research in the field of citation analysis of research papers: citation count to evaluate the impact (Garfield, 1972) and citation content analysis (Councill et al., 2008).

The advantages of citation count are the simplicity and the experience accumulated in scientometric applications, but many authors have pointed out its weakness. One of the limitations is that the count does not difference between the weights of high and low impact citing papers. PageRank (Page et al., 1998) partially solved this problem with a rating algorithm. Small (1973) proposed co-citation analysis to supplement the qualitative method with a similarity measure between works A and B, counting the number of documents that cite them.

Recently, this type researchers' impact measure has been widely criticized. Bibliometric studies (Radicchi, 2012) show that incomplete, erroneous or controversial papers are most cited. This can generate perverse incentives for new researchers who may be tempted to publish although its investigation is wrong or not yet complete because this way they will receive higher number of citations (Marder et al., 2010). In fact, it also affects the quality of very prestigious journals such as Nature, Science or Cell because they know that accepting controversial articles is very profitable to increase citation numbers. Moreover, as claimed by Siegel and Baveye (2010), it is more influential the quantity of articles than their quality or than the relationship between papers with a higher number of citations and the number of citations that, in turn, they receive (Webster et al., 2009).

Other limitation of this method is that a citation is interpreted as an author being influenced by the work of another, without specifying type of influence (Zhang et al., 2013) which can be misleading concerning the true impact of a citation (Young et al., 2008). To better understand the influence of a scientific work it is advisable to broaden the range of indicators to take into account factors like the author's disposition towards the reference, because, for instance, a criticized quoted work cannot have the same weight than other that is used as starting point of a research.

Proceedings of the First Workshop on Argumentation Mining, pages 102–103,
Baltimore, Maryland USA, June 26, 2014.

These problems are added to the growing importance of impact indexes for the researchers' career. It is becoming more important to correct these issues and look for more complete metrics to evaluate researchers' relevance taking into account many other "quality" factors, one of them being the intention of the researcher when citing the work of others.

Automatic analysis of subjective criteria present in a text is known as Sentiment Analysis. It is part of citation content analysis and is a current research topic in the area of natural language processing in the field of opinion mining and its scope includes monitoring emotions in fields as diverse as marketing, political science and economics. It is proposed that this type of analysis be applied in the study of bibliographic citations, as part of citation content analysis, to detect the intention and disposition of the citing author to the cited work, and to give additional information to complement the calculation of the estimated impact of a publication to enhance its bibliometric analysis (Jbara and Radev, 2012). This analysis includes syntactic and semantic language relationships through speech and natural language processing and the explicit and implicit linguistic choices in the text to infer citation function and feelings of the author regarding the cited work (Zhang et al., 2013).

A combination of a quantitative and qualitative/subjective analysis would give a more complete perspective of the impact of publications in the scientific community (Jbara et al., 2013). Some methods for subjective citation analysis have been proposed by different authors, but they call for more work to achieve better results in detection, extraction and handling of citations content and to characterize in a more accurate way the profile of scientists and the criticism or acceptance of their work.

Although work in this specific area has increased in recent years, there are still open problems that have not been solved and they need to be investigated. There are not enough open corpus that can be worked in shared form by researchers, there is not a common work frame to facilitate achieving results that are comparable with each other in order to reach conclusions about the efficiency of different techniques. In this field it is necessary to develop conditions that allow and motivate collaborative work.

Acknowledgments

This research work has been partially funded by the Spanish Government and the European Commission through the project, ATTOS (TIN2012-38536-C03-03), LEGOLANG (TIN2012-31224), SAM (FP7-611312) and FIRST (FP7-287607).

Reference

Councill, I. G., Giles, C. L., & Kan, M. Y. (2008, May). ParsCit: an Open-source CRF Reference String Parsing Package. In LREC.

Garfield, E. (1972, November). Citation analysis as a tool in journal evaluation. American Association for the Advancement of Science.

Jbara, A., & Radev, D. (2012, June). Reference scope identification in citing sentences. In Proceedings of the 2012 Conference of the North American Chapter of the Association for Computational Linguistics: Human Language Technologies (pp. 80-90). Association for Computational Linguistics.

Jbara, A., Ezra, J., & Radev, D. (2013). Purpose and Polarity of Citation: Towards NLP-based Bibliometrics. In Proceedings of NAACL-HLT (pp. 596-606).

Marder, E., Kettenmann, H., & Grillner, S. (2010). Impacting our young. Proceedings of the National Academy of Sciences, 107(50), 21233-21233.

Page, L., Brin, S., Motwani, R., & Winograd, T. (1999). The PageRank citation ranking: bringing order to the web.

Radicchi, F. (2012). In science "there is no bad publicity": Papers criticized in comments have high scientific impact. Scientific reports, 2.

Small, H. (1973). Co-citation in the scientific literature: A new measure of the relationship between two documents. Journal of the American Society for information Science, 24(4), 265-269.

Sugiyama, K., Kumar, T., Kan, M. Y., & Tripathi, R. C. (2010). Identifying citing sentences in research papers using supervised learning. In Information Retrieval & Knowledge Management, (CAMP), 2010 International Conference on (pp. 67-72). IEEE.

Webster, G. D., Jonason, P. K., & Schember, T. O. (2009). Hot Topics and Popular Papers in Evolutionary Psychology: Analyses of Title Words and Citation Counts in Evolution and Human Behavior, 1979-2008. Evolutionary Psychology, 7(3).

Young, N. S., Ioannidis, J. P., & Al-Ubaydli, O. (2008). Why current publication practices may distort science. PLoS medicine, 5(10), e201.

Zhang, G., Ding, Y., & Milojević, S. (2013). Citation content analysis (cca): A framework for syntactic and semantic analysis of citation content. Journal of the American Society for Information Science and Technology, 64(7), 1490-1503.

Indicators of Argument-conclusion Relationships.

An Approach for Argumentation Mining in German Discourses

Bianka Trevisan, Eva-Maria Jakobs
Human-Computer Interaction Center
RWTH Aachen University
{b.trevisan|e.m.jakobs}
@tk.rwth-aachen.de

Eva Dickmeis, Thomas Niehr
German Linguistics
RWTH Aachen University
{e.dickmeis|t.niehr}
@isk.rwth-aachen.de

[In this paper we present a new methodological approach for the analysis of public discourses aiming at the semi-automated identification of arguments by combining methods from discourse analysis with methods from Natural Language Processing. Discourses evolve over long periods of time and, consequently, form a broad database. Up to now, the analysis of discourses is hitherto performed primarily by hand, i.e., only small corpora or discourse fragments can be analyzed. Inevitably, this leads to lengthy and expensive annotation. Thus, there is a growing interest to overcome these methodological challenges by the use of computer-based methods and tools for the semi-automated analysis.

However, there are only few approaches known that focus on the analysis of discourses and the (semi-)automated identification of arguments therein (e.g. Reed at al., 2008; Liakata et al., 2012; Ashley and Walker, 2013). Particularly, approaches that can be explicitly used for the analysis of German-language discourses exist only in initial stages. Therefore, we suggest a fine-grained semi-automated approach based on multi-level annotation that focuses on linguistic means as indicators of arguments. The aim is to identify regularities, respectively, indicators in the linguistic surface of the discourse (e.g. recurring lexical and typographical characteristics), which indicate the occurrence of certain arguments (e.g. premise). In this paper, we focus on the identification of indicators of argument-conclusion relationship: *conclusive connectors* or *conclusiva,* that are typically adverbs such as *hence, consequently, therefore, thus, because* (Govier, 2013; see example below):

Die Campusbahn werde den Individualverkehr verdrängen, weil die Stadt eng bebaut sei. Schon in den 1970er Jahren sei deshalb das Aus für die Straßenbahn besiegelt worden.

[The campus train will displace the individual traffic because the city is densely built. Therefore, the end for the tram was sealed in the 1970s.]

As an application example, a small corpus consisting of 21 newspaper articles is analyzed. The corpus belongs to the interdisciplinary project *Future Mobility (FuMob)*, which is funded by the Excellent Initiative of the German federal and state governments. The methodological approach consists of three steps, which are performed iteratively: (1) manual discourse-linguistic argumentation analysis, (2) semi-automatic Text Mining (PoS-tagging and linguistic multi-level annotation), and (3) data merge.

(1) *Discourse-linguistic argumentation analysis*: First, the data is manually analyzed. Objectives of the analysis are (i) identifying discourse-relevant arguments, (ii) forming argument classes, and (iii) determining the significance of an argument in the discourse (Niehr 2004). To determine the significance of an argument the use by various discourse participants is analyzed and quantified. The argument-use can be categorized as *argumentative*, *positively cited*, *negatively cited* or *neutrally cited.* In addition, to identify arguments and their use in public discourse, the analysis also aims to detect and characterize discourse participants who use similar arguments. For this purpose, the social *role*, *gender* or *age* of an argument's author are determined on the basis of the information given in the text. This allows comparing the argumentation of different social groups in public discourses.

(2) *Text Mining*: Parallel to the manual discourse analysis, the collected data is processed semi-automatically applying the methodology described in Trevisan (2014/in press). Thereby, post-processing is performed in four successive methodological steps. First, the data is tokenized

Proceedings of the First Workshop on Argumentation Mining, pages 104–105,
Baltimore, Maryland USA, June 26, 2014. ©2014 Association for Computational Linguistics

by means of the TreeTagger tokenizer (Schmid 1995). Second, the tokenized data is PoS-tagged using TreeTagger. Third, the automatically tokenized and tagged data is manually corrected. Fourth, the corpus is annotated semi-automatically applying the multi-level annotation model depicted in Trevisan et al. (2014/in press); the annotation is performed using the tool *Auto-Annotator*. Originally, the model was used for the enhancement of automatic *Sentiment Analysis* in German blog comments. The annotation model consists of different annotation levels with various purposes and scopes (token vs. sequence of tokens) of annotation, e.g., the annotation of the morpho-syntactic function of a token vs. the annotation of the polarity (positive, negative, neutral) of a sentence or utterance. Thereby, the fact is taken into account that each token fulfills different grammatical functions, which are also relevant for the constitution of evaluative statements and arguments. The basic idea is, that the interplay and combination of different annotated linguistic means constitutes or indicates an argument and its way of use.

(3) *Data merge:* In a third step, the analysis results from (1) and (2) are merged. By the data merge, it appears, which linguistic means on which linguistic level interplays or often occurs with which kind of argument. The results of the data merge are evaluated regarding the enhancement of automatic argumentation analysis.

The results show that the argument-conclusion relationship is most often indicated by the conjunction *because* followed by *since, therefore* and *so*. In detail, the results show that indicators for argument-conclusion relationship include not only causal conjunctions (e.g. *because, since*), but also concessive (e.g. *although, despite*) or conditional conjunctions (e.g. *if ... then*). Thereby, the conclusiva indicate either the argument (e.g. *because, since, also*) or the conclusions (e.g. *hence, therefore, so*). In the second case, they are still references to arguments that often occur immediately prior to the conclusion. Furthermore, conclusiva occur predominantly as a single token. If they occur as a multi-token they have a reinforcing (e.g. *just because*) respectively limiting or negating function (e.g. *only because*).

The results raise the suspicion that the identified conclusiva are text type-specific phenomenon as the analyzed corpus contains only articles from newspapers. However, we assume that some of the conclusiva may occur across different text types (e.g. *because, therefore*) whereas other (e.g. *for this reason, in the end*) tends to be text type-specific indicators for argument-conclusion relationships.

Moreover, having a closer look at the text data, it is evident that conclusiva only bear evidence *of* argument-conclusion relationships. They do not indicate *where* the argument or conclusion starts or ends or in which sequence (argument-conclusion vs. conclusion-argument) they occur. Regarding the semi-automated analysis of arguments in discourses this constitutes a difficulty. One solution to approach this challenge might be to define the text window, which has to be considered left and right from the conclusiva. In this context, the work of Wellner and Pustejovsky (2007) has to be considered, too.

Future work will focus on the enhancement of the methodological approach and its automation, which includes i.a. the implementation of approaches such as anaphora resolution or pattern recognition. Furthermore, the analysis must be extended to other corpora and text types.

Kevin D. Ashley and Vern R. Walker. 2013. Toward Constructing Evidence-Based Legal Arguments Using Legal Decision Documents and Machine Learning. *Proceedings of ICAIL*, 176-180

Trudy Govier. 2013. *A practical study of argument*. Wadsworth, Andover.

Maria Liakata, Shyamasree Saha, Simon Dobnik, Colin Batchelor, and Dietrich Rebholz-Schuhmann. 2012. Automatic recognition of conceptualization zones in scientific articles and two life science applications. *Bioinformatics*, 28(7):991–1000.

Thomas Niehr. 2004. *Der Streit um Migration in Deutschland, Österreich und der Schweiz. Eine vergleichende diskursgeschichtliche Untersuchung*. Winter, Heidelberg.

Chris Reed, Raquel Mochales Palau, Glenn Rowe, and Marie-Francine Moens. 2008. Language Resources for Studying Argument. *Proceedings of the 6th Conference on Language Resources and Evaluation*, 91–100.

Helmut Schmid. 1995. Improvements in Part-of-Speech Tagging with an Application to German. *Proceedings of SIGDAT'95*.

Bianka Trevisan. 2014/in press. *Bewerten in Blogkommentaren. Mehrebenenannotation sprachlichen Bewertens*. Dissertation, RWTH Aachen University.

Ben Wellner and James Pustejovsky. 2007. Automatically Identifying the Arguments of Discourse Connectives. *Proceeding of: EMNLP-CoNLL*, 92-101

Extracting Imperatives from Wikipedia Article for Deletion Discussions

Fiona Mao
Robert E. Mercer
Department of Computer Science
The University of Western Ontario
London, Ontario, Canada
fiona.wt.mao@gmail.com
mercer@csd.uwo.ca

Lu Xiao
Faculty of Information and Media Studies
Department of Computer Science
The University of Western Ontario
London, Ontario, Canada
lxiao24@uwo.ca

Abstract

Wikipedia contains millions of articles, collaboratively produced. If an article is controversial, an online "Article for Deletion" (AfD) discussion is held to determine whether the article should be deleted. It is open to any user to participate and make a comment or argue an opinion. Some of these comments and arguments can be counter-arguments, attacks in Dung's (1995) argumentation terminology. Here, we consider the extraction of one type of attack, the directive speech act formed as an imperative.

1 Introduction

A large group of volunteers participate to make Wikipedia one of the most successful collaborative information repositories. To ensure the quality of the encyclopedia, deletion of articles happens continually. If an article is controversial, an online discussion called "Article for Deletion" (AfD) is held to determine whether the article should be deleted. It is open to any user to participate in the discussion and make a comment or argue an opinion. Some of these comments and arguments can be counter-arguments, attacks in Dung's (1995) argumentation terminology. A common argumentative attack is a directive speech act suggesting a potential disagreement and a possible way to rectify the matter. Here, we consider the extraction of this type of attack when formed as an imperative.

Researchers are becoming increasingly interested in studying the content of Wikipedia's Articles for Deletion (AfD) forum. Schneider et al. (2013) investigated the difference in arguments from novices and experienced users. Xiao and Askin (2014) examined the types of rationales in Wikipedia AfD discussions.

2 Speech Acts and Imperatives

A speech act is an utterance that has performative function in communication (Austin, 1975). Of the three types of speech acts, Searle (1976) subcategorized the illocutionary act, the act of expressing the speaker's intention, into five sub-groups. We are interested here in the Directives sub-group.

Often, a directive can be viewed as an attack (Dung, 1995), albeit an indirect one, e.g., "Could you provide the source to me?". The user, to whom this directive is made, undercuts (Pollock, 1992) the attack by responding with some sources.

Ervin-Tripp (1976) lists six types of directives one being the imperative. Imperatives express a command. Typically the predicate is an action verb and the subject, often eliminated, is second-person (you). As well, there can be words of politeness and adverbial modifiers of the verb:

- Please do this sort of check in the future.
- Just avoid those sorts of comments and perhaps strike the one above.

Cohortatives (first person plural imperatives) are normally used in suggestions such as, "Let's have dinner together." Some directive sentences from AfD discussions are listed below:

- Add the information, and please give us some information so we can judge these sources.
- Let's avoid compounding the BLP issues caused by the existence of this article, in violation of notability and blp policies, by having it snow-deleted post-haste.
- You must first discuss the matter there, and you need to be specific.
- Perhaps time would be better spent adding more and improving the article rather than just arguing here.
- Instead of complaining, how about finding such content and improving the article?

Proceedings of the First Workshop on Argumentation Mining, pages 106–107,
Baltimore, Maryland USA, June 26, 2014.

Viewing the above examples, some users directly suggest or command other users to do something (the first one). Cohortatives include the user (the second example). The third one is obviously commanding someone to discuss the matter first and to be specific. The first three examples are imperatives. Some commands include politeness, as illustrated by the last two examples. Since the form of this kind of utterance varies, it is difficult to define a rule for recognizing it by computer. In this paper, we only detect direct imperatives and leave indirect imperative recognition for future work.

3 Detecting Imperatives

In English, a typical imperative is expressed by using the base form of a verb, normally without a subject. To detect this kind of imperative, we need to analyze the grammatical structure of sentences.

According to our observation, a typical imperative contains a verb in base form without any subject. Therefore, the basic rule for imperative recognition is to find those sentences with a verb (in its base form) as the root in the phrase structure and this particular verb has no subject child in the dependency structure. Another form of imperative is like the sentence: "You must first discuss the matter there, and you need to be specific". We have adapted a modal directive rule suggested by Sinclair et al. (1975): We recognize the use of a personal pronoun or noun (e.g., "you", "we", or a username) followed by a modal verb (e.g., "should", "must", "need") as an imperative. We used keywords to detect this kind of imperative.

4 Evaluation

In this section, we evaluate the performance of our methods to detect imperatives. Two human annotators (undergraduate students at The University of Western Ontario) extracted imperatives from our data. Agreed upon imperatives became our gold standard. Our system had Precision 0.8447, Recall 0.7337, and F-measure 0.7874 on this data.

Most false positives have an implicit subject "I" (e.g., *Agree with most of the rest of this.*), a writing style found in this text genre. Missed imperatives (false negatives) resulted from parsing errors by the parsing tool and sentences with the form of subject + modal verb, but the subject is a noun (person or organization) instead of a pronoun. Our method keyed on pronouns.

5 Related Work

Marsi's (1997) definition of imperative mood is too restrictive for our purposes here. A use of Argumentative Zoning to critique thesis abstracts (Feltrim et al., 2006) gives no details regarding the imperative sentence recognition techniques, and the language of interest is Brazilian Portuguese.

Acknowledgments

This project is partially supported by the Discovery program of The Natural Sciences and Engineering Research Council of Canada (NSERC).

References

John Langshaw Austin. 1975. *How To Do Things with Words*. Oxford University Press.

Phan Minh Dung. 1995. On the acceptability of arguments and its fundamental role in nonmonotonic reasoning, logic programming and n-person games. *Artificial Intelligence*, 77(2):321–357.

Susan Ervin-Tripp. 1976. Is Sybil there? The structure of some American English directives. *Language in Society*, 5(01):25–66.

Valéria Feltrim, Simone Teufel, Maria das Graças V. Nunes, and M. Aluísio, Sandra. 2006. Argumentative zoning applied to critiquing novices' scientific abstracts. In James G. Shanahan, Yan Qu, and Janyce Wiebe, editors, *Computing Attitude and Affect in Text: Theory and Applications*, pages 233–246. Springer Netherlands.

Erwin Marsi. 1997. A reusable syntactic generator for Dutch. In Peter-Arno Coppen, Hans van Halteren, and Lisanne Teunissen, editors, *Computational Linguistics in the Netherlands 1997: Selected papers from the Eighth CLIN Meeting*, pages 205–222. Amsterdam/Atlanta: Rodopi.

John L. Pollock. 1992. How to reason defeasibly. *Artificial Intelligence*, 57:1–42.

Jodi Schneider, Krystian Samp, Alexandre Passant, and Stefan Decker. 2013. Arguments about deletion: How experience improves the acceptability of arguments in ad-hoc online task groups. In *Proceedings of the 2013 Conference on Computer Supported Cooperative Work*, pages 1069–1080. ACM.

John R Searle. 1976. A classification of illocutionary acts. *Language in Society*, 5(01):1–23.

J.M.H. Sinclair and M. Coulthard. 1975. *Towards an analysis of discourse: The English used by teachers and pupils*. Oxford University Press.

Lu Xiao and Nicole Askin. 2014. What influences online deliberation? A Wikipedia study. *J. of the Association for Information Science and Technology*.

Requirement Mining in Technical Documents

Juyeon Kang
Prometil
42 Avenue du Général De Croutte
31100 Toulouse, France
j.kang@prometil.com

Patrick Saint-Dizier
IRIT-CNRS
118 route de Narbonne
31062 Toulouse, France
stdizier@irit.fr

Abstract

In this paper, we first develop the linguistic characteristics of requirements which are specific forms of arguments. The discourse structures that refine or elaborate requirements are also analyzed. These specific discourse relations are conceptually characterized, with the functions they play. An implementation is carried out in Dislog on the <TextCoop> platform. Dislog allows high level specifications in logic for a fast and easy prototyping at a high level of linguistic adequacy.

1 The Structure of Requirement Compounds

Arguments and in partticular requirements in written texts or dialogues seldom come in isolation, as independent statements. They are often embedded into a context that indicates e.g. circumstances, elaborations or purposes. Relations between a requirement and its context may be conceptually complex. They often appear in small and closely related groups or clusters that often share similar aims, where the first one is complemented, supported, reformulated, contrasted or elaborated by the subsequent ones and by additional statements.

The typical configuration of a requirement compound can be summarized as follows:

```
CIRCUMSTANCE(S)/CONDITION(S),PURPOSE(S)-->
 [REQUIREMENT CONCLUSION + SUPPORT(S)]*
   <-- PURPOSE(S), , ELABORATION(S)
   CONCESSION(S) / CONTRAST(S)
```

In terms of language realization, clusters of requirements and their related context may be all included into a single sentence via coordination or subordination or may appear as separate sentences. In both cases, the relations between the different elements of a cluster are realized by means of conjunctions, connectors, various forms of references and punctuation. We call such a cluster an **requirement compound**. The idea behind this term is that the elements in a compound form a single, possibly complex, unit, which must be considered as a whole from a conceptual and argumentative point of view. Such a compound consists of a small number of sentences, so that its contents can be easily assimilated.

2 Linguistic Analysis

2.1 Corpus characteristics

Our corpus of requirements comes from 3 organizations and 6 companies. Our corpus contains 1,138 pages of text extracted from 22 documents. The main features considered to validate our corpus are the following:
- specifications come form various industrial areas;
- documents are produced by various actors;
- requirement documents follow various authoring guidelines;
- requirements correspond to different conceptual levels.

A typical simple example is the following:
<ReqCompound> <definition> Inventory of qualifications refers to norm YY. < /definition>
<mainReq> Periodically, an inventory of supplier's qualifications shall be produced. < /mainReq>
<secondaryReq>In addition, the supplier's quality department shall periodically conduct a monitoring audit program.< /secondaryReq>
<elaboration> At any time, the supplier should be able to provide evidences that EC qualification is maintained. </elaboration> < /ReqCompound>

2.2 The model

Let us summarize the processing model.

Requirement indetification in isolation: Requirements are identified on the basis of a small number of patterns since they must follow precise

Proceedings of the First Workshop on Argumentation Mining, pages 108–109,
Baltimore, Maryland USA, June 26, 2014. ©2014 Association for Computational Linguistics

formulations, according e.g. to IEEE guidelines. On a small corpus of 64 pages of text (22 058 words), where 215 requirements have been manually annotated, a precision of 97% and a recall of 96% have been reached.

Identification and delimitation of requirement compounds The principle is that all the statements in a compound must be related either by the reference to the same theme or via phrasal connectors. These form a **cohesion link** in the compound. The theme is a nominal construction (object or event, e.g. *inventory of qualifications*)). This is realized by (1) the use of the theme in the sentences that follow or precede the main requirement with possible morphological variations, a different determination or simple syntactic variations, This situation occurs in about 82% of the cases. (2) the use of a more generic term than the theme or a generic part of the theme, (3) the reference to the parts of the theme, (3) the use of discourse connectors to introduce a sentence, or (4) the use of sentence binders.

Relations between requirements in a compound Our observations show that the first requirement is always the main requirement of the compound. The requirements that follow develop some of its facets. Secondary requirements essentially develop forms of **contrast, concession, specializations and constraints**.

Linguistic characterization of discourse structures in a compound Sentences not identified as requirements must be bound to requirements via discourse relations and must be characterized by the function they play e.g. (Couper-Khulen et al. 2000). The structure and the markers and connectors typical of discourse relations found in technical texts are developed in (Saint-Dizier 2014) from (Marcu 2000) and (Stede 2012). These have been enhanced and adapted to the requirement context via several sequences of tests on our corpus. The main relations are the following: **information and definitions** which always occur before the main requirement, **elaborations** which always follow a requirement, since this relation is very large, we consider it as the by-default relation in the compound, **result** which specifies the outcome of an action, **purpose** which expresses the underlying motivations of the requirements, and **circumstance** which introduces a kind of local frame under which the requirement compound is valid or relevant.

A conceptual model is constructed in a first stage from the discourse relations and functions presented above, and the notion of polarity and strength for requirements. Its role is to represent the relations between the various units of the compound in order to allow to draw inferences between compounds, to make generalizations and to check coherence, e.g. (Bagheri et al. 2011).

2.3 Indicative evaluation

The system is implemented in Dislog on our TextCoop platform. The first step, requirement identification, produces very good results since their form is very regular: precision 97%, recall 96%. The second step, compound identification, produces the following results:

	precision	recall
identification	93%	88%
opening boundary	96%	91%
closing boundary	92%	82%

The identification of discourse structures in a compound produces the following results:

relations	nb of rules	nb of annotations	precision	recall
contrast	14	24	84	88
concession	11	44	89	88
specialization	5	37	72	71
information	6	23	86	80
definition	9	69	87	78
elaboration	13	107	84	82
result	14	97	86	80
circumstance	15	102	89	83
purpose	17	93	91	83

References

Ebrahim Bagheri, Faezeh Ensan. 2011. *Consolidating Multiple Requirement Specifcations through Argumentation*, SAC'11 Proceedings of the 2011 ACM Symposium on Applied Computing.

Elena Couper-Kuhlen, Bernt Kortmann. 2000. *Cause, Condition, Concession, Contrast: Cognitive and Discourse Perspectives*, Topics in English Linguistics, No 33, de Gryuter.

Dan Marcu. 2000. *The Theory and Practice of Discourse Parsing and Summarization*, MIT Press.

Patrick Saint-Dizier, 2014 *Challenges of Discourse Processing: the acse of technical documents*, Cambridge Scholars.

Manfred Stede. 2012 *Discourse Processing*, Morgan and Claypool Publishers.

Author Index

Association for Computational Linguistics
209 N. Eighth Street
Stroudsburg, Pennsylvania 18360

CURRAN ASSOCIATES INC
proceedings.com